Beyond the Myth of Dominance
Dominance
An Alternative to a Violent Society

Edwin M. McMahon, Ph. D.

Sheed & Ward

Sheed & Ward™ is a service of The National Catholic Reporter Publishing Company.

Library of Congress Cataloguing-in-Publication Data

McMahon, Edwin M.
　　Beyond the myth of dominance : an alternative to a violent society / Edwin M. McMahon.
　　　　p.　　cm.
　　Includes bibliographical references.
　　ISBN 1-55612-563-1 (alk. paper)
　　1. Self-actualization (Psychology)--Religious aspects--
Christianity. 2. Consciousness--Religious aspects--Christianity.
3. Emotions--Religious aspects--Christianity. 4. Body, Human--
Religious aspects--Christianity. 5. Control (Psychology)--Reli-
gious aspects--Christianity. 6. Violence--Religious aspects--
Christianity. I. Title
BV4598.2.M36　1993
248--dc20　　　　　　　　　　　　　　　　　　　92-38036
　　　　　　　　　　　　　　　　　　　　　　　　　CIP

Published by:　Sheed & Ward
　　　　　　　　115 E. Armour Blvd. P.O. Box 419492
　　　　　　　　Kansas City, MO 64141-6492

To order, call: (800) 333-7373

Cover design by Tim Botts

Contents

Dedication

To all who search for
a way to heal themselves, their children
and the planet

Introduction:

A Twenty-First-Century Renaissance

A YOUNG MAN WHO WAS PILOTING SUPPLIES BY PLANE BACK and forth across Turkey recently told me that from the air he could see the ruins of civilization after civilization below him. Memories in stone of the Hittite, Seljuk, Persian, Greek, Roman, Christian Byzantine, Armenian, and Ottoman cultures drew him to pause and wonder about his own "American civilization," its health and longevity. Why, he asked himself, are these great accomplishments of the human spirit in engineering, architecture, art and sculpture now but specks of dust on the vast Anatolian landscape? What holds a civilization together and what corrupts and destroys it?

Michael Wood, writer and presenter of the PBS series, "Legacy" asked himself the same question and set out to find some answers. For those who saw this remarkable probe into several of the world's ancient civilizations, those that lasted the longest, he found, tried to provide an answer to the deepest of all human hungers—our need to live in harmony and balance with what we experience as conflicting attractions or needs. For instance, to find balance between the pull toward security in material goods and one's deepest security in trusting some Higher Power; harmonizing the masculine and feminine within us in order to be whole; not rejecting either the light or the dark side of our own nature; seeing to it that our needs are taken care of without violating the needs of others and of the planet; nurturing and being part of and contributing to a community while at the same time nurturing and developing our own unique talents and spirit. The list goes on and on.

My understanding of what Wood found is that the more enduring civilizations functioned as a bridge joining these apparent opposites. Much of the enormous energy needed to grapple with these dichotomies could then be turned toward creativity because a harmonious vision of reality and society was provided. They experienced themselves as part of a bigger picture, of a mission that was integral to their ordinary lives. In fact, everything about life was usually connected to the Divine in some way.

How did these great civilizations manage to pull this off? First of all, by providing their people with benevolent, orderly, stable governments that gave them security and the satisfaction of basic needs. Secondly, through ritual that tied together and created a bridge between the human person, nature and some concept of a Higher Power, afterlife, or God. Finally, they created this same bridge in the king, high priest, or great leader of the people by divinizing him in some way so that loyalty and submission to him became religious devotion and one's ticket to the afterlife and to the Divine.

However, the dark side of such a basically closed system of authority residing not in the people but in the preservation of ritual and in the absolute powers of the leader was that corruption and the abuse of people soon wormed their way into the system. Disintegration of the culture was inevitably not far behind. In all these civilizations, there was really no empowerment given to the ordinary person, and thus no lasting source for continuing growth and health in the society. When the power source became corrupt, the civilization fell to pieces.

Our American dream, this young experiment of little more than two centuries, faces the exact same challenge today. Here in America we tried to break with the past by creating a democracy "of the people, by the people and for the people" in order to minimize the danger of too much power in one leader. But we face the same corruption of power now through the monied interests we have allowed to dominate our electoral system. With the demise of the Soviet Union, we now have incredible economic, industrial and military might at our disposal. We are forced into a dangerous role without an ethos solidly grounded in our bodies as a bridge into the wisdom and connection that all nations and peoples have as living cells of an even Larger Body.

It is very easy in an addictive culture like ours to persuade people who are cut off from their bodies, and therefore the wisdom of the Larger Body, to do violence to other people and their environment. Violence inevitably erupts over and over again in a culture that does not have its fundamental character grounded in a body experience of the unity and gift-dimension of all life.

Whenever a unitive ethos or underlying experience is present and alive, it impacts the beliefs, customs and social practices of that society in such a way that a "common sense" abhorrence of violence underlies behavior and relationships. Our children today are not receiving this, and the handwriting on the walls of our cities and the screens of our TV's grows ever more violent. The problem we face throughout Western democracies is that we must not merely reject state-imposed religion and the divinization of our president or prime minister. We must simultaneously empower ordinary citizens, and especially our children, with the conviction that they are that same bridge that can bring into existence a harmonious connection between ourselves, our planet and a Higher Power or God. Before the emerging corruption in our culture further erodes our collective spirit we must, without delay, discover that we are the bridge that unites and brings harmony into human life, *not from outside* but from *within* our own humanity itself. I believe the answer lies at our own backdoor in the human body we all share.

However, to take this step we need to undergo a "revisioning" of who we think we are, and how we perceive we are meant to live, raise our families, govern ourselves and relate to the rest of the planet. And here is the rub. The bridge must come out of ourselves, out of our own inner experience, not from outside through the media, entertainment, laws, politicians, church leaders and the like. We must reown our body's consciousness as the bridge into the Larger Body and its wisdom. We must discover a body-spirituality, a "bio-spirituality" for the twenty-first century, or fall further into the corruption that has destroyed so many civilizations before us.

But how can we do this? Are there historical precedents or models to which we can look for guidance? Is there an already existing "body" of experience that can provide direction?[1]

In the Bio-Spiritual Movement, we have found that Focusing teaches us "how to dwell" in our potentially-destructive feelings in order that they may be "gifted" with change. This provides an opportunity to feel hope in our bodies, which directly diminishes violent behavior. The Institute for Bio-Spiritual Research, as of this writing in 1992, is an international network of over 2,000 people helping each other and their communities to discover an alternative to the violence we perpetuate toward ourselves and the world around us. The following pages share what we are discovering. Let me tell you a bit more about this book by describing a personal experience, something that happened to me not too long ago.

For decades I had experienced a "felt-sense" about the Renaissance that pulled me into exploring everything I came across about that period of history. I was always puzzled by this strange attraction because it seemed so full of contradictions. I found the art not something that expressed my taste, yet I would return to it again and again. The architecture was too overwhelming, but again, I could spend hours in the body-feel of it, especially in Italy. I was drawn to so many remarkable human beings who blossomed during this period, like waking from a long winter's sleep. Thousands developed talents that previously lay dormant, enduring even today not only in the wonder of engineering, masonry, and sculpture but in the literature and sciences then being born. It always felt inside like there was a story in all these incredible achievements of the human spirit. A story waiting to speak directly within me. I could feel the "something," but it never revealed itself until one beautiful May morning on the porch of a farmhouse near Cortona, Italy.

Pete Campbell and I had rented some rooms in this picturesque 16th-century stone building overlooking the Chianti valley. I was reading about Leonardo da Vinci's spectacular engineering feat in draining the valley below me, which previously had been a malaria-infested swamp. Then, on a memorable page of this part history book, part guidebook, the author wrote something to the effect that the Renaissance came into being because a wide-enough threshold of awareness had evolved. A level of consciousness surfaced, sufficient that a movement could be born. What was the breakthrough? People rediscovered the divine within their own humanity!

Suddenly, a massive explosion of self-esteem and human potential "in God" was let loose. I recall the author saying that people again took pride in being "part of God." Dust-covered dreams and the human spirit connected with the Divine, and the impossible became possible. It is this bridge that needs rebuilding in our time.

For the 21st-century not to stumble and lose its way in self-destructive addictions and greed it will need, like during the Renaissance, a self-esteem grounded in the body/ Body or, as St. Paul would put it, "in Christ." As I have so often written in this book, great masses of people through a global bio-spirituality need to experience their empowerment IN the Larger Body. This surfaces the body-feel, not the ideology, of hope, energy, continuity, meaning, purpose and pride to be a part of the Whole Body in its struggle for peace, unity and balance. This sense that "I count and can risk dreaming of my contribution to a better future" is what will make that future a reality.

For me, the connection finally had come. That vague, fuzzy feeling of "something" moved into excitement and an easing in my body. I stood up, amazed at what had happened as I walked thoughtfully down the dirt road toward the walls of the ancient city. My eye caught the magnificent dome of an abandoned church below me, now in an olive orchard, but still greater than most contemporary cathedrals. My mind wandered back to a favorite Gendlin* quote in which he describes how Focusing builds this bridge that once fueled the Renaissance. He wrote: "Your physically-felt body is, in fact, part of a gigantic system of here and other places, now and other times, you and other people, in fact the whole universe. This sense of being bodily alive in a vast system is the body as it is felt from inside."[2]

I thought of the countless workshops I have closed with this quote, telling groups of my telephone conversation with Gene in 1978 shortly after his book, *Focusing*, was published. Toward the end of our discussion he asked, "What are you guys doing with my stuff?" I replied that I had just read a couple of sentences in his book which said it better than I ever could. I got the book, read him the above quote, and then asked if I could re-read it, inserting a few Christian words to explain what I was doing with "his stuff." He agreed, and I read it to him as follows: "Your physically-felt body is, in fact,

---

* Cf. Appendix A: "The Academic Roots of the Bio-Spiritual Movement," pp. 241ff.

part of a gigantic system of here and other places, now and other times, you and other people, in fact, the whole universe. This sense of being bodily alive in a vast system is the Body of Christ as it is felt inside us."

"This sense of being bodily alive," neither alone nor impotent, but IN some Body with a past and a future, with an energy and life-force that makes our sacrifices meaning-filled, is the Renaissance which our disconnected world needs today.

Hope lies not in the mind's ability to understand, nor in the certitude that everything is going to turn out the way I want. Rather, it lies in the *deep-down-body-feel* that what — happens to me now has meaning and is gift. For that to occur, our body needs to feel connected IN some LARGER BODY with a history and story that includes, but extends far beyond my few years here on this earth. Then, my life in this moment, as part of a vast history, *feels precious* and an important chapter in a narrative whose depth and breadth the thinking mind can never grasp.

This is the meaning of "blessed" or "happy" in the beatitudes, which to our culture seems absurdly out of step because scientific method and the myth of dominance overwhelm our view of reality. In order to understand the beatitudes, one must first realize that the Scriptures are not advocating poverty, hunger, nakedness, or humiliation as good things in themselves. Rather, in Jesus' time, "blessed" or "happy" had a special meaning. It referred to the potential we all retain during adversity of touching the mystery of God if we do not "disown" our body and its feelings in that experience—a familiar theme in these pages.

This means that if the body-sense of these painful experiences is not repressed or rejected, but "owned" in our bodies, then a doorway opens into the mystery of God. In other words, what we are calling "the story" in the deprivation (poverty, humiliation, etc.) is allowed to unfold, and in that unfolding opens up into an experience of gift (grace), of Presence, and of new meaning.

"Blessed" or "happy" is connected with a "body-owning-attitude" toward all of life, even adversity, which unfolds into a blessing in disguise. Even though sorrow and persecution were not extolled as conditions good in themselves, nonetheless it was recognized that when "owning" them in the body with openness to God, they could "bless" the recipient with a body sense of God that other human experiences could not. This kind of "faith" was known to be rewarded with the gift of God's hidden purpose and wisdom, often kept from those who rejected this part of life, often railing against such "slings and arrows of outrageous fortune." The beatitude was a prayer that those suffering adversity might be gifted in a way that helped them not break their sacred body-covenant where wisdom breaks through, where the mystery of God's Presence is felt, and where these great gifts can be felt to far outweigh those "slings and arrows."

I believe this most basic process in the development of human and planetary wholeness—"felt-sensing" our tied-in-ness to a Larger Body (for which the Beatitudes pray)—is ignored and neglected throughout our secular and religious education. Moreover, if you do not find it taught in the churches and schools, you certainly will not find it very prevalent in family life. This book describes how we can fill that void.

Our bodies may well be the only rite of passage we ever had. The ancients knew this all along, before we placed dominance and reason on the high altar and worshipped them alone, denying our body as the bridge into the wisdom of a Larger Body. It is time to restore that sacred covenant. Such bridge-building must be anchored in the spirituality of the human body.

Bio-Spirituality is a return to our body as that bridge into the Larger Body, which ancient religious traditions recognized as connecting us with the Divine. Today, the model of dominance as the basis for our relationships with one another, ourselves and with the planet is destroying us. A new paradigm must be found through the shared experience of discovering the bridge-building potential of our bodies as the doorway into community at every level.

We have found that "Focusing" can be used as a way to nurture an openness within the body/Body to the gift dimension of life (which Christians call "grace") so that we then live within ourselves and together in greater harmony, balance and wholeness.

Grace, whether put in a religious context or not, is the essential community-forming force in human society. Our civilization desperately needs to understand and live the psychological components of building "graced community," regardless of any religious connotation associated with the word. The entire globe will benefit from not proselytizing and pushing a denominational ideology, but sharing a bio-spirituality, a global spirituality that can transcend denominational divisions. We all need a viable alternative to relationships of dominance and violence. History teaches that such an alternative must be grounded in a body-feel of the organic unity and gift dimension within everything that exists.

Most cultures on this planet, especially the industrialized ones, are more in crisis than they realize. When we ignore the wisdom of the Larger Body given to us through our bodies, we lose even our common sense, let alone communal and global direction. Increasing violence and a lashing out in indiscriminate rage become the atmosphere we live in as the pain of self-alienation drives us to numb our suffering and confusion. This book has been written to let you know there is an alternative to such destruction.

The time has come for each of us to journey beyond the myth of dominance into the truth of ourselves. There, each will discover the gift of community and, as a wide-eyed teenager said after learning Focusing: "The best friend I will ever have is right inside myself—and this friend always lets me be myself." I might add, it is this friend, yourself, who will meet you with a heartfelt, "Welcome home!"

Chapter 1

What Is Focusing?

"WHAT DO YOU DO IN ORDER TO FEEL BETTER WHEN YOU'RE afraid or hurt?," asked the sixth-grade teacher. Forty pairs of youthful eyes were riveted on him, then gradually grew thoughtful as young minds turned inward to check their own experience. It was their first class on drug abuse and the number one question right up front was dealing with difficult feelings. "I pound my pillow." That came from the back of the room. "I ignore those feelings,"—from an intelligent-looking young man in the front row. "I try to read them away," offered a thoughtful girl in the second row. "I get busy about other things." "I jog or ride my bike until it goes away." The litany picked up speed: "I listen to music, go to a movie, dance, go shopping, play sports, talk to my friends on the phone"—and on, and on.

"What do you do, Elizabeth?" The teacher's friendly eyes picked her face out of the sixth-grade class. She remained still for a moment and then said: "I stay with the feelings. I stop and be quiet with them until something comes that helps them to change." The teacher looked stunned, pondering what she had said, weighing this young response to a question for which he himself had only the shakiest of answers, and then he moved on. Elizabeth has been taught at home to care for scary and hurting feelings since she was five years old.

* * * * *

Yesterday, I walked out along the narrow dirt road that leads into our mountain home. At the end of this winding lane through the trees, one comes to the county paved road and a row of mail boxes. I always enjoy this quiet, seldom-traveled

1

road, especially because I can hear the sound of even the slightest breeze in the needles of the tall pines. As my walk ended and I came to the mail boxes lined up on their individual posts, I was appalled at the sight. Someone had come along with a club, smashing everything in sight, ripping off several containers, throwing one out into the field and bending out of shape whatever else they could not destroy. Why? I stood numbed at such a senseless act. There was nothing there to steal. Why? Who needed to vent their rage or boredom or whatever else was bottled up inside on the nearest thing they could get their hands on? I was surprised at how much sadness I felt for that person's pain and immediately newspaper and TV accounts of recent unexplainable city violence flashed into my mind. Here, no one had been injured. But, I wondered, next time will the recipient of this person's stuck pain be some unsuspecting, innocent passerby?

If I were asked to single out the top priority of my life right now and for the remainder of my years, I would say it is finding a way to let children know there is an alternative to carrying around inside them the rage and pain that destroys us all. Elizabeth's generation has hardly a clue to healing more effectively these wounds than my generation or the hundreds that came before me. And look how impotent religion still is in addressing the hatreds and pain in our bodies—from the ancient wounds of the past in today's violent northern Ireland and Yugoslavia to the disintegrating marriages, family life, and neighborhoods in America. Yet, there is an alternative and it is available to all of us now. Nothing is more important than what we choose right now to pass on to our children.

Rather than explaining in technical terms what Focusing is, I would like to share a story that might give you some feel for this process. You may refer to the appendix for a more detailed description of the Focusing Steps whenever you like. What follows is a children's story, written for a child who was going through a lot of pain and confusion because peers at school, even some teachers and cousins in the family, were pressuring her not to be true to her own precious spirit. They were constantly badgering her to do things and act "their way," rather than appreciating and valuing her as a unique person.

I share this story with you because I have always missed not having my own children and grandchildren, especially at those important times when you want to pass on something you treasure and can cuddle up for a story, creating a wonderful, life-giving moment together. So, for a few minutes if you can put yourself into the world of your own inner child, move into this short story. Here you may discover a body-feel for what Focusing is all about. Of course, we have to begin the story of "The Little Bird Who Found Herself" with . . .

*   *   *   *   *

ONCE UPON A TIME, a tiny bird's nest sat high up in a tree. In this tiny nest was one gorgeous, violet-blue egg. The mother bird was so very proud of it she showed it to all the other birds around her. Then one day it suddenly burst open and out popped this drippy wet, tiny baby bird. The little bird couldn't see too well, felt cold, and was kind of scared, so the mother covered it with her wings to keep it safe and warm while the father bird flew off to find some yummy, delicious bugs for dinner.

After a while, maybe a few days or more, the baby bird began to grow its own downy baby feathers to keep itself warm. Then it felt more like opening its eyes and looking around at everything. But what it noticed most of all was this curious feeling deep down inside.

"I wonder what this strange feeling inside me is," the little bird said to herself. As the days went by, the odd feeling just kept growing and growing and the little bird wondered and wondered what it was all about.

Then one day she heard her mother chirping around the nest as she was tidying up. Suddenly, the little bird knew what the curious feeling was all about. That was what she wanted to do! She wanted to chirp! In fact, the little bird knew she just HAD to do that. So without waiting another moment, she opened her mouth and let out the loudest chirp you have ever heard. Even the children who were playing in the house came outside to see if they could discover what that sound was. The dogs began to bark and the lady next door who was hanging out her washing stopped to look around and listen.

The mother bird, who had not been paying any attention to the little bird as she did her morning chores, was so startled she fell over backwards out of the nest. But since she could fly, she opened her wings and flew right back up to check out what was happening. When the little bird saw her coming back, she felt so good inside. Knowing now what the strange feeling was all about, she sensed it was time for another big chirp, so out it came!

With that, the little bird's father flew over from a branch where he had been patiently waiting to catch a passing bug. Then, over flew the next-door bird neighbors, the aunts, uncles, cousins and friends until all the branches around the nest were crowded with birds looking down at the little bird.

Seeing all this commotion and feeling all the attention, the little bird said to herself, "Wow, I'm really somebody, and this feels so good inside me, I think I'll hop up and down right now." So she did.

But then before the little bird could chirp again, the aunt said: "We don't chirp fast and high like that," and one of the cousins said to the little bird's mother: "You have to stop this," and someone else added: "You need to teach her the right way to chirp." As others nodded their agreement, more and more kept saying things like that to the little bird's mother and father.

The little bird just sat there in the nest looking around. The happy, good feelings inside began to slip away. She began to feel very confused. She began to feel lonely. And she began to feel sadder and sadder inside as all the birds went on and on with their comments. "My chirp is me and I am my chirp," the little bird said to herself. "But all these birds who are older and bigger and smarter than I am say this is not the way a bird chirps." This confused the little bird very, very much, so much so that all the happy, good feelings inside were gone.

The little bird's mother didn't say much, because she also was confused and embarrassed that all her friends and family thought she was a bad mother. And the father bird tried to pretend nothing had happened by going off as usual, getting very busy finding more worms and bugs for lunch.

So that left the little bird very much alone, and not feeling at all like chirping. In fact, she was scared even to try again. Day by day she grew sadder and sadder and lonelier and lonelier inside. Each day she sat by herself on the edge of the nest or on a nearby branch, because by now her feathers had grown in and hopping around on the branches felt like the only fun in life.

Sometimes her cousins would come over chirping and playing, asking her to join in. But whenever the little bird would risk trying to chirp, even as softly as she could, they would say: "That's not the way *we* chirp. Either you learn to be like us or we won't play with you." That would make the little bird so mad her chirps would come out anyhow, and then the other birds would try to drown her out, feathers would fly and all the noise would bring the lady next door running out of her house banging on a pan to scare them all away.

So the little bird stopped trying to play with the other birds and would just sit all alone day after day by the nest. Then one day a wise, old owl flew by and saw the little bird all alone and looking so very, very sad. He flew down next to the nest. When the little bird looked over into the kind face of the big owl, something inside felt safe and right to ask him: "What do I do?"

The old owl gently moved over next to the little bird and said: "When you grow quiet inside, you can pay attention to your body. You can almost hear it talking to you. Listen to it. In all that jumble of feelings, is there one that needs listening to more than any other?"

Quietly, the little bird went exploring down into all the feelings in her body under the new feathers that were growing. The old owl said nothing, but the little bird could feel his reassuring presence and that helped her stay inside herself with her feelings. It didn't take very long before her body told her, "I'm very, very sad." So she shared that with the wise, old owl. Then the owl moved ever so gently even closer to the little bird, saying, "Can you move up closer to that sad place inside yourself like I'm doing with you and let it know that you are there and will listen to it patiently?"

The little bird could feel how to be with her sad place from the way the old owl was with her, so together they were very quiet as she moved even closer to her sad place inside. After a moment or two, the owl quietly said: "Now, let yourself really, really feel in your body what it's like to be next to your sadness like I'm next to you." And then they both grew even more still as the little bird tried to do just that. After a while, in a whispering, very quiet voice the wise, old owl softly encouraged the little bird to stay inside with the sad place saying, "take your time and listen to that place inside, because if you can feel it you know it wants to tell you something."

This helped the little bird be very still and present to her body and the sad place inside. In fact, it even felt like the old owl was right there too, which made it a lot easier since it hurt a lot and was scary.

As the minutes passed, the little bird became aware that the sad, hurting, scary place didn't feel so bad because it wasn't alone anymore. Suddenly, the little bird realized: "It feels better not to leave sad, scary, confusing, lonely places inside me all by themselves. I ought to be taking care of them and playing with them!" And then the little bird said that right out loud to the old owl, who just smiled and replied: "Take some time now to notice how *that* feels in your body." So the little bird paid attention inside to what those words felt like in her body. And almost right away she noticed the sad place didn't feel as sad now. "I think it wants to tell me something else," she said. To which the owl responded: "Just stay in there with how it all feels and listen patiently."

Suddenly, the little bird looked up at the large grey owl perched next to her and said: "CHIRP!" "Yes, that's it, I need to chirp and chirp and chirp and chirp!" So the little bird began to chirp and the smiling, wise owl flew off with the promise to come back again if the little bird needed him. But the more the little bird chirped, the better everything felt inside. So on and on she chirped, day after day, week after week, even when her neighbors would look annoyed and the aunts and uncles would fly by and voice their disapproval. The little bird didn't pay any attention to their scowls, but just kept on chirping the way it felt right to chirp.

Even though the little bird was still all alone on that branch chirping away, inside there was no sadness or confusion anymore. The sadness and confusion were no longer alone, because she had gone inside to be with them and they had become her friends. In fact, they could tell her what they wanted to and so they didn't feel like she needed to be afraid of them anymore. They could say what they needed to say to her now and that changed the way all the feelings felt in her body. Once again the little bird felt very special inside. So special and good about herself that the strange feeling she had so long ago returned again. "I wonder what it is this time," the little bird thought to herself.

As the days passed, the more the little bird chirped away the more that curious feeling grew inside her until she felt like it just had to come out.

Then one beautiful sunny morning as the little bird woke up and opened her mouth to chirp, instead out came the most wonderful sound anyone had ever heard before. The little bird began to sing! Not just ordinary singing, but more beautiful than any of her relatives and bird neighbors. All the birds stopped their chirping and listened in amazement. The dog stopped barking down the street and the children on their way to school came over to listen. Soon the people in the neighborhood would come over under the tree just to sit on the lawn and listen to the beauty of the little bird's singing. She trilled and warbled back and forth between two notes so fast that it sounded like one rich note, which made her singing more lovely and melodious than any of the other birds. So she sang and sang and sang for everyone, but most of all for herself.

All the other birds said to each other: "Why can't we sing like that? Why is the little bird so different?" When the little bird and the wise, old owl (who would come by to listen as well) would hear that, they would smile and wink at one another.

And so the little bird grew to sing more beautifully every day, because she never again left those special feeling places inside herself all alone.

The End.

* * * * *

Before you read any further or distract yourself with something else, you might want to grow quiet and pause. Perhaps close your eyes, giving yourself time to notice if anything inside you needs listening to right now. When you tune into your body this way, it will tell you if something is there that needs your attention. How? Simply because you will feel it. Maybe an anxiety in the stomach, or a restlessness all over, even a calm peacefulness, or a sense of gratitude, or perhaps a sadness behind the eyes or in the heart. Feelings and body sensations like these are part of your body's language. So if you discover your body trying to tell you something through this special vocabulary, then, like the little bird, move up as close as you can to all that is there with gentleness and caring. Let it know that you respect it and are taking time now just to be with it in an unhurried, open, listening way in case it wants to tell you something. Respect your defenses too, if they are there. Do not push into something your body says is not OK to be with now. Let your body also guide you in how close you can come. In Focusing we never force or push beyond what our body says is OK to be with in an "owning" way. When you feel you have had time enough perhaps to identify and even nurture some part of your own story in an inside way, and it does not feel jarring to go back up into the head, then I invite you to continue reading these reflections.

The little girl I wrote that story for is now twelve years old. Out of her growing experience of Focusing, she wrote the following essay—without any adult help—for a school project.

Freedom: What It Means To Me To Be Free

Freedom is a song of glory that comes out of your heart. Reaching its tender hands out to you, it dwells upon you and protects with care. This song is the precious gift that belongs to you.

Freedom may be taken for granted, but some people never experience the glory of being honest and true to yourself and friends. When you're free inside yourself, the song comes out of you. The notes sound richer than the music from Carnegie Hall. There is a different quality to the music that sings out of you, but there is a richness to both songs. When you're peaceful, the peacefulness comes from inside you. The freedom I'm writing about comes when you own what's real inside yourself. When you are able to listen to your feelings without ignoring them or trying to make them feel better, or distracting yourself by doing something else, then you give them a chance to talk to you. After listening to your feelings, a symbol comes to you. The symbol expresses your feelings in a peaceful way. When I can be real with my feelings, that is freedom to me, and when

I'm free inside of myself, I feel like I'm floating or walking on water. When I feel free, I'm honest. I don't feel I have to lie to make people feel better. I know what's real inside myself.

There is a different type of freedom which is the dictionary definition of freedom. When adults talk to children, their idea of freedom is something like this: "You're lucky you weren't a slave in the early 1800s. Some of them were beaten to death or severely whipped. Many died being transported from one country to the next. You have a home and family. You are also healthy and don't have scurvy like some of the slaves did from lack of a balanced diet. Now don't worry. Be happy!"

That is the motto of many people in America. It's their way of telling people to feel free and happy. Telling people to feel happy is not owning what's real inside yourself. Instead it tells us to ignore our feelings and pretend everything is all right. Pretending causes feelings to stack up. When that happens you try to act like people around you. Your goal in life then becomes wanting to fit in with your friends.

This essay has given me the freedom to write what I've wanted to share with people who have experienced the fakeness of pretending to be someone other than themselves. Being in 7th grade, I've noticed classmates who are not comfortable with themselves. They tell me I *should* wear my bangs up, my clothes are out of style, I should shave my legs, etc. You "should" is the key word. Trying to change people becomes an incessant habit for girls in Junior High. This jabber of You should used to make me uncomfortable. I thought I had to change my way of life to fit in with the school. This is what many girls entering Junior High think. At this stage they think that's the only way to fit in. So they lose who they are and enter this other world.

I know *how* to stay with these uncomfortable feelings and that helped me to feel comfortable at school. When I can hold my hurt feelings in a gentle way, the story underneath them breaks through. Then the meaning of my feelings becomes clear. When other girls see that their words don't bother me anymore, they become puzzled. They can't understand why I'm no longer bothered. I'm no longer uncomfortable around girls who tell me what I should do. The freedom inside myself of knowing who I am is the best gift I can ever be given.

* * * * *

Such awesome inner strength for any human being, let alone for a young adolescent! When I wrote the "Little Bird" story for her, I was trying to open up the alternative, the hope, and the direction that lay in the Focusing she already knew and used. I think it might also give you, the reader, some sense for this process, as well as where it can lead a child.

After that, some months elapsed and before I knew it, the once little girl was a teenager, babysitting the younger children in the neighborhood. I have always encouraged her to write, and when I asked her what was happening in her Focusing she told me she was writing a short story of how she used Focusing with one of the children she babysat. Here is a 13-year-old's way of explaining Focusing and Healing Listening as she passes on her "gift" to other kids "on the job." Once again, she wrote this without adult help:

The Golden Hands

Here I was again babysitting my 7-year-old charge, Kirsten. I was watching Kirsten play with her friends when she suddenly turned to me and asked, "Can I tell you something?"

I noticed the urgency in her voice so I replied, "Sure. Would you like to go somewhere private?" She shot me a grateful look and said, "Yes."

Before I get any further, let me tell you that Kirsten has been very moody lately. She enjoys going off by herself and sitting quietly. She never tells anyone how she feels so I assume she relishes being alone. So when she asked me this question, I was taken by surprise. We left her friends playing out front and went into her backyard to sit down. As soon as we were comfortable in our chairs, she broke into deep sobs.

Gently I asked her what was bothering her and she broke into deep sobs again. In between sobs she explained, "It's school. Kids at school are making fun of me. Because I don't do things their way they call me names. Since I don't wear clothes like theirs they call me a dork."

"People at school are making fun of you and it hurts you to be made fun of," I replied, repeating what she told me. It was important for me to hear what she was saying. If I tried to protect her feelings by saying, "It's all right. You know the kids are only saying that because they're uncomfortable with themselves," then Kirsten's feelings would be ignored. I know how often feelings can get ignored, so it was an important step for Kirsten to know that her feelings are an important part of her body.

Kirsten nodded, grateful that I understood what she was saying. She told me when kids make fun of her, she tries to show them that she's mad. Then if they're "nice" they will apologize to her and try to do something kind to make her feel better. Kirsten's parents revolve around the word "nice." She's learned since she was born to ignore her feelings and have "nice people" come and make her feel better. If people don't do what she wants, then they are not being "nice."

I asked Kirsten where in her body she felt this hurt place. She pointed to her stomach, so I told her to gently place a hand on her stomach and slowly rub it. "Can you hold that hurt place like you hold your kitten? Can you tell your feelings you aren't going to ignore them because they are a part of you that needs to be listened to?"

Kirsten suddenly spoke up, "Why are you asking all these complicated questions? What do you mean, hold my hurt place like I hold my kitten? My kitten is an animal. My hurt place is *inside* me. Why do I have to stay with feelings that hurt me?"

Her last question took me by surprise. I never thought *why* I stayed with my hurt feelings. "I do it because it makes me feel better," I told her. She had nothing to say so I went on, "When you place a caring hand on your stomach, do you feel any different?"

"Yes, I feel comforted that my feelings can be listened to. I feel closer to my body when my hand holds my feelings."

"Okay, now let's be quiet for a few minutes."

After 5 minutes, Kirsten told me that it helped to ask her feelings to stay and play with her.

When she said that, I nodded to myself. There are different ways of being gentle with feelings. Some people feel like they are part of water when they listen to their feelings. So when something is bothering them, they stay with their feelings like they swim. Kirsten's way is asking them to play with her. These steps are invaluable.

After nodding, I asked Kirsten, "How do your feelings respond to you when you ask them to play with you?"

It took Kirsten a couple of minutes to talk but when she did she related, "They feel like they want to talk to me." I responded: "Can you stay with that feeling of wanting to talk? Your feelings may want to tell you something."

Kirsten started to fidget. Her hands started to sweat and her forehead creased into a frown as her hand started to slip from her stomach.

I told her, "It's all right to feel what you feel. There's no way you can flunk being with your feelings."

After I said that, the frown slowly disappeared, her hand inched its way back to her stomach and she let out a deep breath that seemed she had been holding for eternity. A smile lit up on her face and she turned toward me. Then she gave me a great big thank you. She squealed: "I really heard you!!! All this time you have been telling me to hold my feelings gently and I thought I had to force that for something to change. When you said it's all right to feel what I felt, something seemed to click. I was feeling so frustrated before you said that. Now I feel terrific!!! A picture came to me when you said that—GOLDEN HANDS GENTLY HOLDING AN EGG INSIDE MY BODY. That egg is the feelings that have hurt me so much. Now I know how to care for them. I can't believe it!"

She got up, gave me the biggest hug and whispered into my ear, "Let's do this more often! I feel as though I'm walking on water."

* * * * *

When I finished reading this, I realized that if a 13-year-old can spontaneously relate to a hurting child in a Focusing way and even teach that child Focusing out of her own experience—and without any formal training or coaching in how to guide another person—then we had better introduce kids to Focusing as soon as possible. They will probably be passing it along to each other while we are still preoccupied trying to unlearn old habits and struggling to process all the neglected stories in ourselves that go way back to when we were their age.

Once we learn how to treat whatever is real inside us, then we will know how to treat others and the planet we live on.

Given the myth of dominance which still pervades most, if not all of our relationships, no generation today is immune from the truth that how we treat ourselves, especially our past —like Kristen was carrying her feelings about the kids at school—is the decisive factor for how we will live our future. That past we carry in our bodies. This is why Focusing is so key to the quality of our future as well as our evolution.

Focusing is about community building—inside ourselves and around us. Focusing is not something separated from our struggle for personal, social and planetary wholeness. But Focusing builds toward group and global community out of our personal wholeness, which is intrinsically a spirituality of the body's movement toward "holiness."

One of the best short pieces of writing to date on the relevance of Focusing to social and environmental issues has been by Les Brunswick.[1] His words may help you situate historically what Dr. Eugene Gendlin termed "Focusing" (and we use the same term), as well as get a further feel for this process as it applies to our whole stance toward change. Brunswick begins by talking about "felt sense," which is a term Gendlin coined to describe not only emotions or feelings and physiological sensations we can "own" by consciously adverting to their presence, but includes as well the body sense for a "more" that is always an intrinsic part of anything we feel.

For example, have you ever been to someone's house for dinner and as soon as you walk in the door, even though you have no data to substantiate it, you *feel* something is "off," like maybe this is not the right time to be there, or something has happened, etc. I had this experience on Christmas Eve a couple of years ago. Everyone was very polite and gracious, but I had this "body feel" that something was not OK there. I've learned to honor these feelings in my body, so once I got some refreshments I strolled over by a window where I could be quiet for a few moments and listen to my gut. Then I noticed the physical sensations of some anxiety in feeling this "more," like sweaty palms and some butterflies in my stomach. These grew as I pondered my confusion as to whether or not I should ask the hostess if it was convenient for us to be there, or if it would be better to come later or at another time in the holidays. When I noticed all the work that had gone into dinner preparations and how uncomfortable she would be if I even brought it up, that only increased the quandary inside me. So it felt right to quietly "own" all of this, pretending to look out the window. Suddenly the words came: "Don't bring it up." That felt right, and by the time I turned around and joined the party again, it felt on target not to say anything and I noticed the anxiety level begin to drop in my body. The direction I needed had come and connected inside and my body told me it was right with the easing I could feel. This is Focusing. The "more" was very real to me in that circumstance and continued to be present for the rest of the evening, but I was no longer anxious about my role or how I needed to carry this feeling. Interestingly enough, a few days later, casually on the phone, the hostess volunteered what had happened in the family shortly before I arrived, which, although no one had said a word about it that evening, I had "felt" when I walked in the door.

Many of you will recall similar experiences like coming into a meeting, or getting into a car, or meeting someone, or going into a certain room or building and "feeling" something, although you have no idea what it's about. That's the "more" our bodies pick up, which is vague and fuzzy—maybe always remains that way, but we know it is real and that we definitely feel something. This "more" is just as capable of being "owned" in our body as is the more easily-identified emotion (or feeling) as well as body sensations we are familiar with. All of these make up what Gendlin calls the "felt sense," which is what we try to "own" in our body when we focus.

Brunswick writes:

"Felt sense" is Gendlin's term for what was first clearly identified and described in the last hundred years by existential and phenomenological philosophers, including Husserl, Heidegger, and Merleau-Ponty. Why was it not discovered before? Heidegger says that, since the Greeks, the assumption has been that Being (reality, roughly speaking) consists only of things that stand out in perfect clarity and exactness. Since the felt sense is always partly vague, it was ignored by philosophers as not being fully real.

This idea of reality being perfectly clear goes with a dominative stance towards the world. If everything is perfectly clear, then you can grasp it all with your mind and even control it. But Heidegger says that Being is actually always partly hidden, mysterious, and not clearly formed. Rather than dominating the world, we need to patiently attend to what is, exactly as it shows itself to us (and if we do this, then more may form than was clearly formed before). Heidegger calls this dwelling, and what Gendlin has done in developing Focusing is teach us exactly how to dwell. Thus, Focusing is not just a method for psychological growth, but has to do with your whole relation to reality.[2]

What an on-target and beautiful phrase, *"Focusing is teaching us exactly how to dwell!"* This crucial attitude is essential for the growth of self-esteem, the healing of addictions, our relationship to each other and the planet, and for the entire approach we take to a spirituality grounded in the body—biospirituality. It is a radical *"incarnation,"* so long neglected by the followers of Jesus that G.K. Chesterton once remarked in an off-hand way that "Christianity really has never been tried!" Brunswick concludes his article with the following social and spiritual implications:

> Modern society's stance toward reality is not a dwelling, Focusing one, but rather is dominating. This dominating stance has led to terrible problems, such as pollution and the threat of nuclear war . . . (but there are people everywhere) . . . working for a world that is peaceful, ecologically sound, decentralized, and psychologically and spiritually healthy.

> I see Focusing as having a key role in such social change because Focusing training teaches the dwelling attitude such a world would need. Especially important here is the issue of separation versus connectedness. In the dominative stance, one tries to be separate from, and be superior to, the rest of reality. But through Focusing, we can regain the sense of being part of the universe as a whole and of being connected to all other people, a sense that is essential for a better world.[3]

What has meant so much to me and to so many other focusers is the experience of "dwelling" which gradually leads us beyond the dominative ways that so condition us in our relationship to everyone and everything. We know only too well the pain and destruction this controlling perception has brought into our lives, so to discover a life-giving alternative not only has great personal meaning but gives us hope for our children's future.

So much of the aggression that begins in childhood has its origin in our inability to listen to, be in or dwell inside the negative feelings that arise when we are youngsters. We become separated from our bodies as a way of coping with pain. Adults around us do not know how to be with their own pain, so they are incapable of teaching us how to be with ours. As a result, we get off track very early in life and only rarely do we ever find the guidance and support to change. Focusing gives us that support.

Gloria Bruinix is a play therapist who uses Focusing with pre-teens. Being with children in this special way has challenged her to care for many of her own neglected childhood feelings. She once wrote me:

> I will give you an example of something I did with my daughter. When I was a child I had long ringlets. I did not want long hair but my mother wanted me to have it. When I had my daughter I said to myself, "I will never make her have long hair the way they made me have it." Unfortunately, my daughter wanted long hair, but I could not hear her because I would have had to face the pain I felt as a child when I was not heard. It's so important to be with how we wanted people to be with us when we were children before we do Focusing with children. Otherwise, we will not be able to hear them.

> I believe each person who is Focusing with a child should spend some time with how they would have wanted to be listened to as a child themselves. If you know that and can feel what it is like not to have been heard, then you will be able to focus with children. Until you know what you wanted yourself, you will not be able to hear a child *when that child wants what you wanted*. Perhaps you will be able to hear quite a number of other things, just as I could. But the real pain in the child will not be heard until you hear your own pain. If the child's pain is around something that you missed as a child, then you won't be able to hear any of that until you can listen to what is unfinished and left over of this in your self right now as an adult.

I asked Gloria whether her own Focusing on painful childhood experiences had revealed anything about how she herself had coped with the pain of not being heard.

How did I go away from myself as a child? I didn't know how to listen to my body; I only knew how to act out my pain and dis-ease. This got me into more and more trouble because *the acting out* was where the adults directed their attention. I had to make a choice as to whether to give up the part of me that still knew what I wanted or to give up another part of myself. I didn't feel very clever in school, so I chose to give up my intelligence. It seemed to be the least important of my attributes, so I decided to become stupid instead of acting out. No one could change me if I was stupid, and I could then keep the part of me that knew what I wanted. I sacrificed my intelligence so that I could one day feel together with my special part that knows what I need. It was worth it to me!!!

One wonders when reading such an account about how many children make such a choice, consciously or unconsciously, in order to insure their survival. I asked Gloria how her own Focusing guided her as she taught her play-therapy children the art of "dwelling" within themselves.

I usually start with a new child by telling them something about me. I do this because so often in my case the parent or teacher sent the child to me to be "fixed." They cannot handle the child's behavior, so they want me to change it. I tell children: "When I was a child, I had lots of feelings but no one wanted to listen to them, particularly the ones where I was sad or mad. Sometimes, I would behave in ways that got me in trouble, and I could never understand why I did what I did.

"Then, I had a dream that when I grew up I would learn how to listen to children and help them understand why they do things. I would not be mad at them, but I would listen." (One eight-year-old boy said: "I am part of your dream.") I tell them, "I have found a special place inside me that helps me feel good about myself, and it also gives me answers." I say, "I ask my body if it is OK to be with what I am feeling and if the answer is 'No,' then I ask my body if it is OK to be with how it feels to say 'No'." I tell them I will always try to listen to them, but if I don't, tell me. Sometimes I don't hear very well. (They often smile when I say that.) I tell them they can stop or start whenever they like. They are allowed to say "No" to me anytime they feel like it. I am just there to listen to them.

From there, we talk together, or draw, or use clay. If I hear something important to them that has a body-feel when they are talking—like maybe they're hurt, or angry, or sad—then I ask if they can be with the feeling of that. Sometimes, they need to imagine themselves setting the feeling out at some distance from themselves so they don't have to be right next to it. If it feels right, I ask them if they can give it a wave or a hug. Then, I ask if they have any pictures or memory that comes.

If they say "No," and resist getting close to the feeling, then I ask if they can be with their feeling of not wanting to get close. Everything is done always with the question, "Is it OK to be with this?," as I think children have a tougher time saying "no" to adults and can easily push themselves to please me. What feels the most important is teaching children to be gentle with how they feel, and listening to what they want to verbalize next.

Children instinctively know how much better it feels inside when they can be congruent. But few adults are with them like Gloria, guiding them into learning in their bodies how to "dwell" and make friends with pain and fear. Instead, child after child, our hope for this planet, is violated and programmed on the road to self and social destruction as the myth of dominance is given the name "parenting," "education," or "religion." So much hope for new life in those little bodies is fed with everything but the pleasure of growing wholeness in discovering and owning themselves.

So their first attempt to be congruent is to act the feeling out, and this gets them in trouble. Then, because this is painful, the only course of action left is to stop feeling their feelings. As we all have experienced, we soon become experts at finding various ways to numb ourselves. That's what the children in Elizabeth's 6th-grade class were already quite adept at doing. A dominative environment reenforces being out of touch—the perfect training ground for low self-esteem, addiction, and ultimately violent, destructive behavior.

Focusing opens another door. It is simple enough to be shared with a child, and this is truly hopeful. But how do you "own" what is fearful or unacceptable in yourself? How can a person "be in" his or her feelings of terror or shame in a way that allows it to change? What is the actual process that goes forward?

Marianne Thompson's story of guiding her 13-year-old son John through Focusing while on summer vacation at a lake may help you understand how we can help each other "own" even the hurts that seem to pierce into the very marrow of our bones. Moreover, the ordinary family setting, as well as her comments on what she did, may clarify some of your questions. Once again, a more formal, complete and systematic description of the "Focusing Steps" is available in the Appendix. Marianne writes as follows:

We were at a cottage during summer vacation on a warm afternoon in July. Before going swimming, we were all relaxing after lunch. I had been listening to some tapes and just wandered into the living room. Lance, my husband, and Elizabeth were quietly reading as I walked in, but I could feel the tension in the air. Lance told me that John and Elizabeth had been arguing about what chair they wanted to sit in. They both wanted the same chair and the noise was building to a frenzied pitch when Lance had asked John to move into the empty chair. He refused and began mimicking Lance's voice. At that point, frustrated, angry and wanting to rest he asked John to leave the room. 'No!,' was the answer, so Lance said he got up, took him by the arm and led him out. I listened as Lance related what happened and tried to reflect back to him his frustration, anger and feelings of having his authority threatened.

I wasn't down at the lake two minutes when John appeared, dressed for swimming. He had a slouched, hurt, tight look throughout his whole body. It didn't feel like either of us wanted to swim. He pulled up a chair next to mine as I told him what his father had said. He started crying as I was talking, so I asked if he'd like to sit with how that whole thing made him feel. He said he did, but "it all felt like too much." There were so many emotions in him and it felt so complicated that I asked what it was in the whole situation that really bothered him. Was it Elizabeth or the chair, or . . . he quickly answered, "no," to those two and said, "It's Daddy."

I asked exactly what in the whole situation bothered him, so that he would have the opportunity to go inside himself and locate in a feeling way one issue in the whole situation. In this way it wouldn't feel so overwhelming to him. Often, when you begin to focus, it's necessary to sort out the different issues that you are carrying inside. If there isn't something that is currently clamoring for your attention, as was the case with John that afternoon, you usually help locate what you want to focus on by asking the question, "Is there anything that's keeping me from feeling really good right now?" As each issue begins to have a chance to surface, you temporarily place it down in order to get a feel for what it would be like inside without it. Gradually, you create a space inside yourself that feels like "there is more to me" than these issues. After you have identified the main issues by taking this inventory, you then check to see if there's anything else that needs attention that is not a problem. Maybe you are looking forward to a vacation, seeing a play, perhaps meeting a friend for lunch, maybe a creative project that's waiting for your attention. You then add that to your inventory. Then you go back to each issue and check in a feeling way to see which one feels like it is number one. Which one hurts the most, has the most excitement around it, which one is calling out for your attention the most? That then is the one you start with.

By asking John to identify what bothered him most in that whole complex situation, I was helping him make this space inside in a feeling way in order that he wouldn't feel so overwhelmed and blocked by all of it. The tears began to come as he located what he wanted to focus on. He grew quiet as I said, "Is it OK to take some time to be quiet with how your body feels all of this? How does that whole thing with Daddy feel inside your body right now?" I always ask the children to check inside themselves to see if whatever they are Focusing on feels all right to be with. This helps them learn to sense from the inside if it feels OK to stay with or if it feels too scary. If its too frightening we may stay with how it feels not to want to go any further. Or if that's still too difficult for them we will go back and choose another issue that feels OK to focus on. It is so important to respect their right to say no. It teaches them that both of us respect *whatever* is there. We all need to learn how our body wisdom can lead us.

He nodded that is was OK; then said in a somewhat agitated way, "It won't work, my story won't break through."

The tears were really coming now as it was so painful and hurting for him. I said, "John, see if you can be gentle and open with all of this hurt, anger and frustration. See if you can let these hurting places inside know that you are going to spend a little more time with them now, creating an open, safe place for them. Maybe when they're ready and feel like you care for them just as they are, they'll tell you their story. They may even want you to spend more time with them this afternoon, like carrying them into the water with you as you swim." He grew quiet as he tried to be gentle with his pain. I often tell the children, when we are talking about this part of Focusing, that it's like preparing a good gravy. It needs time to simmer on the back burner before it's ready to eat. Sometimes our hurting, confused feelings need that little bit of extra time too from us before they are ready to tell their story. When anything is so painful to us, this step of trying to create a caring, feeling presence seems to set the climate better than anything else you could do. It enables you to really own in your body what's there.

Creating this climate toward ourselves seems to be the key learning that the children and I have found is most important in Focusing. Learning to be gentle, open, and soft toward ourselves fosters an attitude of deep respect that more than anything else helps us let go into whatever we feel inside. We walk through the world more lightly when we care for ourselves in this way.

This seemed to take the pressure off John as he again went deeper inside himself. He was letting go into it and just being in all that he felt in this open, waiting way. Within a few minutes he softly said, "Daddy always seems like he's against me." Then came deep, deep sobbing and wailing sounds that seemed to come from the depths of his being. I sat next to him with tears of my own flowing as I felt both the anguish and the release that accompanied those words. During my years of journeying with adults in Focusing, I've heard that deep sobbing frequently as they've gently owned profound pain, but never have I heard a child wail so deeply.

Those words became the symbol that fit exactly how John was feeling about Lance, and they brought with them a deep sense of physical release. Let me explain that in Focusing you let go into the *Felt Sense* of how you are carrying an issue, waiting in this vulnerable way for something to come that fits how this feels. The symbol could literally be anything: words, pictures, tears, laughter, memories. The point here is that whatever comes, comes as gift. We can never *make* this happen! Even though the symbol may sound awful or shocking to our ears or to others, no matter, the symbol is always freeing! John's word's about his father could seem very shocking, but they fit exactly how he was feeling and brought a great release in how he was carrying this inside himself. When a shift comes, regardless of how small the movement seems, we physically feel better, and we never again carry that issue around in exactly the same way.

I knew what a tremendous breakthrough that was for John, but I didn't know what was coming next. Several minutes elapsed before his crying subsided as he remained quiet with his eyes closed for a very long time. He finally said, "That feels better. The muscles in my stomach feel more relaxed, my stomach feels soft, and my awful headache is gone." His eyes were still closed as I asked if he could take some time now to stay with how his stomach and muscles felt. I said: "Notice how your muscles feel now compared to how they felt earlier." This is the simple before and after check to see if in fact there has been any change inside your body. Calling attention to any change, no matter how small or seemingly insignificant, helps us ground and anchor the concrete body feel of grace. Right within your body you can physically experience how gift feels. In more relaxed muscles or easier breathing you can intimately feel this tremendous gift! Over a period of time we begin physically to feel the difference in our bodies between a self-identity that comes primarily out of control versus an even deeper identity as being gifted. Literally we begin to feel a new sense of self being born.

John's eyes were still closed as he sat quietly for several minutes, took another very deep breath and said, "I feel that better feeling going all through my body, it's like it's widening all over me." He took a long time to savor this new awareness, the new gift, this opening up that he felt spread throughout his body. I felt such gratitude for what I knew to be a major breakthrough for John in his relationship with Lance. What is more important to a child than this relationship to a parent; and to be gifted with that inner meaning and freedom at age

13! He still may have to work through more, but he won't have to carry these same feelings around in a blocked way.

I felt the time was right! A gift had come to both of us! This moment was one I had been waiting for for a long, long time. So I said, "John, this is how God feels in your body. Your soft stomach, your relaxed muscles, your headache that's gone *is* how God's grace feels from the inside." He took another very deep breath as we sat in silence for maybe five minutes, while the gift that had been given to us both penetrated into the very marrow of our bones.

Later, we reflected together as I stayed with my feelings of this experience. I told John that I had always wanted to pass on to my children this sense of the Holy. A sense that I've had since I was about his age. This gifted awareness was given to me when I was about 16, while on vacation with my family at Lake Louise in Canada. I was browsing through the lobby of the chateau with my sister when I felt this pull in my body and heard the word, "come!" I was drawn outside the lodge toward one of the most beautiful sights I have ever seen. Before me was the emerald color of Lake Louise with the snow-capped mountains in the background. All of my attention became riveted on that beauty as I lost contact with any sense of time. I have known in my body ever since that this Movement or Process was *leading* me, *drawing* me on to some greater whole, more than my own individual life. Somehow there's been a deep knowing that this Blessing comes to us out of our own body feel of home, family, relationships; our own personal joys, pains and sufferings. And I have always wanted to point to this experience with my children and say, "Look, listen and see."

But at some level too, I've always known that I couldn't *tell* my children about this experience, because I knew that just words without the experience doesn't pass on this deep knowing. It cannot be passed from generation to generation by merely talking about it. *Talking about* this experience is like passing on truths and dogmas of the faith. The words just don't do it. When we can deeply guide children into themselves through Focusing, then the revelation, the gift that we yearn to pass on happens! So, that afternoon I knew in my bones that John had been given in his body that tremendous experience of God. As we learn to create this attitude of gentle care toward ourselves and are gifted in the letting go and own-ing of what is real in our bodies, we break through to the Holy. This is our human way through to this awesome Mystery in our lives.

On awakening the next morning, I became aware of the contrast between what I could have done in that situation and what I did. Getting breakfast, I was reflecting on John's words, "It seems like Daddy is always against me." Just a few months ago, John's feelings and Lance's behavior would have felt like "After all my trying, our family is moving so slowly, what's the use." This wasn't how it felt inside of me now at all. Why didn't I feel that way, I asked? I was Focusing on how it did feel, which was such *a body sense of miracle*. I didn't lecture Lance, didn't even try to get any explanation out of him or try to make him feel better.

It was the same with John. I didn't scold him by saying there were two chairs in the room and you were just asking for trouble fighting over it with Elizabeth, or how could you have such feelings about your father after all he's done for you. Shaming him for his feelings. Or, you know Daddy loves you and you were just pushing him. How very easily I could have done all of that and blown it again. I sat with how all of that felt in my body, especially the *not* doing. Suddenly, it felt like an explosion hit me and the words came: "You didn't do any-thing in this situation, it was all given to you as Gift." The body-felt rightness of that awareness left me weak and I had to lean on a rail in the kitchen for support. A tremendous sense of the More in my life, the Gift that is God when I can move over and get out of the way, swept over my whole body.

I headed for the nearest chair, staying with the body feel of it for a long, long time. A tremendous sense of peace envelo-ped me. What then came home to me was that any relationship where people are going to be able to grow needs this KEY in-gredient in it. Each must give up trying to change or fix, or even understand the other person. When this happens, as it can through Focusing, the experience of "letting go and letting God" becomes the power that brings change. When I can let go of the many, many agenda that I have, not only for myself but for those I love, then God's grace can guide us. Then, and only then, can I pass on the wonder that God is!

Later that day, I shared this story with Ed, who lives nearby. He asked where John was because he wanted to see him. The next day John told me that Ed had found him in the living room, lying on the floor watching television. Ed had knelt down beside him and whispered into his ear, "Happy Birthday, John." John said he looked up, startled, since his birthday was still weeks away. And then he caught it as Ed said, "When something happens to us like what happened to you, it always feels like a birthday inside." After relating this, he stopped for awhile, grew pensive and then asked, "What's that place in France where people go and bathe in water to get cured? We saw a movie about it in school." I responded, "Do you mean Lourdes?" "Yes," he said. Then after another thoughtful pause he concluded, "This all feels like Lourdes to me."

* * * * *

Chapter 2

Childhood Wonder:
A Doorway to the Spiritual

LIFE IS MEANT TO FEEL LIKE LOURDES TO KIDS AND TO US, TOO.
It is meant to be full of miracles every day if we know how to
"dwell" in a non-dominative way "in our own backyard." People
used to call it "contemplation" and thought it was only for monks
and ascetics. Today, we know it is necessary for all of us, just to
be human and not destroy ourselves and the world around us. I
believe this spiritual awareness is deeply rooted in the experience
of childhood wonder. I am also convinced that such experience,
which is available to all of us, can be drawn upon as a resource to
help find a way through troublesome and difficult issues in life.
The purpose of this chapter is to help you learn something about
what to look for in your own childhood that can serve as a very
personal guide and inner resource for spiritual growth and adult
problem-solving.

Wonder has become an important doorway to spiritual experience for me because it brings something saving into my life
over which I have absolutely no control. When I know all the
reasons for uncomfortableness about some issue, and then
through Focusing am surprised by a completely different resolution or direction, one that allows feelings and not just my
thinking to change, then I sense wonder rising within. "I
didn't do this. Where did it come from? How did it happen?"

I know that I find God in my adult experiences of wonder.
When I'm surprised by grace, like the gift which can come
through Focusing, I seem to catch glimpses of another world.
It is a world where I am not in control but a greater Mystery
happens within me. I want to write about some experiences
that have helped develop in me a *body-felt-attitude* of openness

to the adult surprise of grace—especially an openness to grace in the more painful issues of life. My hope in writing is that you, the reader, may be encouraged to tap your own childhood resources in order to find similar nourishment and direction for your spiritual journey.

As a boy, growing up in a small town in the Sierra Nevada mountains of California, I was surrounded by such incredible natural beauty that habits of allowing myself to sink into the sound of wind in the trees, or birds and insects in the fresh grass of spring came quite naturally to me. Summer swimming in a nearby river canyon, walks along the streams and in the woods, trips near high, snowcapped peaks invited everything in me to open and be present.

I remember vividly one special vacation place we called our "Sunset Rock." For weeks at a time during summers when I was very young, mother would take my sister and me down the road from our cabin toward a river tumbling and splashing through giant boulders as the higher snowpack melted and rushed toward the sea. We had a regular ritual. Almost every evening after supper and just before the sun was ready to set, we would head down that road. Arriving at the river's edge, we would then climb a gigantic, smooth granite dome which to my youthful eyes was the size of a small mountain. On top we could see far down a twisting canyon toward the western horizon where soon the sun would set. Scrambling over the weather-worn surface, we would go directly to our favorite spot. It was a natural indentation, like a carved bench, where all three of us could snuggle up against the rock's radiating heat as the chill of evening settled quickly in the high mountain air.

My mother would then encourage us with "mousy quietness" to open ourselves to the warmth of the rock, the roar of cascading water and the changing patterns of the clouds and color. These were exciting moments of expectation. Then it would happen! The whole world went fiery red before mellowing to gentle pink as that glowing ball left us with an unforgettable finale behind the darkening silhouettes in the valley far below. This was experience a child soon learns never to disturb with thoughts or words.

Years later, after endless semesters of "education" and university degrees, I would return to this learning for direction and a solid footing for further growth. My time as a child on "Sunset Rock" always seemed a miracle to me. The magnificent colorful finale which closed each summer day encouraged a special openness. The sunset could not be changed, only contemplated. In that contemplation I came to appreciate a different kind of knowing in my body. It wasn't a "fixing up" knowing but a learning to "be with." For me, this was an important first step toward what was later to come through Focusing.

Attention to this "different kind of knowing" is the first important point I wish to make. Something in childhood wonder told me that my sunset rock experience was beyond all words and thinking. Over the span of years since that time, what yet endures with energy is not simply the memory of "what" I saw, but the *feel* of "how I was present" in that childhood spectacle. The vibrancy of this incident stems not from information which my adult mind can now recreate and verbalize. It comes, rather, from some awesome mindfulness in the body, making this incident present once more not merely in mental remembering but through representing the bodily-felt knowing of that special moment.

The spirituality of this experience lies in the fact that such bodily-felt knowing somehow transcends the chronological limits of time. It is recalled, not as a pale specter of its former self, but with all the vibrant resonance and tonality as the original. It has the same timbre. The *feel of it* is what endures. That is what brings excitement into memory. The incident itself, historically limited and now frozen in time, served as some sort of graced moment for the breaking through in bodily-felt knowing of a more enduring awareness that quite literally transcends chronological time. In such moments of fuller presence, we find ourselves caught up *through our bodies* into an awareness that flows beyond past, present and future. Once experienced, this more contemplative "being in" kind of knowing endures, quite literally, *forever*. A small piece of "The Mystery" has broken through into human awareness.

The "fixing up" kind of knowing associated with the need for control is always bounded by temporality. It ultimately breaks down and must be superseded, as does ultimately every form of control. But the "being with or in" kind of knowing, which is born during moments of childhood wonder, draws us toward some deeper Mystery of Presence which, in the words of scripture: "Eye hath not seen, nor ear heard, nor has it yet entered into the mind of humankind to conceive." Our bodies are the link to this incredible world of Spirit.

Moments of childhood wonder, then, stand as permanent resources through which one can grow beyond the tyranny of reason. Such special moments endure in our bodily knowing. *They are still present*, now, and abide as privileged reminders of a wholeness beyond all thinking and control.

As a first step toward making this learning real for yourself, can you recall an incident or special moment in childhood where the feel of it still remains vivid inside you? Most of us easily remember times of trauma where the ache of terror comes rushing back like tearing the scab off a wound. But let us set that kind of remembering aside for now and direct attention toward experiencing where you were filled with wonder, awe, opening in delight, "letting go." Most of all, can you recall a time when the feel of a situation or event carried you totally beyond the need for any thinking about it. You were "in it" in a bodily-felt way, like relishing the rush of being on a swing and delighting in nothing more than the swinging itself. Take time right now to recall some such childhood experience.

As you do this, can you notice "how your body is feeling the experience," not just then but now as well? What is it like inside, allowing this "past" moment to fill out and be known? How is your body in this remembering? What's going on in your head?

I recall once, during a workshop, asking for some reaction to a simple exercise such as this. One participant responded immediately that her body felt relaxed, open, totally present while her thinking head was "out to lunch!" We all laughed at the humor of her observation, probably because the response was so accurate. None of us at the time was attempting to downplay the vital role of reason, only to locate it as an important part of human awareness. We all know in our bones that there is yet another world beyond thinking and control. The way into this lies through that special knowing in our bodies which has already begun to surface during moments of childhood wonder.

Now, what's the point of all this? After many years teaching adults to focus, I know most have had "letting go" type experiences into the beauty of nature, so wonder is no stranger in their lives. But so often adults fail to realize that such experience can be a helpful step toward Focusing on painful issues that they block or avoid when trying to focus. What I have found is that if an adult can, once again, regain a body-feel for "letting go" by beginning with something not so threatening, such as experiences in nature of special childhood moments of delight, then this provides a concrete body-sense for allowing muscles to relax and emptying the head of chatter. Such an exercise in no way forces grace to happen, of course, but it creates a climate of body-openness. This can be compared to reactivating the feel for typing or skating after years of neglect. *Our bodies know the right way, the best positioning for wholeness,* but so often our heads are filled with "catastrophic expectations" and these, unfortunately, rule the day. Rather than attending to what our bodies really know about some current situation in life, we dangle, instead, like helpless marionettes from the rabid firestorm of fear raging in our brains.

Yet, the experience of how to do it already is in us. Recalling experiences of wonder from childhood can re-present the more open physical posture and feel of being present, of "letting go" without thinking or verbalizing. With that familiar learning renewed, attention then can be turned toward "putting your arm around" some painful issue being held at arm's length. This is the "Caring-Feeling-Presence" step we often need in Focusing. Sometimes having another person lead you also helps. Support like this often makes radical breakthroughs possible. Feelings that have been stuck for years finally get a chance to speak and be heard. I would hope that recalling some of my own searching to understand these steps may clarify them for you as well.

I believe wonder is a great grace, especially in a child's life, because it implants a deep hunger and direction for later living. It is a first critical step which, if nourished, can lay a solid foundation for future spiritual growth. But as adults, we need to take further steps and I have had to labor not to lose, but deepen and grow from these learnings of my youth.

For most of us, life invariably brings painful and frightening experiences that we react to with strong feelings. Since we rarely have been taught to be with such feelings in a Focusing way so they can change, we continue for years to carry them around inside like open sores. They may be small wounds, but even an insignificant cut needs to heal properly or the body's continued well-being can be jeopardized.

For years, I kept wondering why my wounds were not healing, given all the praying I was doing. The frustration stemming from this output of effort with such negligible results led me to begin searching elsewhere for clues to change. Some inner voice kept telling me there was a healing resource in my childhood experience of "just being in" and not trying myself to fix or solve things, laying my "control trip" on God. But how to proceed? How could I deliberately let go this way into feeling something that really hurt or scared me? I could find no invitation or openness in myself to be with what was painful in the same way I was drawn toward just being in the beauty of nature. How could I do this with something difficult when my immediate response was to push away or try to distract myself from it?

Then one day while attempting to focus and at the same time finding that I was resisting the process, a childhood image from some idle, long-gone summer came to mind. In it, I was lying on a rubber raft, sleepily floating near the lake shore. Gusty breezes kept pushing me further out into the deep where I didn't want to go. Finally, the tiresome effort to keep holding myself near the edge of the lake combined with the drowsy warmth of the sun began taking their toll. I said: "to heck with it." No longer struggling, I allowed myself simply to be in what was happening—breeze and all. I then drifted on the lake, taking direction from the wind which blew me where it willed. With this came an indescribable breakdown of barriers and a profound sense of oneness. The sun, wind and water felt like they were as much *in* me as outside me.

As this experience came back, I recalled how I had felt inside as body tightness eased with the letting-go of thinking and willing it. It was like all my pores could open and allow whatever surrounded me to get inside. I remember how reassuring it felt to bring this back once more. Beauty and nature had always been easy to open into this way. No desire came to name it, figure it out, change or analyze it. No longer trying to control but being open, caring, and to that extent "vulnerable,"— all these important clues which felt on target.

Yet, at the same time something more still was needed, a further step beyond this bodily-felt letting go. I knew I had to abandon trying to "fix the feeling," just as I had let go of trying to fix the wind and hold my position against the current on the lake. That part of the image and memory felt right. But how could I do this with painful, difficult inside feelings that I was accustomed to holding at arm's length? Over and over I asked myself: "Is it really possible to let go into *negative* feelings and fears in the same way I have done all my life with nature and beauty? Is there some way to risk not controlling pain, not pushing away the scary things, the self-doubts and the incomprehensible in life as these are present within me right now? The shadow side is as real as beauty in nature *but I'm not owning it or letting it speak to me.* What must I still do in order to let this happen?"

Then months later, during a Focusing session on this same gnawing problem, the image of a crying child came as an answer—a child simply needing to be held lovingly without words. I followed through, trying to create the *feeling-climate* I would want to communicate to a hurting child, but now around issues and feelings in my life that would surface while I was Focusing. These were feelings I instinctively resisted letting go into. But now I tried to imagine the issues I was Focusing on, yet also holding back from, as a child who needed to *feel* my presence of openness, gentleness, tenderness, patient caring, listening—all without words or thinking. I tried to create an atmosphere of feeling-presence around the whole thing, not just thinking with my head but letting my body communicate this message. Sometimes I would even image myself holding or rocking the hurting or scared feelings like I would hold a crying child. I found it helped to place my hand in a gentle, stroking, caressing way on the part of my body where I could feel it the most. *It worked!* A crucial, perhaps the most important piece of the puzzle had fallen into place.

I found when creating this "Caring-Feeling-Presence" around an issue that I could risk letting go bodily into fear or pain just as I had opened to the wonder-filled childhood experience of nature. This friendly, gentle, tender touching of my own hurting place by me made the difference! Within this climate I could let go into really holding them, feeling how I carried them inside me and allow them time, eventually, to tell me their stories and personal meaning. Holding these negative experiences like I would hold a hurting child seemed to be so concrete and real for me that it eased the resistance to being with them in Focusing.

I realize each person must find his or her own way of owning and listening to the shadow side of themselves. We all try to hold this seeming "demon" at arm's length, yet maturing wholeness can never grow in us without some sort of "friendly hearing." Whenever this happens, there is always a quantum leap in personal/spiritual development.

I hope these learnings from my childhood encourage those of you who work with or have your own children, grandchildren, nieces or nephews to nourish their appetite for wonder—an important doorway to Focusing and spiritual growth. Maybe you can help them find that special place in the garden or by a window on a rainy day, in the park or with a school project where letting go might happen. Letting go into the mystery of some flower or silhouetted spider web, a creative risk or some snow-etched branch may penetrate and teach that child more than all your ideas or words could ever convey.

Learning to let go into nature, beauty, excitement and wonder are a child's doorway into Focusing. With this foundation of trust and enlarged-self to fall back on as they grow older and the "slings and arrows of outrageous fortune" begin to hit, they can be guided to use the same letting-go process with hurting, scary places. Children, today more than ever, need the personal, caring presence of adults. This tells them something about themselves in their body that nothing else can.

It is always worth taking time to lead a child to the doorway of Mystery and then wait there together in wonder. My hope is that what I recalled and reflected upon in these pages may support some parent's lonely struggle to penetrate and balance the overwhelming noise and constant busyness that dulls our presence to children. Perhaps you, too, will be moved to invite some child into a world more exciting than all this clutter—the world of wonder in that child.

Chapter 3

Focusing: A Process of Gifting Our Children with Themselves

How Adults Can Journey with Young People

ONE AFTERNOON TOWARD THE END OF A SIX-DAY "BIO-SPIRITUALITY Through Focusing" program, a young woman stopped me in the hall and asked if I had a few minutes to talk. She identified herself as an elementary school principal and told me one of her jobs was dealing with problem children. Then she quietly looked at me with tears in her eyes and said, "I just want to say, thank you, for all the children you have reached this week." I guess I looked a bit confused so she continued.

> I am in charge of a school in an upper-middle-class area, largely populated by professionals. Hardly what anyone would call a "deprived" class of people. These kids appear to have everything. Yet, this week I have realized more than ever before just how deprived they really are, which is something I have been suspecting for a long time, but just couldn't put my finger on. Gradually, as this week unfolded, I have come to understand what a very special little boy said to me only a couple of weeks ago. This child is so bright, sensitive, and promising, and had always been a top student when things started to change a few months ago. Increasingly homework is neglected. He is becoming a troublemaker with other children, even in his family as well, and his parents are mystified and asking me for help. In the classroom his behavior and cooperation is deteriorating every day. Just a couple of days before I came here, I called him into my office again, not really knowing what to do. As he sat there before me with his eyes cast down and his shoulders slumped, in desperation I said: "Can you tell me how I can help you?" Without looking up he shrugged

34

an "I don't know," but seemed to go deep inside himself for a long time. I didn't break the silence. Then ever so thoughtfully, out of some place deep down, he said: "Inside me it feels like a mistake that I was born, because everybody wants me to be somebody else."

I stood there stunned, as my eyes watered up, too. Finally she broke the silence. "I suppose another reason I stopped you was to tell you and Gloria that I now know how to be with him so maybe he can find support for holding on to himself. Maybe through me he will feel someone does prize him for who he really is. Perhaps, someday he might grow to feel inside he isn't a mistake."

Even deeper than the fear of starving, of being abandoned, or of never being able to grow up because of some war or environmental disaster lies the fear of never being able to grow into being who I really am. Children the world over, but especially in the more affluent, technological societies, feel deeply afraid and confused by this fear. Most often they are out of touch with it at the conscious level, even though they carry it in their little bodies. As they grow up carrying this fear and confusion it affects entire cultures, like our own, because all their relationships—family, school, community, work—are affected. It tones everything with an underlying tension and violence, continually erupting on the surface in personal and social destruction. The little boy in the principal's school is no isolated example.

Without in any way tuning out the cries of millions of suffering children whose hunger, neglect, chemical addictions, appalling lack of health care and educational opportunities are a scandal in our country, I am trying to be a voice here on behalf of an even more pervasive pain. This is an agony carried in all children, even those whose basic needs are well answered, when they are deprived of their own spirit.

When we are small and helpless, totally at the mercy of our environment, we submit to all the more powerful persons who tell us in a million ways that it is not OK to be congruent with our own unique spirit, let alone live this realness as the way a human being is supposed to grow up and live with other human beings. But what a price society pays as the more deeply deprived lash out as soon as they gain some power, if only with larger and stronger bodies.

It erupts not only in rage and violence as they grow older, but in paralyzing fears and the inability to be creative, grow and change in relationships. Sometimes, as adults, this inner deprivation manifests itself in an unaccountable and mysterious lack of energy, a lethargy; or in just the opposite extreme in compulsive, obsessive activity.

Through the women's movement, many women have grown to recognize this profound deprivation in their lives. But men are still largely unaware of what this loss is doing to them—and to the rest of us. Over my lifetime as a companion in growth for many people, the most significant loss I have noticed in men I might describe as follows:

It seems to me that boys and young men need to absorb from an older man's body-presence a "permission," a confirmation, even a felt "his strong arm's around me message" that to be "my own man" I have got to go on what may be a risky, even frightening inner journey. Boys need to feel from the older man, "this is the way men find their strength and courage by walking through this dark night in themselves." In fact, the young boy needs to feel bodily the older man's presence and support as he risks this primal venture into his own self-awareness. He needs to feel in his body that it is time to set forth and that he is not alone. This is almost totally missing in our culture, because it means being very vulnerable and open to all of one's fears and limitations as an appropriate male role in order to "own" them and to find in that "owning" process one's true male identity and strength. Older men must not only model but physically accompany boys and young men on this journey for as long as it takes. Unless they do, these boys as they grow up will not find their true masculine identity in learning how to carry in their bodies the burden and pain (as well as joy and strength) of the inner freedom that comes with bodily "owning" their own unique masculine spirit. This is not something that can be taught from a book, nor by a woman. Without it their body lacks the inner strength, the "toughness" which is absolutely necessary for male moral and spiritual leadership. In any healthy society there must be men and women who are life-givers, not just life-absorbers. There must be people who discover in their bones that opposition, adversity, not having answers, not being understood, etc., are not walls that block life and growth, but, in fact, are doorways if we carry them and listen to them in the right way in our bodies. Early in life, having been guided on this journey by an older, more experienced person of their own sex, they find their own unique male or female way, not to be frightened of life and what they feel. Then, as adults, they carry in their bodies that deep, inner resource and its energy, instead of a debilitating inner war or emptiness. This sustaining emotional reservoir, rooted in the body's experience, can absorb rejection and pain without falling apart or resorting to addictive, numbing behaviors. That person has found and bodily "owned" their own unique spirit and has learned that within the very feelings of fear or pain lies the doorway. As St. Paul would put it, "when I am weak, then am I strong." The male in our society continues to be taught by the acceptable male model to deny or hide weakness, especially from himself, and in this lethal role never discovers his real strength. This is a cultural disaster, emasculating male spiritual and moral leadership in parenting, politics, business, religion, health care, and education.

How well I remember the hundreds of hours I spent as a high school counselor in a college prep listening to the confused pain of this profound deprivation in so many of the boys who came from fine backgrounds and were being given one of the best educational opportunities available. Yet over and over again I was hearing confusion and pain as every cell in their being was telling them they were born on this earth to discover and be true to their own spirits, while the whole world around them seemed hell-bent on blocking that journey.

When any of us are taught to deny, reject or in some way numb out what we feel because it "doesn't fit in," (which is not the same as "acting out") it feels like the very core of our being, the whole organism's feel for why one exists at all, is being violated. Great masses of the world's helpless children feel trapped, helpless, profoundly violated and denied their very identity by the way our adult world rapes their spirit. They feel frustration and rejection of their unique and precious journey into themselves, a gift to them by life itself and held within the consciousness of every cell of their being. Day after day, they are told, "this is who you are," instead of being journeyed with to discover that for themselves. Day in and day out home, school and church tell them not to "own" what their body knows is real for them, but instead to forget that and listen to whom we tell them they "should be."

The cry of the children of this planet is not just for food and health and safety to survive. Not just for a body that is not abused, but for a spirit that is not violated by what we call parenting, education and religion. We adults who carry those wounds of violation in our bodies today must become the voice of protest for the children whose helpless pain, whose rage and sense of hopelessness can only find a crusade for change in us. Their confusion and despair as it touches our bodies must create a new world around them that says: "it's not only OK for you to discover who you are by "owning" your feelings but it would be exciting and fun for me to be with you on this journey. Then together we both can enjoy the story of who you are as it unfolds."

Most people really want to love children. It is just that all they know is what they were taught—the myth of dominance. We must be that voice from the inside, not only to care for our own inner child but for all the children. A voice that says loudly and clearly—"there is an alternative."

Nothing so stirs us to act than the abuse, neglect and deprivation of children because we know without even needing to think about it that they are our future. What happens to them now is happening to our body as it will live on through them into the years ahead. Their bodies are our physical presence on this planet after ours have withered away and turned to dust. What legacy have we given them? What wisdom and life-force have our body-presence to them invited into their hearts? What will they carry of us in their bodies into the future? Have you ever stopped and asked yourself: "What is going to be passed along to the next generation and maybe the next and the next in the bodies of the children I have interacted with during my life?"

Gloria Bruinix and her husband, Bill, who are Focusing Companions, have been so graced through Focusing that they are passing on this gift to neglected, abused and troubled kids in the "Focusing way" Gloria continues to describe here as we go further with our conversation.

Gloria, what have you learned most from Focusing that we adults need to know about helping children?

We have to teach children to believe in and know there is a special place inside each of them that has the answers they are looking for. This is where our adult teaching must be centered. There is a special place inside each child, inside each one of us, where we can listen and receive answers—answers that are very different from the ones we normally get from outside. These answers fit each of us just right. They are our very own personal answers.

You spoke earlier of the choice you made as a little girl for survival, a choice to play stupid, to give up your intelligence. That is a major decision for a child. I wonder how many children are forced into similar choices in order to survive. Right from the start, they are pushed away from their own unique gifts and direction in life. They are really denied their own spirit.

This is how children lose their own felt sense of themselves. We tell them how they should feel, when they should feel it, and why. Sometimes we even tell them what they should feel.

All of us as children start out really in touch with our bodies. We are able to cry when we are hungry, laugh when there is something funny to look at or when someone responds to us, express discomfort when we feel it. Then the adults come along and say, "you are spoiling that child," or "she rules this house," or similar statements. So, instead of responding to the child, we start to "know what is best for it." When it cries because it is hungry, we say, "sorry, not until four hours are up," or "you just ate; you can't be hungry." Perhaps the child is crying to be picked up and comforted but we "don't want to spoil it" so we let it cry. I hope that if I went to my family or friends and said, "I'm feeling lonely and want some company, help me to laugh and feel better," I hope they would respond to me. Or, if I said, "I'm not feeling quite right, I don't know what it is, but I would like to be given a hug right now," I believe they would listen to what I have to say and respond somehow. Even if it's just to acknowledge how crummy I feel. We do not always give babies that privilege. We say, "It spoils them."

What a privilege it must be for you to help children re-own their spirit by finding their own unique body-feel of themselves.

I am so excited about what's been happening with the children I work with. Even friends of mine are starting Focusing with their children. The son of one of them was stuck on a project for school, so she focused with him and he could feel that the subject he'd picked was boring. He changed to one that he could feel a lot of excitement with and everything then came easily. What a difference! All it took was listening to what was important to him as he felt it in his body.

Have you ever reflected on what makes the difference in being present to kids in a Focusing way? Your responses seem so ordinary, so simple. Can you share something from inside yourself about how you are "with" children that makes the difference?

As a child, I could feel two levels of being with people. One was I wanted people to be WITH me. I can think of an instance with my own son, Michael, when he was two and a half and I was a very busy mother. I can picture him sitting on the side of his bed and I was putting his socks on. The feet could have belonged to anyone. I was just putting the socks on. What a difference it could have made to both of us if I had been WITH him when I put his socks on. We would be doing it together. *It is acknowledging the person that mattered, not the act.*

How many times do we do things FOR our children because we are busy or want to be a good parent or whatever? It takes a little longer to be WITH a child, but it makes such a difference inside when the WITH acknowledges both of us. I would have let Michael pull them up himself and watch while he did it. I would have been able to listen to what he was saying as he did it. When I did it for him, I couldn't hear what he had to say. It was just another task. Both of us missed out. But, as a parent, it was up to me to know how to be present. The strange thing is, I don't think I would have been as tired at the end of the day because the stress of doing things for people wouldn't have been there. I would have received something, too. It is so empty to just DO.

Would you say more about being WITH a child? How does that feel inside you as an adult?

One of the questions I ask myself is: "Am I allowing that child to express him or herself, or am I standing in their way." If I am in their way, I promise myself to sit with that later in a Focusing way. If I am allowing them to be with what is real in themselves, then the next question for me is: "How can I help them to feel it inside?" One of the hardest things for us adults is to see the child as they are. One of the most plaintive cries from my own inner child is: "Can't you see who I am?" Maybe even more important: "Can't you feel who I am?"

In school we are taught to "think." But if we were allowed to learn facts with our body involved, we wouldn't have to go solely into our heads. All my life I've wanted to learn crocheting, but each time I tried, the instructions overwhelmed me—chain, double chain, slip. I was completely overwhelmed by the instructions. I tried so many times but gave up baffled. Then, just a couple of weeks ago my daughter, Jennifer, was crocheting and I told her how much I always wanted that. She said: "Watch how my needle goes and tell me what you see." I said: "You wrap, stick it through the hole, wrap it, take off 2 stitches, wrap it, 2 stitches—and then do it all again." I'm making my first-ever afghan blanket and it feels so precious to me because I was heard *at the level I needed to be heard at* by my daughter. She gave me such a gift.

Somehow I feel I had to wait all my life for that, and now I don't feel so impatient with myself if I don't catch on because I just haven't heard whatever it is the way I need to hear it. Now I can spend the energy looking for my way, rather than beating myself up for being stupid. Wouldn't it be wonderful if all children were taught through their way? How easy school would be for them.

Just the respect for a child's unique way of body-learning—that in itself is a gift. If only more parents could recognize this in their children, and in themselves! What have you learned about your own unique way of body-learning?

I am a pencil! This came in a Focusing I did. I didn't want to be a pencil. I wanted to be a computer that is complicated and can be rearranged and have magic inside that makes it hard for people to be with it. Or at least a quill pen with a wonderful feather. Something with class. A pencil is so ordinary. So mundane. So dull. Not a pencil! But the image would not go away, no matter how much I wanted to change it. So I stayed with "I am a pencil" for a while. There was a shift for me then, and I saw a picture of a very young child using a pencil and a very old person using it and everyone all ages being able to use it. It was not like a computer where there was a certain level of intelligence required. It was not like having a quill pen where having ink available was necessary. Anyone could use it, and if they made a mistake, they could erase it right away. It did not freeze up in the cold or melt in the sun. Too often we were asked as children to be radically different from who we really were. Our own uniqueness was taken from us and ignored. We were expected to conform but in a way that did not allow us to be who we really were. Focusing has made it possible for me to go back and listen to my pain and anger at being treated like that. I can now rejoice in "being a pencil." What a difference Focusing is making in my life!

Most of the time the things kids need help in "owning" in their bodies are very mundane, issues we would think unimportant.

Yes, but not unimportant to the child. For example, I often sit with them around what it feels like to be at school. Perhaps they have issues with teachers or children at their school, or even on the school bus. Before, I thought I had to fix all the things in their lives, but now I can just spend time listening to them, letting them hear for themselves what it really feels like for them. I find this so satisfying! Such joy! Every time they share themselves with me it feels like a little miracle. I've always known I can't change their situations. But helping them to know how they really feel about these situations and how they feel about themselves when they connect up to that special place inside themselves is so special and worthwhile to me.

You know, there is such respect for the child in what you are doing, Gloria. You honor the child's inner life. That is so rare. Part of that respect seems to be honesty. Authentic communication. It is important for adults, but doubly important when we are relating to children.

As a small child I can remember being open and wanting to share myself with other people, but sometimes they didn't want me. I could not see that their life was going in another direction and it didn't have anything to do with whether they did or did not love me. All I knew was I wanted to share myself with them and they said "No." Perhaps they were reading a book or just felt too tired, but adults rarely say where they are with children. They just say "No."

I was reading a magazine where a young mother was reviewing children's books and she wrote about a book that was a favorite of her daughter's. To illustrate how often her daughter read this book, she told a story. Her daughter wanted her to read it to her one more time, but the mother confessed in the article that she had read it so many times she did not want to read it again. What brought tears to my eyes was what she said to her daughter. "Sit over there in the chair and read it like a big girl." What a confusing message to that little girl. Her mother could have just shared how she did not want to read that book today because she had read it so many times, but perhaps another day she would feel different. This leaves the little girl the choice of reading the book alone or negotiating with her mother around a book that her mother would like to read. Maybe it was just the sharing with her mother that the little girl wanted!

You have told me many times that parents and teachers need to be free enough inside themselves to risk guiding, even if they do not do it perfectly, or they will never get started. As an adult trying to learn how to be with children in a Focusing way, you have had to Focus on your own fears of failing and the "shoulds" you were carrying.

This is so important. When I attend to the story in my anxiety about failing and all the "shoulds," then I am much freer to continue growing personally with the children. I've learned the hard way how essential it is that I listen to myself as well as to the child. Just last week I didn't do that with a little boy. I was very tired and didn't want to carry the video equipment up three flights of stairs, but thought I "should," so I overruled my tiredness and was out of touch with what I had done to myself. Because I had not listened to myself, I really listened to him very poorly. Then I felt the frustration after the session. I could feel how uncomfortable I was with what I had done and how ineffective it was. When I went home, Bill, my husband, asked me if I wanted to be with that in a Focusing way and I said, "yes." There had been a lot of imagery in Focusing around my relationship with this child. But in this instance, the words that came and fit were: "I was not with him because I was not with me."

What happens, Gloria, when a child is misbehaving and for the sake of order you have to intervene with some kind of discipline? How do you do that in a way that respects a child's feelings?

One of the sentences I use when a child is misbehaving is, "I do not blame you for what you are doing, but I am confused about what you need. Can you ask that special place inside what it wants to say?" If it feels quite long for me to put the "I do not blame you" part first, I simply start with "I am confused" or just say straight out, "What do you need?" *The key to any change in destructive behavior is staying with what the child feels in his or her body.* What do you need? When in conflict with a child, step back and ask them this question. They are fighting for something very important to them and so are you. Asking "What do you need?" helps us to NEGOTIATE instead of command and confront. Negotiating always takes in both people, which is so different from one winning, one losing.

One lady I knew spent Focusing time with a boy and just by staying with what was in his body, he didn't destroy toys the way he usually did. Instead, he put one together. He's always felt so frustrated before. But when he could be in touch with what really mattered to him and how it felt in his body, he didn't want to break anything.

Violence is a non-verbal way of expressing our outrage at what is happening to us. If we can allow our children to verbalize their outrage by helping them focus on how their bodies carry such anger and frustration, they will not have to resort to violence toward themselves or others.

When you recall your own experience of misbehaving as a child, what learnings can you draw from this experience?

I know what made me misbehave as a child! I was not allowed to say "No," but I still had "No" inside me, so I had no choice but to find a devious route so that I could still say no. We hear two-year-old's when they are going through the "terrible twos" saying "No" and are told by everyone we must not "let them get away with it." *We are trained NOT to listen by not being listened to when we were two.* This is where we start to lose ourselves. Our "No" is strong, but if we say it, we will be in trouble. I did a Focusing and I could feel "empty" in my stomach. It was a huge ball. I was doing an inventory, so asked it if it would be OK to put it aside for a moment. It started to shift, but as soon as it moved, I could hear this terrible scream coming from under it. I quickly put it back but it was too late. I had heard the scream and the word I was screaming was "No."

How many times as a child had I wanted to tell people "No"? No, I didn't want to do it, or go there, or behave in a certain way. It felt as if all the times I had wanted to say no were under this ball and it was now built up to a tremendous scream. I have a weight problem and I know it is because I eat the wrong foods. *But if I couldn't say "No" when I wanted to as a child, I can't say "No" to myself as an adult.* I either can or cannot say no. There is no way of saying "No" to myself unless I can say "No" to the people around me. If I bury the "No" I want to say to them, it is not available to me to say to myself, even if I need and want to say it to myself.

Instead of becoming upset the next time a child is misbehaving, think about what happened recently to him or her where s/he wanted to say "No" or where someone said "No" to the child. It may be something as simple as your saying "No" to a cookie or having to go to bed at a certain time. I am not saying you should not say "No" to children but, rather, recognize when they have a "No" inside them they are not saying, *and let them say it.* Let them be with their "No" and help them to feel it inside. Ask them if it would be OK to be with the "No," or whatever sentence they have, in a caring way. Then ask them if it has something it wants to tell them. This is the "more" we all want to experience inside ourselves. We don't want to be stuck in our behavior or just feel our feelings. We want to know the story of ourselves. The "more" of ourselves. Who are we? Why do we behave like that? This is the important part of our lives, and we can help children be there by listening differently to their behavior, instead of just seeing what they are doing and reacting to it. We can know they are trying to say "No" and help them find their own words. Their own story. This was what was missing in my life and this is what I wanted so desperately to have someone help me with. Children cannot be there on their own because at two years old, we train them not to be. All over the world, there are children going "No," and no one even acknowledges the "No."

One of the most discouraging things I experience is how families keep passing along destructive ways of being with themselves and one another. It's like a virus.

I dreamed there was a man in a boat kept there by handcuffs. He was in the water and I could hear him groaning with pain. I looked in the boat and his captors had put a heater in the bottom of the aluminum boat so that *the source of his comfort becomes the source of this pain.* He needed heat to survive, but it was torturing him to have the heat. Every now and again, he would go over the side of the boat to clean himself off. They brought him food regularly. When he was first captured, he would sit on the edge of the boat when the heater turned on. Then, as time went by, his spirit became more and more dejected and he would look after himself less and less until, finally, he just lay in the bottom of the boat and moaned. This is what I think happens in families. A family is the only source of comfort on a regular basis for a child. So, if it is very painful in that family, children are worn down until they can no longer find ways of not feeling the pain. They then endure until they can have a life of their own. When they do find their own life, they have no choice but to keep the pain going because by then their spirit is so far away from them they don't have any other choice.

I think this happens in adult relationships, too—marriages, religious communities, among priests in rectories, young adults in medical school or graduate studies, etc. Just a couple of weeks before Norman Cousins died, I read that he told an audience: "The important thing is what we do while we're alive. The great tragedy of life is not death, but what dies inside us while we

live." I think Focusing teaches kids as well as adults that whatever is real inside them does not have to die while they are alive.

Yes, so much dies inside children as they grow up. This is simply because they are not taught how to listen to whatever is real in their bodies and, of course, they rarely have anyone to journey with them when they come across the scary places. For example, Bill and I spend a lot of time Focusing on our old childhood nightmares. Our nightmares really fit our lives and the struggles we have had through them. For instance, my nightmare was a terrible fear of zombies. I would be petrified to be where I thought they could be. Mine lived at the top of our garden and at the top of our stairs. They were guaranteed to be there but they could also pop up somewhere else at any time. As a child, I was manipulated into not expressing my anger or my sadness. This made a deadness in me. Zombies are living dead! Now, I can say to myself, "Am I behaving like a zombie here?" My body knows when I am not feeling everything I feel, but before I spent time feeling my nightmare in a Focusing way, I was not aware I was deadening myself.

I believe that a child's nightmares are the body's last chance to try to keep that child in touch. My body was aware that this was the last chance to get my attention and help me listen to myself again. If I didn't listen, *then I had no choice but to become what that nightmare was!* My body wanted me to have the chance to be together again, so it gave me nightmares as a clue.

What a strange paradox that most adults try to comfort a child with a nightmare, which ends up communicating "Don't feel what you are feeling, it's only a bad dream, not real." Whereas, if the child had been taught how to create a caring-feeling-presence around other scary feelings, then the parent could suggest the same attitude here and help the child stay with the body-feel of the nightmare until it had time to tell its story. The body's attempt to clue the child in to something important would not have been lost.

I believe we could all benefit from listening to our nightmares. Our contact with ourselves is through everyday experiences, and until we learn to listen to our bodies we have no choice but to repeat unfinished experiences over and over again until they change in the way our body carries that unfinished-ness.

Even if I listen to my life as it is now, I will still, eventually, have to go back to where I split myself off from my own body wisdom and decided to go along with society or the family rules. What a difference it would make in our adult lives if, as children, we were helped to hear the message in our nightmare and did not have to carry that unfinished story around for years.

I did Focusing once with a 7-year-old boy and I just asked him if he felt safe enough to tell me about his nightmares. He said he did, so then I asked him how far away he needed to put the nightmare so it would not scare him any more. He said he would put it in the closet with his wrestlers and they would take care of it for him. He sat with that for a minute, and I asked him if it would be OK to bring the wrestlers and the nightmare over to the room we were in. He said, "Yes." I said, "Would it be OK to put it on the table?" "Yes." "Could you give it a hug the way you would hug your favorite stuffed animal?" "Yes." He then told me that the bad dream was about someone coming to chop off his father's arm. Then he said how scared he was when his father was drunk. He said he really was scared when he was in a car with his father when he was drunk. This had happened three times. "People should not drive when they are drinking." The next week I asked him if the bad dream bothered him anymore, and he said he did not have to sleep with his older brother anymore.

It is so hopeful to me that you are helping children learn to find meaning and direction in their pain, rather than running away from it.

When I was a child, I could see the pain that kept my family where it was. Everyone thinks they are escaping the pain by not feeling it. But, actually, *by not feeling it, it runs your life.* I did a Focusing with an ache in my stomach and the image that came was of me in a damp, dark, dismal prison. I could feel the "Why me?" in my body. I was gentle and caring with that and looked up when the warden came in. The warden was me. I was kept in the prison because I did not want to feel. As I looked out the window, I realized there were no bars. My worst fear is to have freedom so close but not be able to be free.

I was a prisoner of my own pain, but I thought I was free by not feeling it. It is the exact opposite. Freedom only comes when you allow yourself to feel the pain—otherwise, you are a prisoner of yourself. You are the worst warden imaginable because you know EXACTLY how you can torture yourself better than anyone else. For me to look at freedom rather than be free is worse than any pain I could imagine. We do this to ourselves because it takes this kind of pain to make us pay attention. Anything less and we could tolerate it or ignore it. It has to be the diabolical pain that is just right for us and only we know how to be the warden for it.

We are taught to push our worst fears away, but I believe that our worst fears are the body's way of telling us WHAT WE ARE DOING TO OURSELVES. If we listen to our worst fears, then we will know how we are perpetuating the misery in our lives. Such fears are our friends, not our enemies.

It must be so satisfying just to be with children in their real feelings and not be compelled to "save" them or try to "fix" their lives. They know their own answers. I am sure you find there is sometimes great wisdom in a child.

Yes. Just today I focused with a boy named Scott who was able to talk from inside about his grandfather being in the hospital with a heart attack and how scared he is that he'll die. I tried the approach of "just the two of us keeping his bad feeling company for a while." He sat with that for a while and then talked about a movie and a TV show where someone had died and the person blamed himself. We sat together for a few minutes and he just said, "There really isn't anything I can do." Something definitely shifted in him.

How important that experience was for Scott. We all know how children tend to blame themselves for death, divorce, and other family trauma. So many adults still carry that guilt inside them even years later. It goes on affecting their relationships, sometimes for their entire life. In closing, Gloria, is there anything you want to add to what you have already shared, any personal reflection or experience?

Yesterday, when I was at the hospital with our daughter, Jennifer, I could really appreciate Focusing. I felt as though I was on three levels. One level wanted so much to be a mother to Jennifer and tuck her in and comfort her, stroke her face and tell her how helpless I felt at not being able to alleviate her pain. The second level was a rage at not having a mother when I was young who was really there for me when I needed her. The third level was seeing my mother in bed suffering and me feeling helpless, but not knowing how to say it. It felt good to be able to put the second and third levels on the back burner and be really present to my daughter.

Afterward, I sat with how all that felt, and the sentence came: "Gloria, you take my breath away. You do what you need to do in spite of the pain. You know that being a mother to Jen will really, really hurt but you do it anyway."

I thought to myself, "What kind of drawing would I have done if someone who knew Focusing had helped me then?" What came were flames and the devil with his pitchfork in the corner. I would draw hell. That was what I live like when I can't say what I need to say that hurts so much inside. I could feel also that it would be a good place to stop drawing so that I could spend some time living the reality of my life. So, I urge someone who is doing Focusing with children, please to check when they come to an "unpleasant" or "ugly" drawing, to check with the child *and with themselves* as to whether they should go forward or whether to stop. I felt very content to stop, then, realizing I had a lot of listening to do around the "hell" I have lived *and it would have been wrong to rush me to a "nicer" place!*

Please be aware of *yourself* at all times as a guide because you have a tremendous responsibility to be with children *where they are.* If you feel uncomfortable about what they are drawing, own it and tell that place inside yourself you will come back and listen to it as soon as you can. *Then, listen to the child again. Be really present*—don't push, don't worry. Where they are is very comfortable as long as we facilitators don't get in the way. Remember, the body is very wise and won't leave us in places we can't handle unless we are pushed there by someone with a different agenda than our own. Let children be where they are and feel safe enough to share that.

As a child, I was stuck behind the pain of not being allowed to speak, trapped by the rules I had conformed to. If someone with Focusing had been around, what a difference it would have made to me. Instead, I had to build a wall around me because I wanted to say these sentences so badly, I thought they would just blurt out and I would not be able to stop crying and would make a fool of myself in front of everyone. I would be out of control, and I was frightened by the thought. I had so much built up inside that I couldn't say the sentence I needed to set myself free. There were people in my life who would have listened and probably given me a hug and a cuddle, but the pain was too much for me to handle and much, much too scary to go near by myself.

As I sat with the feeling of all this, a memory came of myself as a three-year-old child and how excited I would sometimes get. My mother would say: "We are going to take the bus to Bournemouth," which is about seven miles from where I lived, and I would run around getting myself ready and singing and just felt so full of life. Helping my mother get my little sister ready, I was so excited because I was going to see the sea! We lived near the English Channel and on the bus ride, just as we arrived in Bournemouth, we would come to the top of Bath Hill and there it was, the sea—glittering and blue, huge and wonderful. It has never failed to take my breath away, no matter what the season or the weather. I loved to go there in a storm when the waves were huge and roaring, with tremendous surf spraying us with a fine mist, even when we stood a long way back. To go there in the summertime when we could swim was ecstasy. Digging in the sand with hardly an inch between bodies. Fathers sitting in deck chairs with hankies on their heads with knots tied in each corner so they would stay on. Playing in the sea until I turned blue and my mother made me come out. I even have a photo of myself on the sand with my hat and coat on, it was so cold. But it was a place of wonder and excitement to me. And, if we were very lucky, there would be an ice cream cone that would melt all over me. The pure pleasure of just licking it. My sister, Paula, and I would see who could make theirs last the longest.

Sometimes, there was a Punch and Judy show to watch. I found the puppets rather frightening, but I was fascinated by the story each time. But what happened when I became excited was *my mother would start to get tired.* She'd say, "You make me tired to watch you, Gloria. Sit still, stand still. Stop." And I would see her droop. Then she would say, "I can't manage to go to Bournemouth, I don't have the energy. But we could go to Wimborne, instead." Wimborne was five miles away and not at all as exciting, but they did have a market there where they sold animals and flowers, and had a van where we could buy a cup of tea and a bun. But it was not the same as the sea for me, and I felt really sad that I had spoiled my chance to go. I would still be excited, though, and still be running around.

Sometimes, my mother would then say, "I am too tired to go to Wimborne, but we can go to Cannon Hill and have a picnic with the teddy bears." I really enjoyed this, too, but it was not the same as going to Bournemouth. We would put my sister in her pushcart (stroller) and walk about a mile to the woods near us, taking along extra food so that the teddy bears that lived there could have a picnic after we left. We would let them know the extra food was theirs by joining hands and singing the "Teddy Bear Picnic Song." This was a lot of fun, too. I was sure they were there because the food would be gone the next time we went.

Some days, my mother would be too tired for even this by the time I danced around and wore her out and she would say, "Now, I am too tired and we have to go to the green pit for a picnic." This was just at the top of our street and I knew the fairies lived in the green pit, so it was a special place to go. It was a little hollow and was very green and pretty and was the only place around that looked like that, so it made sense to me that fairies, elves and goblins lived there and I could make any wish I wanted to come true there. Sometimes, I would wish that I could go to Bournemouth.

It is so easy to blame children for how we are, how we feel, and what we do. After a while I stopped showing I was excited and tried to contain myself, so mother would not be tired out. I tried to learn to walk slowly and only do the things she wanted me to do. I learned not to show myself because then, maybe, perhaps, I would get what I really wanted. I felt it was my fault when I didn't. I couldn't see my mother as tired, sick, or just plain worn out. It was *my* fault and I could control the good things in my life by behaving better and listening better. But it was not as nice, as there was a piece of myself missing.

Not long ago, I spent some time Focusing on how it felt to be in the different places, and what made Bournemouth and the sea so special was the connection with my body. When I looked at the sea, something inside of me said, "This is life. This is really how life is. It just goes on and on. Sometimes in a raging mood or sometimes in a calm mood. You are born and you die." It was so calming and real to hear and feel this inside me. It was not at all the usual petrified or nervous way I habitually felt. I felt real there. I could hear the "more" of myself there.

In the other places, I was with people. But in Bournemouth, *I was with myself* and listening to the MORE of me. That was why it was so special. I could feel my own specialness there.

As a child, I felt like Eensy Weensy Spider climbing up the spout, and the rain that came and washed me out was an adult telling me I couldn't do or couldn't have what I so desperately needed. But each time, after I was washed back down the spout, I would climb back up again. This is to acknowledge the perseverance, courage and determination that I had as a child and that you all have in you. Even when there really isn't much hope of reaching the top of the spout, we all must try again and again to obtain what we so desperately need. My body never gave up on me to do what was right for me.

Each time we deal with a child, we can wash them back down the spout or help them reach the top. It all depends on whether we are willing to face the pain of not being seen, heard and acknowledged ourselves as children.

What a priceless opportunity we have to give birth to the Spirit in the spirit of countless youngsters. Our group is actually teaching both adults and children how to become whole not just by opening their minds, but by "owning" and thereby healing the destructive, hurting feelings they carry in their bodies AS THEIR WAY TO GROW SPIRITUALLY. In our culture, the parent, teacher or religious educator who is not terrified by all this is rare, indeed. But the religious and social implications of what we are risking are also staggering.

It sounds like we end where we began, with that special place inside each one of us.

Yes. I remember the first time I Focused in one of your workshops. What came and was connected to what I felt was a parade. Bands were playing, soldiers were marching, people were riding in cars and on horses, drums and bugles and bag-pipes with huge crowds lining the street. There was cheering, yelling, dancing and ticker tape falling from hundreds of windows overlooking the parade. And the message that came loud and clear was: "Inside yourself, Gloria, *THE WAR IS OVER!*"

My ultimate dream is that one day, children will be able to do Focusing with each other. And then the wars really *will* be over!

Chapter 4

At Last, the Missing Piece!

I WRITE WITH A HEAVY HEART AND A DEPTH OF SADNESS this January 1991 morning. An ache in the whole center part of my body cries out, not only for the suffering of all people caught up in another war as our planes and missiles begin to strike at Iraq. But inside there is a weeping for our planet, and what we continue to do to each other and to the gift of life we all share.

I had to hold these feelings gently and patiently in Focusing for a long time this morning before I could write. There was so much story in them that needed to be heard. What came first was the memory of a man who, like myself, sat at his desk in the English countryside in the 1940s as the German bombers thundered overhead toward London. He, too, was overwhelmed by the repetition of this madness as tons of bombs reined down on his beloved country and rumors about what was happening to the Jews of Europe slowly made their way across the Channel. The imminence of invasion hovered over his every waking moment. The man's name was Lancelot Law Whyte, a renowned physicist/philosopher and author of many books. He felt that his life work had brought him to a point where he understood enough of what was going on in the world and in human nature that he could accurately describe the psychological mistakes we all make that lead to violence and war. As a writer, he set out to propose an alternative for survival on this planet.

I got up and pulled his book from the case. For a long time I just sat at my desk looking at the cover, holding the body-feel I carried of those planes heading for Baghdad. Then the words came: "Look, over 50 years ago Whyte brilliantly exposed the terrible consequences of societies and relationships organized around the myth of dominance. Who listened to him? He knew what was off and where we had to change as he wrote his book, *The Next Development in Man.*[1] Today, the sexist title would be changed. But still, who even knows of this man? Where has his profound insight gotten us? How many people over these past 50 years have even read his book, let alone tried to build on it and implement his vision in the practical order?" Those discouraging words felt connected with how this new war sat inside me. So, I stayed with my feelings, of how pointless and fatiguing it all felt to continue with my own book. The feeling kept saying: "Life is so short, I'm getting old. There are so many other things I still want to do. I give them all up day after day to stay with this writing. . . . Why?"

And then the body-feel suddenly changed as the words came: "It's me he has changed, because everything I have done over the last 40 years has been to clarify, to go a step further and better implement how I carry him and what he said. The rightness of it, even his devastating critique of Christianity inspired me to give my life trying to get the church back on track. I wasn't discouraged by what he had said. In fact, I even went on to be ordained into the middle of the mess I knew the Church was in. So he *did reach somebody,* . . . and maybe my book will reach someone . . . and long after I'm gone someone with the talents at organization and communication which I don't have can take it the next practical step until the 'hundredth monkey' gets the message and we have a global shift that really makes a difference."

Needless to say, a few minutes ago as I sat with the body-feel that the above words try to describe, I could feel heaviness and sadness move into energy and an eagerness to write on. And then, as I was savoring these feelings while putting paper in the typewriter and rearranging my desk, the final piece clicked in. "I believe we have the missing piece that Whyte was unaware of 50 years ago. The piece to the puzzle that can make a real difference!" The experience of Focusing and the Focusing Companion relationship has taken us beyond theory into extraordinary changes in our lives. In a practical way, Focusing has given us access within our own bodies to the "Cosmic unification process," to use Whyte's phrase. That is the missing piece. We can move from lofty ideas and ideals of religions and philosophies to living them in the Body. We can move from our heads into our bodies with a healing process where the fears, hurts and violence lie. I sat stunned, looking out the window, but deep inside feeling what I already knew in my bones but did not yet understand until that moment.

Back now at my typewriter, I want to share in more detail what I just touched on. During the 1940s, Whyte could only analyze the problem as a scientist and philosopher, pointing to a rational alternative. As I write in early 1991, public television is airing guidelines for parents whose children are exposed to this new war. In them Mr. Rogers of "Mr. Rogers' Neighborhood" counsels parents to tell children they will be cared for, taking time to listen to their fears and encourage them to share whatever they are feeling. This is a big step from the neglect of the 40s and is certainly good as far as it goes. But today we can help parents understand that there is a unique personal story within each child's feelings. Children can be helped to own these feelings in their bodies, because being safe or cared for may not be the personal story these feelings actually stir up in the child. Who knows? Even the child does not know until such feelings have a chance to tell their personal meaning. Then, they shift inside in their own way . . . not because of parental reassurance or the imposition of their adult interpretation on the child. Obviously, young, helpless children are not going to reject their parent's attempt to comfort them. But that is not necessarily helping each little boy or girl process the unique personal experiences they carry inside themselves about this war. There is another critical step that must be recognized. One that moves us light years beyond this best-intentioned expression of the old myth of dominance as we again tell our children how they are feeling or should feel.

So often these days, as I experience the sincerity of Mr. Rogers and listen to what support groups do when they gather together, I cannot help but say: "So close, and yet so far from what we all need in order to turn this whole dynamic of dominance upside down." A listening that does not interrupt, advise nor interpret creates a safe atmosphere where sometimes we can spontaneously go inside and own what we feel. Sometimes, too, a memory, words, or something else might connect with the feelings and our story unfolds a step or two further. But until we understand how this process of congruence or wholeness actually goes forward inside us, and then recognize the supportive role of a certain kind of listening, we easily interfere with this process by what we say or do. For this reason, the process of congruence is haphazard at best, even when those around us are trying to help. Focusing provides a much more precise and accurate knowledge of how we can help each other to grow more whole.

Given the world that Whyte lived in 50 years ago, all he could do was to analyze and think it out. Now, although it's a well-kept secret, we have the "body technology," so to speak, to reclaim and reown the wisdom of our body. Today we know how to allow our body to guide us into the gift of unity inside ourselves and between each other. We have the first practical, although probably primitive steps, for implementing not through endless talk, but with our body presence to ourselves and each other, the vision of global unity, of a united nations.

Technology, in the sense of applied research, is not just coming of age in the world of computers, medicine, genetic research, electronics, etc. It is also occurring in the realm of human relationships, like our Bio-Spiritual Movement, where we are discovering ways of accessing the wisdom in our own bodies as integral cells of the Whole Body. Today we can take advantage of these practical steps, beginning to turn around the momentum of social and self destruction within our bodies that leads to war. In the book, *Bio-Spirituality*, which Peter Campbell and I wrote in 1985, we said: "People who are out of touch with themselves have no alternative except constantly to prepare for war."[2] Within us, around us, and even globally such out-of-touchness keeps repeating itself over and over again. And it will continue to do so unless our body-consciousness evolves beyond the myth of dominance. That quality of awareness is what Whyte called "unitary consciousness." It flows out of the changed perception and behavior we have toward one another and the world around us when wars inside us are healed. Focusing is the most practical and significant step I know of for healing inside wars and launching us into non-dominative models for all levels of human relationship. If we are ever to restore our sacred covenant with this earth, we must first begin with our own body.

This may seem a small beginning from the place inside us that feels so powerless and vulnerable. Yet, it is precisely within that place where two or three gather together in mutual vulnerability as Focusing Companions that invites the empowerment. The power that wholeness unleashes in us when we can risk owning bodily what is real among ourselves always amazes me. We do have an alternative that teaches us how to access the body/Body's ability to guide us toward unity and peace!

I am not saying the technology, technique or "teachable steps" dimension of Focusing is ever enough in itself to bring about the needed change. There is always the X-factor over which we have no control, the gift that enables us to risk entering into ourselves using these steps in the first place. We have no name for this "X-factor" that I know of, except for one drawn from religion. That name is "grace." Moreover, as I wrote in Chapter 3, the technique is never the same as the wisdom given to us in and through the body/Body. The technique does help us more effectively to create a climate of openness and listening, so we may be disposed to receive the gift of this wisdom.

But who among us wants to risk that vulnerability even on occasion, let alone as a way of life with each other? There is endless talk, as history repeats itself, about the ideal of peace. While churches lead their people in prayers for the miracle of peace, the wars rage on inside us, unattended, and ignored. No one seems to see the connection. We continue to behave as though the answer were always in some form of dominance, somewhere out there in the God we create for "our side" or in "smarter" bombs than the other side can get hold of.

Whyte was right in his awesome critique of our vain pursuit of ideals. They simply bypass "owning" how our body carries the opposite of the ideal and dissociate us more from what is real. Then our energy goes into protecting and maintaining this split inside ourselves. Incongruence becomes a way of life in the name of the ideal. Rather than face the imagined terror of actually opening to one's inner fear or hurt (step 4 of the Focusing process), we escape into an addictive quest for solace by absorbing some ideal which we imagine will enable us to overpower our inner demon. But the fatal flaw in pursuing ideals is that we never own the opposite of that ideal within ourselves, as well as tension between the two within us. When the process of wholeness is divided into its conflicting opposites, instead of owning the whole together with the tension as this actually resides in our body, we fuel the inner war. The denial of our fears, hates, anger, and hurts sharpens and preserves them inside us, while their body acceptance ("owning") transforms them through the healing power of grace. By striving for the ideal, we suppress the opposite in us. Eventually, this violence to ourselves boils over in destructive behavior. As Whyte put it: "Ideals which seek to deny their shadows eventually exhaust their own power, when the dissociated balance becomes unstable and the dark component seizes control."[3]

Whyte understood and could articulate this terrible dilemma. But at the same time he was unable to offer an effective psychological process in the body, one that could facilitate human wholeness. If he were alive today, he would recognize Gendlin's "Focusing" as the process of his "unitary consciousness." But he would be appalled to see the religions of the world still unaware of this "unification process," still contributing to the self-alienation that ironically spawns the violence they denounce. As Whyte wrote of Christianity:

> For all its superb aspirations, Christianity has not lessened war, disease, or hatred. It could not, for compassion is dishonest in the dissociated person; there is no honesty where unity is lacking . . . dissociated people deny their potential unity and lack the vitality to recover it; they find balm in the service of others. But the logic of fact is relentless. In rendering their own dissociation tolerable, they tend to perpetuate it in others. When self-sacrificing service expresses flight from personal despair, it is abortive, for it works to achieve its own doom.[4]

How well I remember 40 years ago as I entered the Jesuits, believing that if only I showed them what Whyte had written, then together we could work toward turning this whole thing around. They were intelligent men, and my vision was that we could begin guiding religious orders away from their inevitable decline and self-destruction. How little I knew at that time about the body's role in change.

Gendlin shows that by penetrating rather than fleeing from feelings of anger, hostility, or other negative feelings, one eventually can be drawn through to their hidden meanings. Then the potentially destructive energy we carry in these feelings is defused, loosens up, and softens in its power to destroy. The path to constructive change lies in bodily owning whatever is real, not in using some ideal to neglect, deny, avoid or repress how we carry the opposite inside us.

How often we still hear parents telling their children that "a *good* little boy or girl wouldn't feel that way toward so and so." This is where so much self-alienation gets passed on. Since nobody can ever measure up to ideals that are set before them, especially by religion, the insidiousness of a culture based on ideals is that it also feeds feelings of failure, low self-esteem, and self-hatred. We are disempowered and separated from an experience of the sacred within ourselves. We lose our own spirit. That precious inner companion is discovered precisely where we find ourselves poised for the next step, feeling the tension of two conflicting pulls, of transition, of unresolved problems. It is in this place of uncertainty, change, challenge, "call" that we are most alive and most in touch with our unique spirit's unfolding. But we have created religion as the refuge, the security blanket, the safe haven where we are not threatened—quite literally—by our own spirit struggling to be born in the Spirit.

What irony that we baptize as "spiritual" that which sprinkles holy water over this retreat from our own spirit, from "process," rather than valuing whatever plunges us into that which is "in tension" in our bodies. Given such brainwashing, it is no wonder that owning in one's body the terror of not having an answer, or the pain of being pulled in two directions, the scariness of being confused, or the helplessness of not knowing where to turn feels like the enemy to be run from, rather than the birthing process of our own spirit. All such cultural programming, much of it coming out of religion, erodes creativity and the energy we need in order to be open and available for new directions and answers.

This morning I received a letter from a public high school principal in which I could palpably feel the fatigue and confusion of being surrounded by a system that has disowned the birthing process of spirit. He wrote about the intensity of being immersed in the "dumping ground for all of society's ills," describing how it was getting harder and harder for him to walk into this day after day without any answers. "We used to teach Math, Science, English and History. Now we need to be some kind of miraculous midwife who assists in the birth of their values, their life-purpose, their ethics—even a powerful wisdom Presence that will free these kids from their addiction to self-destruction."

I paused with his words, thinking back to three little kids (who will soon bring their wounds into a high school like his), eyes red from crying, quiet, afraid, as I walked in on them at home a few weeks ago. Their mother had just told them "Daddy is going to move out and we will probably get a divorce." I think of the long, painful years that preceded this sad day. Endless talking, trips to counselors, trying to reason it out, third parties being brought in to hear both sides and explain each to the other. Desperate attempts on both sides to *make* things right. Yet, none of this seemed to do any good.

This is what I see all around from personal struggles and domestic differences to international conflict. Our cultural pattern is to put an end to conflict without ever risking an actual letting go into how it feels in our bodies. We "stuff" it, rather than opening it to the healing of grace. Most people seek a solution to the tension of opposites by trying to control the situation more effectively, instead of opening their body to a resolution in how they carry the conflict. At the level of body-feeling, this just builds higher, thicker walls between the conflicting parties as efforts to control one another intensify and each person feels the other's lack of vulnerability and availability. The procedure being used violates body language and the body's need for invitation and dialogue in order to avoid harm. It is like *telling* somebody "to relax," further fueling confusion in the message and mistrust in the relationship. Most interhuman problems flow out of this "body-feel" of someone excessively needing to control something important to someone else—like food, shelter, freedom, self-esteem, sex, work, family etc.

I have spent most of my professional and social life with well-educated people. Maybe it comes from years invested in education, or perhaps it is just a human trait, but we "schooled" people assume that we know what to do in most situations. Therefore, when a problem arises within ourselves or with others, our well-learned, educational patterns kick in automatically and we immediately start manipulating the problem into its proper solution. Control—either with our head, money, political clout, brawn or a combination—is our knee-jerk reaction. This is what education has taught us. Whether we do it with a veneer of propriety and manners or use more brutal force, this myth of dominance now imperils our very existence on this planet. The harder we try to operate this way, the worse it ultimately gets in the long run. Our children, however, are ready to be guided into an alternative which I call "letting the body-feel of gift (grace) guide us toward answers." In our pluralistic society, the whole thing can be secularized in education and taught from the earliest years as the "creative process," or "finding your own answers from the inside," or "letting your body guide you in learning." Religion can still call it "grace."

Over the years, I have seen the myth of dominance grow worse and worse as people struggle to save relationships in conflict, especially marriages. Their rejection of the body is as powerful as the excessive rationalism of Western education organized around the scientific method. Both have blocked and continue to block access to the body as a valid source of community building and as the vital human link which connects us to the wisdom of the Whole Body.

I think back to the Mom and Dad of those three children and how they did everything but be truly present in their bodies to how they carried the pain, fear and disappointment of their relationship. They refused to value these feelings as having anything to do with "fixing" the marriage, so deeply programmed by the myth of dominance was their approach to change. For them, not "working at fixing each other" was to give up on the marriage. Tragically, that was what destroyed it.

Most conflicts are only temporarily alleviated by control, and are usually made even worse as time permits them to boil beneath the surface. Where change is the next step, personally or socially, there will always be the tension of two directions—holding on to the past or going forward. It is intrinsic to life. We can find it in a timid child in class proudly knowing the answer and wanting so badly to raise her/his hand and at the same time feeling the fear of "What if I'm wrong and look stupid, or the kids laugh?" It is present in a retiree isolated within the security of a comfortable condo and enjoying no financial worries, being able to indulge a very self-centered lifestyle, and yet still feeling deep inside a pull to reach out and be present to the needs of others less fortunate. The tension between polarities that we feel in our bodies has its own way of signaling us that it's time to grow, to take another step forward in life. But we have never been taught to understand that tension is a friend, not an intruder; to discover it as a creative companion who will never leave us, rather than a nuisance or an enemy.

This is the next crucial step, and I call it "Learning to create a caring-feeling-presence" around this tension so you can risk owning whatever is real in your body. Most of us know nothing about the exciting new world this will open for us, because the myth of dominance so permeates all that we have been exposed to.

As one of our workshop participants wrote in her M.A. thesis,

> I believe our culture, scientific and industrial, in the Church and in the New Age Movement, has fostered an "out of body" experience. Not just the New Age Pollyannas of "love and light," (that reflect the ancient mind/body split) but also the insidious mind of the ordinary man (who considers himself grounded in the reality of the material) which is really fixated and addicted to the material *outside* his body. There is a denial of the body, especially the feeling/body in almost every corner of the Western world. This orientation has escalated to the point of almost total annihilation of our largest body, the Earth . . . you need only look in your experience to know that what we all do in the face of uncomfortable feelings *in our bodies* is deny them, run from them, stuff them with alcohol or food, blame them on someone else, or destructively express them in the form of neglect of our children, indifference and rage at our spouses, or global armaments and war with our brothers and sisters on this planet.[5]

It is not only neglect of our children, but the emotional, physical and sexual abuse of them that flows out of this inner-body denial as our pain and confusion pour out upon the weakest and most vulnerable around us. Groups like Covenant House speak of more than 300,000 kids on the streets of the United States alone, running away to escape this exploding deterioration of family life. These homeless kids, sometimes as young as 8 or 9, living on the streets alone, unloved, often abandoned, scared and so vulnerable to drugs, prostitution, alcohol, even murder are but a tip of the iceberg of this cultural disaster in our midst. Seldom are they abandoned nor do they run for reasons of poverty, as is often the case in less affluent countries. They run away trying to save their own precious spirit from the lethal effect of dominance gone berserk in their homes. It is hard to conceive that every few minutes, given the number of new homeless kids on the streets, a child runs away from home into even worse situations, hoping to save him/herself. The momentum of this destruction is not unrelated to a country which pours its human and material resources into armaments and war.

My thoughts go back as I write to a few months ago when a young mother came up to me filled with excitement and amazement, saying: "I finally get it!" I wasn't sure what her exclamation referred to, so I asked and she replied:

I have noticed that when my ten-year-old daughter gets a good grade in school, she immediately brings it to me in order to get my support and approval. She seems to need that from me, and I have been wondering about that. I tell her how proud I am of her and she just beams. I used to think this was my role. But lately I have been growing increasingly uncomfortable with responding the way I do.

Experiencing how Focusing feels inside me must have opened another option. I'm wondering if my approval when she gets good grades isn't being translated from her perspective as "good grades equals good person, loveable person, valued-by-Mom person. Poor grades mean unloveable person, something wrong with me, not a valued person." I notice she never shares anything about the projects and assignments she doesn't do so well on, and I think it is just as important that she knows I love her and value her even when things at school are not going that well. Now, I think I know how to open that kind of sharing and possible bond between us. I've decided that instead of giving her my approval for the good papers, I'm going to ask her if she would like to sit down with me and quietly take a moment to notice how getting a good paper feels inside. Then, I'll invite her to share that with me if she wants. I wonder whether my gradually showing her that what I really value is *her* having whatever her feelings happen to be, as well as our companionship in sharing what is real, that this will help her value herself for who she is—getting good grades or not getting good grades, feeling OK or not feeling OK.

The conviction in her voice told me how important a breakthrough this was for *gifting* her daughter with something she knew was not happening.

Children who learn that there is an alternative to dominance in their relationships by being introduced to Focusing know in their bones, after a time, that the kind of community they want in their lives does not come from control. This story about a thirteen-year-old boy who has been Focusing with his mother since he was six comes to mind.

One afternoon just before last Christmas, John was riding his bike around the neighborhood looking for his pal, Zach. He found him in a field, quietly watching for birds, which they both love, along with all kinds of other animals. Zach and John are in the school orchestra and the two of them share many sensitive interests together. John joined Zach and they hiked down into a wooded canyon to see where deer had rubbed their antlers on some trees. After roaming around together for a while, John left Zach and went back to get his bike. When he returned, two other neighborhood boys had joined Zach and the three of them started yelling at John and letting the air out of his tires. John told his mother later that all three kids were doing this to impress each other and show who was the toughest.

John left the group and returned home, feeling very hurt. He told his mother the details as they sat down together on the couch so he could be with his tears and sad feelings in a Focusing way. He was used to doing this when things were not going well. After a time he said: "I feel so hurt, so let down by Zach, so mad at him for being my friend and then acting like that." His mother noticed the relief that came with those words, but the story was still unfinished. Nothing else came with a little more sitting, and since it was time for her to prepare dinner, she asked John if he wanted to continue his Focusing on the kitchen stool while she started the evening meal. He knew something still felt incomplete, so he moved quietly into the kitchen with her.

After several more minutes she heard him say, ever so gently: "Sometime when we're alone, I'm going to let Zach know how hurt I feel. I'm going to ask him why he acts that way." That was the unfinished part, and when he had said those words, his feeling of incompleteness left. He went to play until dinner was ready, feeling very different from how he had been when he first came into the house. As time and circumstance permit, his mother is now introducing John and his brother and sister to a special nurturing period at the close of Focusing where the gift dimension and sacredness of bodily-felt change can be experienced by the child and then connected with their Christian faith tradition. This is an organic passing on of the faith within the healing and change children can experientially know in their bodies.

As the two of us look back to when we were thirteen, Zach and his buddies were a familiar scene, as bullies have been throughout recorded history. What young men, and increasingly today young women, do not feel the pressure to carve out their own nitch of dominance—through athletics, through the use of their wits, the beauty of their bodies, their brains, their ability to clown, etc., etc.? They are told by their environment a hundred times a day: "To be somebody is to dominate something or someone else in your little corner of the universe. Get busy with learning how to do it, and do it well, because you don't want to end up a nobody."

In 1988 the American Council of Education and UCLA's 23rd annual survey of 300,000 college freshmen and women entering 585 schools showed the most anxious and emotionally unstable group ever measured. The study found that the new college students reported more depression, feeling more overwhelmed and feeling less emotionally healthy than ever before. They also smoke more and 72% said, "Making more money" was their big reason for pursuing a degree. The myth still eats into generation after generation.

But imagine the self-possession, the development of an "OK-ness" with owning negative feelings rather than denying or running away from them that is growing in John. He does not have to dominate or be on top of what hurts him inside in order to be somebody. So there is no need to relate to the world around him in that way, either. If he can be in community within himself, chances are that this will flow out to everything else in his life, including the way he will want to learn. In what marvelous place within himself must this child stand at the tender age of thirteen in order to risk the vulnerability of sharing what is real inside himself with his neighborhood playmate who could reject him, laugh at him, or take advantage of

John's openness. Even for John to contemplate sharing his feeling openly, let alone feeling secure enough in being someone worthwhile with such feelings, takes an inner freedom and maturing self-identity lacking in most adults in our society—not to mention, teenagers. The implications of "family Focusing" for building healthy community and diminishing violence boggle the mind. This kind of strong self-identity grounded in feelings that might be ridiculed, especially by his peers, is a solid foundation for this boy's future—and for ours, if more of us could join him. What a priceless gift out of which any human being would be proud to act and choose.

Perhaps Zach and many others will reject John's outreach to create a different kind of community with them. It will not be easy for him, and it may be a lonesome trail. But the fact that this book can be written means that John is a lot more likely to have companions on his journey than we could have hoped for when we were thirteen. I am not worried about John. He knows now in his bones, even at thirteen, that there is an alternative. He has tasted that hope to which we are all called, and he will never be satisfied with the myth that destroys us.

The reason so many of us continue on this endless merry-go-round of destruction is because the value transmitters in our culture—like religion and education—are part of what brainwashes us into separating from body-knowing. They teach us instead to perceive that the answers to all problems in life lie somehow in fixing what is wrong, either fixing it ourselves, especially by thinking it out correctly, or getting a more powerful or intelligent fixer like God, teachers, counselors, clergy or parents to do the job for us. Money and political clout would be added to the list of "professional fixers" by many as almost indigenous to our culture.

The myth of dominance has so infiltrated both education and religion as we know them that by the time we are seven or eight years old, we have become addicted to fixing and know of no other alternative for problem-solving or searching for answers, even from our churches, who turn God into the "Super Fixer" in this same addictive mold. One of the reasons for this is that generous, dedicated people in education and religion who genuinely want to be open and grow do not know how limited and limiting the "scientific method" of cognitive understanding, prediction and control really is. All these various systems of dominance are so interlocked and interdependent with vested interest in retaining the status quo, we are overwhelmed.

Our educational system, which now has become the predominant cultural approach to learning anything, is based on this method whose aim is ultimately control, dominance. Our religious educators and leaders are for the most part well-educated products of this system, which permeates even the seminaries and religious formation programs. This has an enormous impact on their approach to religion, especially spirituality, because they are taught in a million different ways that fixing is the goal in whatever we do—children fixing, poor-people-fixing, injustice-fixing, self-fixing, praying-to-get-God-to-do-the-fixing, etc. This today is simply taken for granted as what we are all about if we are concerned, caring people. We are meant to be fixers as good Americans or good Christians—or both. It simply never dawns on us that there is a whole world of unexplored understanding beyond our "fixing ideals" that is available to us if we would listen to our bodies.

And the irony of all this, of course, in terms of what has happened to so much of religion, especially Christianity, is that this is the world within which we are meant to "know," in the Biblical sense, the reality of God's grace. This is the realm of knowing within which we let go of the clarity of clear mental concepts, prediction and control. This is the kingdom within, where one finds the pearl of great price in just owning and being in what is real. This is that place of wisdom beyond books, the center of learning in ourselves within which we are given the body-wisdom that makes it possible to evaluate what we come to in our rational thought processes. It is that dimension of human knowing that not only provides us with the means of personally evaluating as "on target" or "not on target" what our heads come up with. It is the other half of the "knowing equation" that makes integration of "mind and body" into life-giving wholeness. Without nurturing this vital life-enhancing wisdom that our body "in the Body" knows is necessary for wholeness, we make decisions that destroy us. And we become addicted to that destructive decision-making process.

I use the word "addicted" here intentionally, meaning by it the use of anything or anyone (including God) as a substitute for a growing congruence with the truth of myself—i.e., with what is real in me. In other words, how almost inevitable it is for a small child, as Gloria has said, to be told not to feel what they are feeling because it does not fit in, bothers someone, or does not match the moral or religiously-acceptable ideals that adults perceive the child should have. Very likely something does need to change; for example, children acting out their frustration in destructive behavior. But the starting point must be to help them (and any of us) own what is real inside us. Then once that is known and can tell us what it wants, very often what was fueling the behavior simply disappears or a more constructive alternative surfaces.

Helping us into body congruence with what in fact is real in our body and then continuing, if necessary, the same way with destructive behaviors is not yet a religious or educational value. Control through fixing is. No wonder, then, that at a very early age generation after generation get hooked on by-passing this owning process called "Focusing," and launch into patterns of destructive, addictive behaviors. The price tag in human suffering is incalculable.

Yes, there are social, economic, political, sexist, racial injustices. There is destructive human behavior all around us that needs to change. But the starting point for our effectively contributing to that change in such a way that we do not simply perpetuate addictive behavior by manipulating people and the environment in the name of righting the wrong must be an honest standing in the truth of ourselves. Daily we need to know exactly what is real in us and what we need to care for and listen to within ourselves before we do anything else. If we are out of touch inside, it is so easy to be doing the "right thing" for the wrong inside reason, ending up making ourselves and the whole situation worse. We can fall into this pathology individually, as families, as churches, even as nations when our culture, including our religions, leads us into living a lie. A lie in one area of our life leads to denials and lies in others unconsciously, especially under the self-deceptive cloak of religion or patriotism. There is simply no substitute for owning what is real in our bodies personally, as well as collectively, to live healthily, socially, spiritually and in every other way. It just makes sense.

Any alternative to the myth of dominance can only be experienced in the body, not merely described with words for the mind. This is because the alternative that we now write about touches our body-knowing of a situation, not our mental analysis of what needs to be fixed. Perhaps you can begin to feel this more embodied alternative to the myth of dominance by reading an account written by Elizabeth's mother, Marianne, as she guided her eldest son, David, in Focusing several years ago:

The minute I saw David across the school yard that fall afternoon three years ago, I knew immediately that he hadn't made the soccer team! I had come to pick him up on this last day of tryouts. As he walked toward the car with head down and his whole body slouching, I felt so bad for him. He had been excited about trying out and was optimistic about being chosen for the school team, but as he got in the car that day all he could say to me was, "Why is it taking you so long to start the car?"

On the way home, I was very tempted to say the usual things a mother says when she wants to comfort her child: "It's not so bad, David, lots of kids didn't make the team; there will be other tryouts and other games; this one really isn't all that important; just go out and play when we get home and you'll feel a lot better." But I didn't. An awareness that is growing stronger in me every day brought my attention to my gut area as I realized the best "comfort" I could give David right now would be to invite him to go inside himself and gently embrace the realness of his pain.

Because it hurt him so keenly, he was somewhat reluctant when I asked if he'd like to sit quietly for just a few moments with how he felt. But I could see him decide, even before we drove into the garage, that maybe he should try. I know he is learning that this way feels better inside. We went into his bedroom, sat on the floor and he talked awhile about the other kids who didn't make the team, how he didn't play very well that day and then he grew quiet and very still, and with the pain on his face came the tears. I suggested that he might be really gentle "with what it feels like now." After what seemed like a longer time than usual, he said so quietly, "I'm really going to miss the fun of being on the team."

What came to him was so simple, and he seemed so relieved! I asked if there was anything more inside that needed some attention and all he said was, "It feels so much better now." My own feelings were much more complicated. I thought he would feel rejected, not want to try out for any sport again, somehow be scarred for life. But as a child of 14, he told me his story and it was so simple and so different from what I expected.

As I sat with myself after David left, I realized that philosophically it's OK to say, "Oh, that's really not very important, David. After all, it's just a game." But on another level, an experiential level, there is much more involved than not making the soccer team. On that level there is a story waiting to be heard. Without gently allowing his story to surface, it can develop into an issue that blocks rather than frees him. It's so easy for all of us to dismiss these incidents as minor and not important, so that the ordinary stuff of childhood experience turns into a process of self-alienation rather than one of self-possession.

In a few weeks, David will be 15 years old. My hope is that he is learning another way of *being in* his hurts and disappointments. I believe that just as many of us were taught ever so gradually during our childhood to avoid, fear or distract ourselves from painful issues, David is just as gradually learning *a new pattern*. He is getting a *body-feel* for another approach to life's experience, a knowing to which he will be able to return over and over again during his teen years and for a lifetime. The learning for him that comes from, "It feels so much better now," teaches him that there is another, more hope-filled way that feels good.

It's always a blessing for me to see the results of our children's Focusing experiences. David went outside that afternoon, worked in the yard quietly by himself, stood tall as he walked around, and then talked so freely with us at supper that night. His story was allowed to move forward so that he could be more present to the rest of us. It freed him to grow rather than get stuck in sulking or taking it out on the other kids. This kind of growing creates life-giving community in our whole family.

* * * * *

Chapter 5

Focusing: The Body's Inner Climate for "Dwelling"

DAVE SAT UPRIGHT BEHIND THE WHEEL OF HIS CAR. SUDDENLY, he realized what was happening. Driving down the main street of town, he had paid little attention to traffic or any of the stoplights. Automatic reflexes took care of that for him. What riveted his gaze, though, again and again, were the faces of old people.

Dave, an athletic, middle-aged, successful businessman became aware of growing uneasiness. His eyes carefully noted everything about each aging figure, the unsteadiness, the loss of vitality and power, the canes. All this registered in a felt way as it never had before. The realization overwhelmed him so forcefully that he blinked to make sure he was awake. But the feeling in his stomach was too real to ignore. Dave knew that feeling very well. He'd known it many times as an officer in Vietnam. Fear of sudden death was one thing. But this was different. This was the fear of growing old. He shuddered at the similarity.

Talking with Emily that night did little to ease his uncomfortableness. If anything, it just made him argumentative because she really had no answers for his distress. Her friendly, comforting words made logical sense to his head but failed to soothe the troublesome mixture of fear, anger, and helplessness that just looking at old people had raised inside him.

It was at this time that Dave and his wife were scheduled to make one of our "Bio-Spirituality through Focusing" workshops. Here he learned how to be in touch with the way he carried this important life-issue in his body. He realized that he did not just think meaning in his mind, but carried it in his body as well. Gradually, as he focused, he began to understand that "felt meaning" was the hidden motivator in many of his relationships, career choices, business decisions and outlook on life.

In a nutshell, Focusing involves learning to hold the body-feel of what lies inside you in a more caring, open and gentle way. It is growing close to the inner-felt meaning that needs to be heard so, eventually, it can unfold and you carry it in a different way. That is important! Sometimes, external issues that disturb us remain the same. But if we carry them inside in a way that allows them to change and even surprise us with fresh meaning, that makes a real difference in how we feel. This is especially true of things we cannot change—like growing old, for example.

Generally, it helps to get your first experience in Focusing with someone who already knows how to focus. Such a person can help you attend more carefully to aspects of felt meaning you might overlook through inexperience or lack of attention. All I intend in this chapter is to provide a general idea about the process and help you identify something of what you are looking for inside yourself.

Let us turn now to six useful learnings which will help you create this different body-climate called "Focusing," in place of the old "fixing" or "numbing" with which most of us are familiar. These learnings may help you to begin dwelling inside yourself as you really are, and not merely as you think you are or ought to be.

Nurturing a Climate for "Dwelling"

1. Learning to sense how an issue *feels* in your body, not just what you think about it.
2. Learning to have a *"Caring-Feeling-Presence"* toward difficult issues inside you.
3. *"Owning"* your issue so it can tell its story.
4. Learning to tell when your issue has spoken and changed.
5. Learning never to push or force your issue to move (this is an important doorway into the life of Spirit.)
6. *Nurturing* the movement of Spirit in your body.

1. LEARNING TO SENSE HOW AN ISSUE FEELS IN YOUR BODY, NOT JUST WHAT YOU THINK ABOUT IT

Most of us spend so much time *thinking* about problems that we almost forget to be in touch with how we *feel* about the problem or how our body is carrying the issue. In fact, we sometimes place little value on this. "I need solutions, not more wallowing in my hurt confusion," is what we say. Such a sentiment is understandable. But it overlooks a very important clue about how change occurs in the way we feel about things.

Have you ever been in a situation where you felt bad about something, say, an unguarded remark that hurt someone or made you look silly? You felt embarrassed. Then, maybe a friend gave you all the reasons why you should not feel bad. Perhaps, this person even made an excellent case for the way you acted. Your mind assented to the accuracy or logic of what you heard. But you still went on feeling embarrassed or hurt. Have you ever experienced something like that?

This illustrates how the realms of *thinking* and *feeling response* not only differ, they do not even connect sometimes. Rational arguments rarely change your feelings. How your body feels about issues will not go away just because you think them out logically.

Dave felt uneasy and fearful about growing old. None of Emily's soothing, logical answers touched that. Neither did Dave's, for that matter. He could not *think* a solution to the uncomfortable meaning he carried in his body. So, the uneasiness remained locked in place and began to affect all of his relationships—at home, work, etc.

Focusing does not begin with a search for solutions. The starting point is not thinking out an answer to some difficulty. Instead, you set a more modest goal.

Turn your attention from the feverish search for answers and try to get in touch with what it feels like in your body to be carrying the particular issue you are Focusing on. Notice the texture of "feltness" that may be there. What can you sense physically as sensations in your body, if any are present? Is there tightness, heaviness, hollowness, perhaps a feeling of tears? Where in your body do you notice your body saying something in your breathing, eyes, muscles, digestion, bowels, etc.?

Then, be aware of whatever else is noticeable in a felt way about the issue you are Focusing on—uneasiness, loneliness, excitement, fear, distrust, anger, embarrassment, humor, warmth? Allow yourself quiet time to notice how you carry in a felt way the issue that holds your attention and interest. Remember, too, that Focusing is not just for working with difficult things. It is a way of being with anything that is important to you—creative projects, relationships you cherish, problems, challenges, new directions, disasters, disappointments or the beauty of nature.

The reason it is crucial to spend time with the body-feel of what is happening to you is because the unique meaning that is there, the "felt meaning," can only reveal itself when you are present and "owning" it. There is a marvelous resource of meaning, direction and surprise inside your body knowing. But it rarely gets a chance to speak unless you create a climate for that to happen. Focusing allows this to happen.

It is like setting the table just right for someone special who is coming to dinner. You do not throw things together any old way. You put out your best china, the silver is polished, the tablecloth clean, the flowers are just right, the wine carefully chosen. We need to be that way with ourselves sometimes, careful and attentive.

What Focusing teaches is that we can move beyond the dominance model when relating to ourselves if we are willing to try letting go of controlling everything with our thinking and understanding. In other words, if we will let go of trying to bring about changes in our feelings by thinking it right and, instead, utilize another knowing potential which Dr. Gendlin calls *"felt sensing."* What Gendlin has found is that we do not just think meaning in our minds, we carry it in our bodies as well!

Focusing teaches a practical, simple way of putting aside for the time being our principal mechanism of dominance and control—thinking and problem solving—and allows us to move into an entirely different process. This is an extraordinary step for most of us because we are so programmed to believe that thinking is the only way to be human and bring about change. What we fail to realize, however, is that the deeper answer to a problem often does not lie in its solution.

If you would like, at this time, stop reading for a moment, and see if you can touch the feeling side of some important issue in your life right now. Don't try to solve this if it's a problem. Just allow yourself a brief space in which to sit back, perhaps close your eyes, and notice how different issues feel inside you. Often it is easier to begin with something not painful or scary, like a get-together with a dear friend, an anticipated vacation, or something similar. Notice the special quality of these feelings. Next, try a problem area and let yourself become aware of what it is like to be carrying that inside you. Notice when you quietly attend to different issues in your life how they are being carried with their own unique body-feel or texture.

2. LEARNING TO HAVE A "CARING-FEELING-PRESENCE" TOWARD DIFFICULT ISSUES INSIDE YOU

This brings us to a very important part of Focusing. Often what you focus on may be scary, painful or difficult. Sometimes, the felt meanings which most need to be sat with are those that have been hidden for a long, long time. They are so unsettling, we do not want to get near them. We are afraid of being caught in a maelstrom of emotional wallowing that goes nowhere and just makes us feel worse.

But there is a strange paradox about the way we are created inside. It is a paradox which Dr. Gendlin clinically verified with numerous clients in the laboratory. What causes emotional blockage is neither past pain or trauma, nor our fear that this will gobble us up. Rather, it is being cut off from the body-meaning this has in our lives, being out of touch with what one might call our unique, personal "story." This is an amazing discovery.

The fear comes from *being out of touch* with the unknown, unavailable to hear the story in our catastrophic expectations. Whatever is down there *is you!* It is a pained, hurting, sometimes fear-filled part of your being, wanting to be respected, cared for and listened to by you. It does not want to be treated by you like the enemy.

Can you find some way to be gentle and caring, perhaps even a little bit friendly with some place like that inside yourself? Is there any image or inner posture that will help you be a little more welcoming of what you find so difficult and hard to live with in yourself? Some of our workshop participants have been helped by the question: "Can I be with this painful issue like I would be with a hurting child, perhaps holding it with care on my lap?" Once a woman in our workshop found this just too close, so she imagined patting it with her hand as it sat next to her. That was her way of trying to show openness and caring. Others have imagined sitting down as close to their pain as they can get, then letting go into the body-feel of not running from it. One laughingly admitted, "I can't let myself get anywhere near it, but at least I can wave as it goes by and hold the body-feel of doing that!"

Use whatever approach helps you be a little more open, gentle, and caring with your hurt. Be there in a way that is different from your usual attitude if perhaps you have ignored or pushed it away.

With difficult things, it is always helpful to ask yourself: "Is it OK to be with this?" Never try to bulldoze or push your way through to such closeness. If it is too scary, back off. Your defenses are there for a reason. Respect them. See, instead, if you can be, not with the issue that frightens you, but with the feeling of how difficult it is even to get near such pain. Find something in all of it with which you can be a little more open, even gentle, and start there.

Focusing is filled with respect. It never forces itself or you into inappropriate places. That is why finding your own way to be caring and gentle is so important. If you find even this is too scary, then you probably need someone who knows more about Focusing to sit with you while you try again.

"*Caring-Feeling-Presence*" is how I describe an alternate way of being with hurting places inside ourselves. Instead of running from or trying to control them, we look for a body approach that is different from pushing them aside. This is not a mental operation, like "thinking" we will be nice to them. It is sensing whether we can find any body-feel of openness, understanding, respect for, or gentleness toward feelings that we routinely ignore or reject.

One of the hardest things is finding a positive way to be with difficult feelings inside ourselves. Most of us were never taught how to do this as children. So we imitated the adults around us who routinely ran away from, numbed, or ignored their negative feelings. In this way we took on their addictive patterns and, if we are not careful, we will pass these same addictions on to our children. There is no time like the present to reverse this trend, and Focusing offers a way to do it. Chapter 7 will go into much more detail on how a Caring-Feeling-Presence teaches us how to dwell in whatever is real in our bodies.

3. "OWNING" YOUR ISSUE SO IT CAN TELL ITS STORY

When Dave made the workshop, he did not stop growing old. But the way he carried, and eventually "owned," his aging began to change. *"Owning"* is being in your body's awareness of an issue in a way that allows the body-feel of the whole thing to tell its story and thereby to change in the way it feels inside. Being caring and open with fear, frustration and helplessness put Dave in touch with an untold story in himself. How you carry an issue in your life *needs to tell its story.* What do we mean by that?

Did you ever look forward to hearing stories when you were little? You probably still enjoy them even now. What holds your attention in any good narrative? Certainly, not just the information. Above and beyond any content, there is the delicious sense of being caught up in some ongoing drama, the movement, the flow. You are sometimes surprised by unexpected twists and turns which carry you down unexplored avenues. Enticing doorways beckon. That is where the real spice of a story lies. It is in the irresistible sense of being drawn forward along some path of adventure, romance, mystery or scientific inquiry.

Felt meaning in your body includes just such a story quality. It is meant to move, to unfold, to lead you forward. Much of the pain in life occurs when body-meaning becomes blocked and cannot go anywhere. That is when we feel stifled, trapped, or "burned out."

Part of Focusing, then, is learning to recognize and respect this story dimension in your body. Any transformation in the way you carry an issue does not arrive because you think out some solution in your mind. Rather, Focusing creates a body attitude toward an issue so that in being allowed to tell its story, the blocked tension can release. Not *"solution"* but *"resolution."* That always feels better and eases stress.

But how does this happen? How can you create a climate for "owning" within which forward movement occurs?

It is really quite simple—*let go into the body-feel of whatever you happen to be Focusing on.* Your body tells you what to focus on through feelings and physical sensations like anger, joy, tight muscles or butterflies in the stomach. Your body gives you the priority when you take the time to listen.

What does that mean? Let us use an analogy. Do you know what it is like on a warm Spring day to be basking on a grassy hillside and just lying back to soak up the sun? Do you know how it feels to let go into the taste of a delicious hot fudge sundae or some other treat you especially enjoy? Most of the time you are caught up in it, wanting to be fully present so you can enjoy and savor every moment of it. You are not thinking or analyzing the experience. *You let go into the body-taste of it.*

Now, can you do a similar kind of letting go into the body-feel of whatever it is right at this moment that needs Focusing? Can you be in this without thinking or trying to manipulate or change it? Can you just be in your body's sense of whatever is there, like you would be in the warmth of the sun, the sound of music, or something similar?

Of course, it is natural to let go into things we like. Feelings of love, warmth, challenge, excitement, inquisitiveness, humor—most of us find it relatively easy to surrender into how our body carries these more positive experiences. But what about anger, frustration, loneliness, fear, jealousy, confusion? Can you let go into the body-feel of experiences such as these? That is more difficult for most of us. Yet, this is the path we must walk if their underlying story is ever to unfold.

Most people run away from being in their negative feelings because they have found from past experience that whenever they try to do this, they just wallow in their misery and go nowhere. The same feeling keeps repeating itself over and over again without changing. As a result, they are usually pretty gun-shy about getting near any negative feelings, because this just means more pain. So they keep repeating some addictive escape pattern that has numbed their hurt and kept them out of touch.

What Gendlin found was an important clue that unlocks the mystery of how feelings change in people. He discovered that our bodies hold the key to transformation *when we can allow felt meaning to unfold and tell its story.* Emotions like anger, fear, confusion, jealousy are just the more-recognized tip of how our bodies carry felt meaning. People usually spend a lifetime blown about by such emotions, trying to control them in various ways. Dr. Gendlin's research proved this is pointless and a waste of time.

Gendlin discovered a deeper layer of embodied knowing that lies beneath the more-readily-noticed emotions which float near the surface of body-awareness. When we can have a caring-feeling-presence for this deeper part of ourselves, allowing it to tell its story and move forward, then the jumbled emotions that sit on top of this can change as well. The secret lies not in *"having power over"* but in really *"listening to what your body has to say."*

How do you do this?—By first allowing yourself to be aware of whatever feelings you carry concerning an issue in your life—let us say, anger over something in your relationship with a significant person. This is where most people get stuck and just wallow in their anger. But in Focusing you ask yourself: "How do I feel about always being angry in this relationship?" A question like this allows the body-feel to widen inside you. It lets a kind of stillness grow around the sharp, white-hot point of anger so a broader body sense of *"all about me in this relationship"* can surface and be felt. The potential for change in feeling lies not in your anger, the tip of awareness, but in being drawn down through this anger into the wider *"felt sense"* of the whole relationship.

Your body already feels a lot more about this relationship than you can ever think in your mind. The trouble is that you rarely gain access to this wider knowledge (this "felt meaning," to use Gendlin's phrase) because you get side-tracked and caught up in the anger that sweeps all else aside. Anger is surely part of the picture. But it is *not the entire picture!* The potential for changing your anger (not just gaining control over it, repressing it, or escaping from it) lies in the broader felt meaning that your body carries. Focusing offers an opportunity to be in and own this wider felt sense to which we rarely attend.

Let us move now to the fourth learning which describes a little more what Focusing is all about.

4. LEARNING TO TELL WHEN YOUR ISSUE HAS SPOKEN AND CHANGED

Your issue speaks like a story *by moving forward* in the changing body feeling of it. The body carrying of what you are Focusing on feels different. You will usually notice this difference when a symbol comes and connects with your body's feel of the issue. Dr. Gendlin refers to such transformation as a "felt shift."

Whenever you take Focusing time to be with your body sense of an important issue in life, you give it an opportunity to speak. This is done through an *interaction* between some symbols, like a word, image, memory, tears, literally anything which spontaneously comes and connects with the body-feel of the issue you are staying with. Maybe it will come as tears or a bubbling sense of humor somewhere inside you. There is no set rule about how this body-meaning of yours will express itself. But, when a symbol does come that is right and "connects," you will recognize it by a physical release—e.g., in muscles, in slower breathing, easing of discomfort in the stomach, etc.—which says: "Yes, that's it, that fits with what this is all about." The connection may not make logical sense to your head, but it makes "felt-sense" in your body. Thus the "felt shift."

Difficult issues sometimes need to speak many times before there is any significant change. They do this by taking little steps, one symbol after another. For example, you might begin with a general feeling of *anger* about some relationship. When you sit with how that feels in your body for a while, you begin to notice a lot of *uncertainty* mixed in with the anger. Sitting with the body sense of uncertainty may reveal a further feeling of *helplessness*, followed by other steps and emotions as you are drawn further into the story that is you. This is the way your story unfolds, through a flow of symbols interacting with the current body-feel of the issue, changing the "felt-sense," step by step.

5. LEARNING NOT TO PUSH OR FORCE YOUR ISSUE TO MOVE

You cannot make your story move forward. *It moves itself!* You have absolutely no control over this process. The truth of this is the lesson we all refuse to own in our bodies over and over again, especially when we want to write the script our way. Focusing is like climbing into a canoe at the edge of some great river and paddling out into the middle. At first, you do a lot of the work. You paddle. You direct the canoe. But upon reaching the middle of the river, you place your paddle inside the canoe and allow the current to carry you where it will!

The surprising twists in direction, resolution of painful issues, the fresh meaning and direction which can emerge are *in no way* due to your power of manipulating the canoe. This is out of your hands, completely. Whatever comes is *grace*, a gift.

For most of us, Focusing is not complicated, just unfamiliar because the body feel of grace is so unfamiliar. The myth of dominance that we have been taught to live by, even "religiously," has seen to that. We resist the nakedness of such inward presence and its risk of deep faith. Something in us rebels at the vulnerability of letting go into the body feel of this truth in ourselves. Our very identity feels threatened. When this happens, *be gentle and caring with your resistance!* It is *a doorway, not a wall,* if you respect and own it in a caring and Focusing way. Remember, an untold story waits to be heard within that part of yourself.

6. NURTURING THE MOVEMENT OF SPIRIT IN YOUR BODY

When you stop Focusing, for whatever reason, always pause to take stock inside yourself. If no movement has yet occurred, then promise your unfinished place that you will return, and not reject or neglect it. Sometimes, asking how it needs to be cared for and carried in the interim helps create a bond of kinship.

If a "felt shift" or perhaps several shifts have occurred, then recall how it first felt inside as you began. After that, come to how it now feels in your body. Notice if there has been any difference, like easing of muscle tension, deeper breathing, pain subsiding, heaviness lifting, etc. We call this a "before and after checking."

Second, take time to savor this physical change: time to become anchored and grounded in the new body-feel so you can come back to it again, if appropriate, or simply return to be nurtured there.

Third, while you are allowing yourself time to become familiar with the body-feel of this inner landscape, let yourself become aware that your physical feel of this change toward more wholeness is the body-feel of grace. It is your personal and unique experience of a sacred gift within where you may dwell, as well as say, "Thank you."

The Depth and Breadth of Focusing

Body knowing is a rich, vibrant, untapped source of human meaning and direction in life. It contains a story hidden in the marrow of your bones—a story that connects you with the mystery of life and everything that exists, a story that, when unfolding, plunges your self-awareness deep into a Presence and Power of Life in your body that you will instinctively recognize as sacred. Focusing draws us into the mystery and gift of our body with a depth and richness we can never clearly understand or express. St. Paul tried to describe this "felt sense" of his own body being an integral cell "in" some Larger Body with the often-used expression in his letters, "in Christ." He even wrote of his own experience, "I live, no longer I, but Christ lives in me."[1] And he speaks many times of each of us being living "membranes"[2] or cells of this Larger Body, which he calls the Body of (the Whole) Christ. In the Acts of the Apostles he writes, "In him we live and move, in him we exist."[3] Focusing teaches us how to be inside ourselves in a way which opens us to this mystery, to the gift of our own existence and our profound cellular connection in the One Body with its meaning for our own individual lives. Irrespective of religious affiliation or interpretation, our shared humanity through our bodies can be made one in the body-experience of grace/gift. By entering our own bodies in a non-dominative way, we can discover who we really are, that we are not alone, nor impotent in our weakness, pain and struggle to grow. Rather, in Paul's language, we recognize ourselves as the "groaning" yet empowered Body of God in this world . . . Christ.

Focusing has taught me and those who are sharing their story in this book that we can move beyond the dominance model in relating to ourselves if we will let go of trying to control everything with our thinking. In other words, let go of trying to bring about change in how we feel about something through thinking it right and, instead, utilize another knowing potential we all have which Dr. Gendlin calls "felt sensing." This teaches us a practical, simple way of putting aside, for the time being, our principal controlling mechanism—our cognitive thought process—moving us into another process. Most of us are programmed into believing that thinking is the only way to be human and to bring about change. We are afraid to be with ourselves in any other way. Our culture has conditioned us into believing we will self-destruct when we let go of trying to control with our heads. We need to counteract this with a life-style, and a spirituality that teaches balance. It is OK not to control by thinking all the time.

Focusing has also taught us that understanding does go forward, even when we let go of trying to make it happen with our minds. Change does happen both intellectually and in our body, especially our feelings, when we let go of trying to control everything with cognitive thought. The understanding that comes in Focusing is often beyond containment in some idea or concept beyond just a cognitive grasp of its meaning, moving one's whole being with a depth and breadth far surpassing what any concepts or words could adequately express. In fact, this quality of understanding often feels like one has a toe in the door of some great mystery.

I remember, years ago, at the end of a workshop when an old man came up with a twinkle in his eye and gave me these words. He said they described what Focusing meant to him and were written by the poet W.B. Yeats. I have never had time to verify the author. Whether Yeats actually did write them or not, they do express so well a wisdom and balance Focusing can bring into our lives. With apologies for the sexist language, I share them with you.

> Guard me from the thoughts men think in the mind alone
> The man that sings a lasting song
> Thinks in the marrow bone.

Has there ever been a time in human history when the stakes were higher and the call more urgent for each of us to take time daily to dwell and listen in the marrow of our bones? Yeats' words are a timeless reminder of the song we all hope our lives might leave behind us—some wisdom that encourages others to "think in the marrow bone."

Rich Meanings of Focusing

As you have been reading and perhaps glanced at the steps in the Appendix B, the thought may have occurred to you, "This word, 'Focusing,' seems to refer to different emphases or facets of a process. It appears to stand for several things."

My response would be, "You are right." As I use it, first of all, "Focusing" is the word referring to a specific technique for facilitating body-awareness. It describes various steps (primarily developed by Eugene Gendlin) which help a person contact and hold the "felt sense" of something. It is an organized, highly-researched method for processing body-consciousness. Although over the last 30 years, through Gendlin's research and that of others, we have all learned a lot about technique, there is always more to learn. Focusing, as a technique of body-awareness steps, can evolve and can be improved upon. I do not claim my way is the only method or the last word.

Secondly, Focusing is here used as a term to describe the process of congruence. By congruence or wholeness I mean being able consciously to feel the "felt sense" of something physiologically and being able to let it symbolize itself accurately. That is what I often call "owning" in this book. This meaning of Focusing refers to the absolutely essential psychological body-process all human beings must participate in to grow into greater wholeness. It is not something we have a choice in if we want to become more integrated, individually and communally. It is the basic psychological dynamic of community—inner and outer. As human, we do not have a choice in this any more than we have a choice if we want to stay alive not to eat or sleep or to see without eyes. In this meaning, Focusing refers to the basic meat and potatoes of human development. Therefore, all exercises or lifestyles, whether in or out of a spiritual context, undertaken with the goal of healthy, human wholeness, cannot bypass this essential body-owning movement.

Thirdly, Focusing, as I use it, is a term referring to a wisdom given us in and through our body. It is a wisdom we discover on a journey no one can take for us or excuse us from making. We find it in our body because it is precisely our body that connects us to the Cosmic Body or, in St. Paul's language, the Body of the Whole Christ. This learning grows in us as the bridge grows, as we reconnect more organically with a Life Force, a flow of energy in this Larger Body within which, as Paul would say, "we live and move and have our very existence." This is the Christogenesis and Cosmogenesis of Teilhard de Chardin.

We can neglect or reject the gift of this wisdom by the way we choose to "own" or "disown" our body. For most of you who read this and can still connect to some degree with your body, Focusing, as Dr. Gendlin has found, concretely helps you reconnect so deeply that you can feel this bridge-building process physically. It is so much more than any idea or ideal, religious truth or vision. This actual physical feel gives you an experience of solidly reestablishing deep, conscious ties to your own body, to its wisdom and to your personal story in the Whole. Soon this experience expands into a "knowing" beyond intellectual knowing that, indeed, "my body IS the avenue of entry into the Mystery." Feelings of hopelessness, helplessness and isolation also dissipate as this covenant with your body "in" the Larger Body is renewed. Why? Because this wisdom of the Larger Body can now begin to flow in you since you are living a "yes" again to that most primal and sacred covenant we were all blessed with when we received our unique body-spirit in the Spirit. In this sense then, Focusing is a process of revelation in which we are gradually given the wisdom of the Body/body.

Fourthly, anytime you Focus, you take ownership of your own life. You take responsibility for discovering your own answers, for being true to and honoring your own spirit as it reveals and expresses itself through your body. Such action is a clear political and social statement against any system that does not support such a process of liberation. Focusing, as our group shares it with others, is an alternative to systems of oppression, co-dependence and manipulation which alienate us from the power of the Spirit within our own body-spirit. Therefore, it is intrinsically a social statement of liberation proclaimed through our body as we become more whole (holy) together.

Lastly, Focusing is a process of ongoing personal and social conversion in the sense that it becomes an alternative lifestyle moving us away from the overwhelming hegemony of dominance in all our relationships. It is conversion away from our tendency to write the script for everything ourselves, pushing, fixing, manipulating and trying to control what ultimately is the gift of personal and social wholeness or community. Focusing is conversion as a process of surrender, of letting go into whatever is real in our body-awareness in order that a power greater than ourselves may bless us with direction, answers, new life, unity. In Christian language, it is a body way of disposing or opening ourselves to the gift of God's grace, which always puts our lives a lot more on the line than doing the same "letting go" only mentally. It takes a lot more courage and believing that one "lives in Christ" to let go into the body-felt truth of oneself with the no-strings-attached attitude we try to cultivate in Focusing than to do this surrendering as "mental prayer."

Chapter 6

The Starting Point is Owning Bodily What Is Real

IF THERE IS ONE PIECE OF WISDOM, ONE LEARNING THAT I WOULD single out above all others in what Focusing has taught so many of us, it would be the title of this chapter. Why? Because body-"owning" turns the lie we often live in ourselves, with others or with the world around us upside down. It reverses the whole destructive dynamic of denial and moves us right into the truth of what we actually are carrying in our body.

Note that I have not said anything about this conforming or not conforming to "the facts" as others might see them. Nor have I said this is necessarily in conformity with whatever "objective" analysis might conclude. The reason these are not of concern here is that the truth that is our starting point for any change involving more than an idea resides in the whole human organism. In other words, how you are bodily carrying your interchange with the world around you, coming from the past as well as the present, is an enormously important part of who you are right now.

Getting in touch with who you actually are by discovering what your body knows and wants to tell you is essential for your own wholeness, as well as providing you with the only truthful launching pad for the next step in life. If you do not know where you stand, it is impossible to know how to live authentically, being true to your own spirit, or what your next step should be. "Where you stand" is always your own unique interpretation and body-feeling of the events and circumstances in your life. Sometimes it matches what other people think. Very often it does not. That is really not the issue when your life needs to move forward, as it must day by day. That starting point is your being congruent with what is real in you. That is the only sound psychological platform upon which to transcend limitations, as well as actualize the growth potential that is you.

In my experience, most of our interchange with the world around us, especially the interpersonal, ignores this. In varying degrees, these relationships are based on a lie—a projection, wishful thinking, someone else's perception, some script we have written years ago—all of them very often an organismic denial of what in fact our body knows is real. Our culture creates and supports this charade, which in time becomes so painful it propels us into addictive behaviors of all sorts to numb the hurt.

As I write, I cannot help but think back to the hundreds of times I have been accompanying someone in Focusing whose marriage or relationship to their church, job, or religious community was in trouble, and who, when they focused, found out that they were actually carrying needs from childhood mixed into this relationship. For example, I vividly remember Janet, a talented and attractive young woman in her late 20s, married only a few years. She wanted very badly to start a family and to put her career on hold for a few years until the children were older. However, she came to Focusing terribly distraught because her husband said she was driving him crazy and was not sure their marriage could last. Therefore, he did not think it right to bring children into this unresolved conflict. He complained about her over-solicitous care and constant fears that he would not come home from some work accident.

As she focused on her "felt sense" of the arguments and trouble that was erupting in their relationship, what came and fit this body sense was a memory. She clearly recalled how as a teenager one afternoon, her father, whom she loved very much, had given her definite instructions just before leaving on a business trip about when she was to come back from a party she was planning to attend that weekend. She had yelled at him, becoming angry with his restriction, made a scene about it, and had refused to kiss him goodbye as he left to catch his plane. On the business trip he suddenly and unexpectedly died of a heart attack. She never again saw him alive.

With that came tears, and I encouraged her to be gentle and caring with how that memory felt in her body, giving it time to be owned. It was not long before the words came, "Maybe it was my fault that Daddy had the heart attack, because I got him so upset when he left." I then asked her to check if it was OK to be with how that felt in her body, and since it was, she stayed with that in silence for several minutes. The tears subsided and she appeared deeply connected. Then she sighed as her body and breathing eased noticeably. Without leaving her deep in-touchness, and with her eyes still closed, she whispered: "Yes, that's it. I've been using Rick without knowing it to try to work through all this."

Again she paused, savoring the rightness of how these words now felt in her body. Then, opening her eyes and glancing my way, she commented:

No wonder he can't take it anymore and doesn't understand what's happened to our relationship. I've been afraid to even have an opinion around him for fear of disagreeing and having an argument. I've withdrawn into the fear that he would have an accident on the road or at work, and I never knew why I was so preoccupied with that. I've been dumping this unfinished thing about Dad's death and my guilt on the poor guy.

I did not have to suggest she stay with the feel of these words because they just drew her down into her body again. Closing her eyes, she fell silent again, taking time to relish the release this new step brought her. After a time, with a realness that I could feel in my own body, she concluded:

It feels like an enormous pressure has gone out of me and that I don't need to relate to Rick the way I have been doing. It feels also like my body is asking for time . . . lots of time . . . to be with this new place inside myself . . . time to get to know myself this different way and time to create new options. I think I should stop now, leave, and carry this home with me as a place I will care for and listen to!

So often, when I have the great privilege of journeying with people like Janet, because I am a priest and they openly discuss their spirituality with me, I find that religion frequently has become an accessory to this dishonesty, baptizing it as "religious" or virtuous in some way. When this happens, religion in that person's life becomes part of the pathology, feeding the breakdown of wholeness and community.

This reminds me of a workshop participant active in the peace movement telling the group after learning Focusing how he now knew why there were so many angry people in the peace and justice ministry of his church. He said this had always bothered him, experiencing how it ultimately undermined their dedication and commitment. "The same is true for so many in the women's movement," a woman sitting near him said.

> I have been active in working for women's rights for years, and I can see now what a difference it would make in our effectiveness if we were as committed to caring for and listening to our own anger and hurt as we are to this important cause. I think it would change the "feel" people have when they encounter many of us, as well as our tactics in trying to bring justice and peace to the world.

Nurturing a caring-feeling-presence around whatever is real in our bodies and giving them time each day to tell their story must become a way of life for all of us. This is a lifestyle of "invitation" to the grace that heals, changes and brings inner peace. It is this peace within us that ultimately brings healing and peace around us.

Conscious of the enormous social implications of what I am saying, the most incredibly exciting and hope-filled learning that comes from daily starting with bodily owning what is real is that one finds it is not necessary for things that are not all OK to be all OK in order to feel good about ourselves and at peace inside. For those of us who never even heard there was this alternative, the discovery feels like being born again. What is necessary is to be in touch with whatever is real bodily in a caring, open, listening way so that a kinship and trust can develop. One does not have to deny or run away from what the body feels in order to numb pain. Then the unfolding story that each of us is meant to be can go forward—warts, hurts, frustrations, and all. Our story is a human story wanting to unfold in the only way it can—humanly, with all the imperfections, disappointments and frailty of human existence. By blocking the pages turning and denying our only starting point—what is real—then emotional imbalance, addictive and destructive patterns of behavior, confusion and hopelessness invariably arise.

Because of our programming, we simply cannot believe, until we experience the opposite, that the starting point for effective and lasting improvement in our lives and that of others is not getting busy right now fixing everything and everybody, including ourselves. To break this pattern of dominance is extraordinarily difficult for the caregivers, the socially and environmentally sensitive, the religiously and ethically conditioned, and those whose lives are largely motivated by some "cause." People like that, and I certainly include myself, have absorbed with our mothers' milk an ideal, a myth grounded in an interpretation of Christianity that tells us how we are to live our lives, what spells success or failure according to this ideal, and how we are to proceed in living up to this goal. Deep down in us something tells us we need to be "fixing" (which, of course, we call caring, nurturing, teaching, counseling, etc.) in order to be what we "should be" and feel good about ourselves. The problem lies not in the model or life of Jesus, but in losing touch with owning bodily whatever is real as sacred and religious living, rather than assimilating dominance as the means to live and relate as Jesus lived and related.

Through the centuries, Christianity has developed a finely honed spirituality of control, sprinkling holy water over the myths of dominance and incongruence until they have become indistinguishable for the average person from Christianity itself. We baptized living a lie as Christian spirituality. Today, with our technological advances giving us massive ability to manipulate each other and the environment through the media, nuclear power, chemical production, global economic cartels, climate alteration, etc., millions of thoughtful people instinctively know something is wrong in Christianity or any other religion that feeds the dominance model. We can no longer risk the clear danger and destruction which this fuels in unsuspecting people, people who in their need and pain reach out for help and guidance to sick religions. Their disease is too lethal and contagious. The confusion this spawns is profound and universal. Within Christianity, for example, no person in history has so called out the best in people as Jesus Christ. Yet on the other hand, millions, even within the Christian churches, feel something is radically wrong at the very core of Christian life and spirituality. There seems to be some kind of untruth or unknown deviation at the core of things. Few have the time to figure it all out, so they reluctantly "hang in for the sake of their children," leave in disillusionment or anger, create their own version, wander into something that feels more "in tune," like Buddhism, or stay linked in some way with a church or religious community in order to follow through with their vocation of service. But inside there is so much suspicion and uneasiness that something is off track. I have heard this constant theme throughout my entire life as a priest.

The astonishing experience which Focusing teaches is exactly what St. Paul was trying to teach the early Christians about where to look for the reality of Christ—in the truthful owning of their own humanity. Teilhard de Chardin's and Eugene Gendlin's research, corroborated by many others, boils down to the same conclusion, although in very different language. Namely, that when we reject being congruent with what is real in our bodies, we fall off the track of human evolution's direction toward global and cosmic unity.

I know that owning what is real in my body, especially when I have the script written differently from what is actually happening, remains my most difficult challenge in life, even though I am committed to it and have been trying to live it for a number of years. But when the chips are down, everything in me still wants to rally around victory for my agenda. This is especially true if I perceive it through the eyes of my own conditioning as a "holy and just" cause. Not too long ago, I was struggling with letting go and really owning how I was carrying my relationship with a church group with whom I was working. I sat with it in a Focusing way several times, finally noticing resistance that I must not have wanted to let myself feel. Carrying the body-feel of the resistance around all day without anything happening, I took it to bed with me, letting it know I was not going to neglect it any longer and would try to listen. I drifted off to sleep, with this growing kinship as my last waking attempts to create a caring presence around it, when suddenly a few hours later I woke up feeling the need to write this down. These are the words which came to me, fit my body feel of the whole thing, changed that feeling as they were scribbled on the note pad by my bed, and brought to the surface what was previously completely unclear to me about why I had been resisting the owning process. What I had been feeling as "off track" and blocked in the group was also blocked in me and in need of telling me, as well as the group, its story through these words:

Maybe if Jesus were among us and speaking to us, He might say something like this: "Oh, you of little faith. Have I been with you so long and you still don't realize that you deny me, that you give me no place in the Inn when you not only deny your brokenness, but then go on to create me as the ideal parent, the loyal friend, the tender lover, the caring spouse you haven't had?

"Oh, you of little faith, how often you have created me as the fantasy of your unfulfilled dreams and pushed me away as I am, refusing me a place in your heart. Instead, you grasp at anything that keeps you from embracing me as I really exist in you. Even in my name, you use prayer to deny me room in your heart. How long will it be before you give me the acceptance, the caring, the open gentleness I long for within the fears and pain and incompleteness that is you?

"Oh, you of little faith. Do you not yet know that I am that terror of loneliness in your body? I am that emptiness that you feel. I am that sadness in your heart. I am those tears of frustration and anger. I am that place inside you where you feel there is no answer. And yet, when you feel me, you still push me away and do not understand.

"And you who claim to lead others to me and to know me, instead of knowing me in your own brokenness and then lovingly guiding others to find me in their brokenness, instead you use their needs and confusion to gain power for yourselves. You are like whited sepulchers. You give laws and words and pageantry and promises of the future, instead of the companionship of your own vulnerability which invites me and the power of my Spirit into your hearts. Woe to those who rape the pain of others with their power, their words and their false comfort, leaving them helpless, addicted in dependency and alone on their journey.

"Yes, the pearl of great price, the kingdom of heaven is, indeed, inside each of you if you do not run from it when you are fearful or pained in your body. I have emptied myself into your body, into all that is real in you—incomplete, unfinished, weak as you may be. And it is there and only there that you will find me as I really am—in my crucifixion and in the power of my resurrected Body. My Body now is your body. Your body now is my Body, which is being given for the life of the world. And so I pray that your inward eyes may be illumined in faith, that you may find me in owning my crucifixion in your own body. Then the Spirit will come and dwell in your hearts, and you will know the power of that hope to which you are called."

* * * * *

For a long, long time after putting down my pencil and pad I just sat on the edge of the bed, stunned and awed at the felt "rightness" of the words that had just been given me, words so personal and yet so universal in what has gotten off track in Christian spirituality.

Perhaps what matures in owning the real in our bodies is an experience of grace enfleshed in consciousness. The Word becoming flesh and dwelling in us. Our own self-awareness become enfleshed in Spirit. We have the opportunity, perhaps for the first time, of our body's consciousness becoming the bridge into the Mystery of God-with-us, Emmanuel. We become the heartbeat of the crucified and resurrected Body of the Whole Christ. The pulse of our humanity in all its incompleteness and brokenness, by its surrender to what is real in the Body—our body—is transformed into the Holy, the place of new beginnings.

But we can't recognize that place of new beginnings in us so long as we avoid owning what is real in ourselves, especially how we bodily carry the things that feel hopeless. Usually we have either given up on these, which is very different from actually owning them and allowing them to tell their story. Or we are killing ourselves and what is left of our relationships, frantically trying to fix what feels so bad. Without a mental health approach or a spirituality grounded in something like Focusing, we are never given the opportunity to discover an alternative route to change. Least of all would we ever be given the chance to find out for ourselves that the "bent-out-of-shape" things in life, many of which are simply an expression of the human condition and are not going to change anyway, can, in fact, when their story in us is listened to in the owning process, feel OK. In our culture, even religious people are so deprived in the body-feel of grace, that we need to be helped to discover it again in our bones in order to know we do not have to be fixers to feel good inside about ourselves. We do not need to name it religiously, but we do need to experience it enough that we know there is an alternative we can opt for.

Denial of what is real is the culprit, not human frailty, because it unleashes a blocked-up energy that lashes out in its pain, destroying everything in its wake. What sucks the life out of relationships is not human limitations and brokenness, but that depth of denial which penetrates even into the tissues of our body with a defiant rejection of what is really there. This disdain for our own body and its integral tie to the Larger Body echoes out into the cosmos with unfathomable reverberations. St. Paul writes of this rejection of what is real in our body as a rejection of the Body of Christ. This is a profound truth for Christians and non-Christians alike, if they understand Paul's meaning of Christ. It pierces to the core of our being in its implications for spiritual and planetary survival.

I am not saying that there is not a proper time and place for action. If our goal is to grow while living or working with someone, sometimes we have to own and act upon another's refusal to own what is real in themselves. We have to do this because their denial is not only blocking their growth, but ours as well. We need to plan, build, make changes and come to decisions, often painful ones, because part of the human condition is that people around us will refuse to grow and change, even when their behavior is destroying the very things they want and value in life.

But when we do make important decisions and action becomes necessary, then this needs to flow out of an in-touchness with the truth of ourselves. Because our bodies, if allowed to grow, want to guide us into wholeness—individually and together with all that exists. If the starting point in the "doing" part of life is an expression of our separation from this graced guidance, which is always a gift given us through the body/ Body, then we usually make judgments and decisions that express this separation and are destructive in building wholeness and restoring unity. Whatever we seek to change must be guided by our body's graced "felt sense" for wholeness in and around us. The starting point for Focusing—being in the real— nurtures this bio-spiritual way of living, because the energy of life is not directed toward doing something alone, but toward acting out of a body-feel for the harmony within the whole.

Over and over again, I have seen in my life that whenever one or more persons live in denial of what their bodies really know, all their relationships are threatened. I can recall countless times when poor performance on the job was directly the result of not bodily owning something seemingly unrelated. Or, blocked creativity in some important project was, after Focusing, clearly connected to not owning what the body was carrying unlistened to from years past. A man whose success in sales depended on his clients feeling they could trust him reported his boss told him people said they felt he was hiding something. His reputation, work-record and integrity, however, were impeccable. Over the weeks, as he began to own what was real in his body through Focusing, his personality actually changed. Colleagues and his wife commented that there was a different "feel" to him. He felt more open, present, and available to the people around him . . . which in fact, he now was. One of them even said he "felt more real," and as a consequence, his sales success improved considerably, as did his family life.

I will never forget the young woman, well along in medical school with excellent grades, whose dean had recently confronted her with the faculty's serious reservations as to whether she should be allowed to continue. As she sat with the pain and confusion of their telling her it was her "way of relating to patients," her "bedside manner," her "inability to relate well with people," etc., a whole scenario of put-down memories from home and school came. Each fit her body's "felt sense" of this situation, which threatened to shatter all her hard work and dreams of someday being a doctor. Bit by bit, I encouraged her to own each new memory or vignette from the past and to let each piece have its say. Gradually, the story emerged of a bright, talented, ambitious little girl whose brothers, as well as some important relatives and teachers, for whatever reasons, thought it was their role to dump cold water on her dreams. She was "only a girl" and should get interested in "girl things." As she gave herself time to own how she carried all this inside, there were lots of tears, anger, resentment and loneliness. What also felt good was that she not only survived, but had been true to her dreams. Finally, toward the end, she said, "The dean, faculty and patients aren't putting me down. They are not my enemies." Then, after a long pause, she concluded: "Maybe if I don't feel that way inside, then I won't be so suspicious, so guarded, walking around expecting somebody to cross me or dump on me."

Owning what was real inside was finally beginning to open new options for changed behavior on the outside. It was encouraging to get a letter from her some months later, telling me how she did not feel the need anymore to be looking over her shoulder. Moreover, the dean had told her reports were coming back much more positive about her "attitude change."

As I have journeyed with hundreds of people like these, a familiar pattern emerges. It is one that seems to be the theme of much of the world's great literature—that deep desire to let go and be whole versus eternally confronting that intense drive to manipulate and control. What human life does not forever play out that theme in some way or another? In fact, it appears that not only is this drama played out in the very cells of our bodies, but that the only way to bring about any harmony and constructive progress is precisely to recognize where the conflict and tension lie.

Yet we have been so conditioned into believing that if we own the hurts or fears we feel in our bodies, we will self-destruct. Even the thought of doing this together in order to strengthen a marriage, build a ministry team or create real community seems dangerous and absurd to most of us. Often when I propose such a step, I get that panicky look in the eyes that says: "Oh no, this will jeopardize whatever we still have left in this relationship. Don't rock the boat!" However, the exact opposite is what we find happens whenever we Focus together in mutual vulnerability. We have found that it is the inability or neglect or refusal of people to be real together in this grounded body sense of owning that blocks life-giving relationships from growing. A living lie, no matter how well disguised, even as spousal/parental care or as religious, cannot be the foundation of community, as Janet learned by eventually owning what was real in her body.

No question about it, there is a leap of faith for any of us to risk being real. But that is why "Focusing companions" who bring their Christian faith to this process are gifted with a depth and experience of Christ and his message that is beyond words, even beyond the narrow church categories used to express this ancient faith tradition. Often, in training sessions where people are learning to guide each other, we hear them say: "This feels so holy, so sacred. What a privilege to journey with someone this way." Or, "It's suddenly hit me what such and such a text from scripture really means."

Religious people in particular have a great deal of difficulty in growing beyond a prayer model taught for centuries in which they enlist God as the "super fixer" of what they feel impotent to fix by themselves. This kind of conditioning not only leads to an addictive use of God and prayer, but misses the mark completely, both theologically and psychologically. It is damaging to a healthy faith development, as well as to good mental health. I recall trying to explain this to a couple married long enough to have bumped into some of what was real in each other. They were in a lot of pain and confusion over it, struggling with what this all meant for their marriage. Both were cradle Catholics, knew Focusing, so I could write them as follows:

There is absolutely nothing comparable in my experience to the graced empowerment that grows between two people than what happens when they Focus together in mutual vulnerability. The reason I say this is because the hope or feel of a future in any relationship does not lie in everything being all okay according to the scripts we bring into the relationship. Rather, what Focusing teaches is that we can come to an inner peace about a relationship when the way we are carrying our script in that relationship can tell its story.

It is the script you bring to the relationship that gets in the way, as well as your trying to fix the relationship or fix each other or trying to get God to do it, instead of together "owning" what is real.

Owning what is real is given to us as gift, as a grace. Somehow it changes the whole feel of the relationship and of the way we carry our own agenda in that relationship. This is not just mutual resignation, but a peacefulness that comes when living that quality of shared truthfulness and realness together. Most people, to some degree, live a lie in their relationships. To find someone who helps you be real, and who is reciprocated by your helping the other to be the same, creates such a deep bond of love our bodies say: "Hallelujah" and "Amen." Our old scripts no longer feel the same because in the grace that comes through Focusing together, mutually owning what is real has created a new priority in the relationship. What begins to emerge as a much greater value than fixing the other person to match each other's script is the mutual realization that in the other person, as that person is right now, is someone who is willing to journey with me as together we own what is real. This is the only place of new beginnings, where our bodies are transformed into the One Body, the Holy. That is community of grace. This is the agape communion of the New Testament where the transformation of the broken and crucified Christ in our bodies is physically changed into greater wholeness. All because together we are willing to be real—a cry out of our deepest longing for the gift of wholeness and roots in the Body. A call that echoes out into the Cosmos to return a hundredfold in the miracle of a human relationship that is becoming more and more the "Real Presence."

I believe today in Catholicism the growing shortage of priests is providential and necessary. I don't believe its sole purpose is to widen the active priesthood by including married clergy and women, as valid as this may be. Rather, an even more profound value is that in the absence of priests, all of us will be forced into searching for a much deeper experience of Eucharist than what we have been conditioned to by the emphasis placed on the ritual of the Mass. Left only with each other and our relationships, no longer able to fall back on ritual to tie us together, this could turn us toward examining what quality of presence we actually have in our Christian gatherings. This is the more important issue we haven't faced about Eucharist.

Needless to say, I think we will be appalled at what we find and what we call Christian. Out of this vacuum, while still carrying a rich Eucharistic hunger and theology, can emerge a depth and breadth of Eucharistic faith and community never before known in Christianity. Then when the ritual can be celebrated, it will be in the relational context within which it rightly belongs and has its true meaning.

I know of no more effective way for real community to happen than through the experience of mutually shared Focusing. We are so brainwashed and conditioned into imagining that what will improve a relationship is to change the other (or get God to do it) that we miss the incredible power of two people simply owning in themselves what is real. Given our backgrounds as Christians, we were never taught to own what was real in our bodies but to turn everything over to God, asking God to fix it all. This kind of denial and dissociation developed destructive mental health habits and plays havoc in the lives of millions today. It is still being taught, because most Christians can't believe that something that old could be so wrong until they actually experience it. We simply cannot imagine how hope or the feel of a future isn't somehow connected to being fixed, whether by God or by ourselves. Needing to be all okay or perfect has been indoctrinated into our bones from childhood.

Even common sense tells us that we are destined to go through life unhappy, upset most of the time, and moving in and out of relationships unless we can find some way to live peacefully with human frailty and limitation. Nothing I know is all okay and perfect. Many situations simply cannot be changed. However, because of our brainwashing in the dominance approach to change, and our inherited spirituality of control as part of it, we go on trying to fix and change endlessly. As a result, we miss the key faith opportunity where grace actually enters into relationships.

Aside from all of this, experience also teaches that there is nothing more attractive and appealing in every way than someone who is real. Wholeness draws us together, and married couples who focus together tell me, "Wow, this is really sexy." Somehow the limitations, defects, and human frailty of each other fall into perspective, overpowered by the grace of God that is now part of the relationship where two people risk owning together what is real in their bodies.

In my experience, it is ultimately denial of what is real on the part of one or maybe all involved in a relationship that destroys it. Nothing blocks growth more than denial. Nothing feels so hopeless, frustrating, helpless and dead-ended as the experience of this dishonesty and incongruence in someone you love or want to grow with in a relationship. This is as true in a working or ministry relationship as it is in a family, friendship or marriage. The body-feel of hopelessness and frustration is so acute. Human frailty is not what destroys relationship. It is stubborn denial and the refusal to own whatever is real in our bodies in such a "contemplative" way that God's grace can empower that relationship.

What we have learned through Focusing is that denial is not just a refusal mentally to acknowledge something—like a destructive behavior—but a refusal to own the body's "felt sense" of it all as well. It is only this more organic or holistic starting point, when shared by all in the relationship, that brings about real change and the bonds of community. The bond that ties relationships into community is the grace of owning together what is real in us, not denial.

Nothing else I know of is more important than the daily owning of what is real in our body if we want to live creatively, grow in wholeness, contribute to building healthy community, carry in us the inspiration for genuine non-dominative problem solving, and deepen our intimacy and bonding with all that is life-giving. There is nothing more destructive than living a denial pattern of our own truth, refusing to own what is real in our organism's knowing of reality. It launches us full steam into addictive behaviors, excuses, cover-ups, defensive maneuvers, poor judgments, and confusion over what our own organismic "right" and "wrong" guidelines actually are. The list of problems that flow out of not bodily owning what is real is literally endless.

Because owning what is real in our body is not part of our cultural heritage, especially religious, denial and neglect of "felt sense" are considered normal behavior. Most people, including myself at one time, feel very suspicious of this owning, saying to themselves that if it were so all-important, then it would have been on our menu at home, in school and at church. Most of us, particularly men, have been trained into a kind of implicit, if not explicit value system that equates body "owning" with reckless, potentially-destructive playing with fire. This is because we have been given only a dominance approach to sexual integration. We know nothing of a "graced" process in sexual wholeness, because control in sexuality is also part of our inherited spirituality of control. I will write of this more at length later in this book. Sometimes, owning is also equated with the intuitive or "feely approach" to life, which is not considered masculine by many males. The socially-acceptable, safe, and intelligent way is to work things out with our minds. This is an all-pervasive, deep conditioning in our culture for both men and women. Even those of us who try to grow beyond this conditioning are amazed at how deep it still resides in our bones.

Not too long ago, a large group of our Focusing facilitators gathered to plan changes for the years ahead. We had started our four-day meeting by Focusing on what was real in our bodies, breaking up into small groups to help each other own and listen to what each of us found. As I told the group when I proposed to them that we start this way:

You have all been sent working papers to study, as well as the main questions we need to discuss. And there is a time and place for getting down to these practical details, for getting a consensus and for making decisions. This has its proper place. But the starting point for something truly original, for any creative project that calls for inspiration to launch us beyond past models into the unknown, that starting place is bodily owning what is real in each of us right now. That is our primary agenda in the Spirit and therefore our group priority in the Spirit. What is really number one in you may have nothing to do with these study pages or the proposed goals of this meeting. It may be worry about your health, or the frustrations of your job back home, maybe a deteriorating relationship or what the future holds for you. Whatever it is, that is what is real in you in its unfinishedness and need of your owning it "in Christ." What is real in each of us and needs grace to tell its story is the only starting place for any person or group who want to be guided by the Spirit—not ideas or an agenda imposed on you, as valuable or appropriate as these may be.

Although we are all Christians, many of us sisters and priests, it never dawns on us that when the task at hand is one that depends on inspiration, we must each become that invitation by helping one another own what is real in our bodies. This always has a story to tell, needing grace to unfold the next page. It is time to let our bodies open to the graced story we are meant to be, and to let our presence to each other be prayer. During these days together, we must be that mutual vulnerability which is invitation to Spirit, creating in us the sacramental community we have gathered here to better understand and carry back to our ministries at home.

After these words and the group's positive response, we decided to break up into smaller groupings to expedite the shared Focusing. It was then that a sister came up to me with tears in her eyes and said, "I can't believe this. I just went through the most painful and discouraging week of arguing, hurt feelings, and impossibly different opinions at our annual staff planning sessions. We are all trained Focusing facilitators and not one of us thought to start by helping each other own what is real. What creative ideas, community building and healing might have come out of those agonizing, divisive days if our starting point had been owning bodily what was real."

When what is real in each of us is programmed out of the picture by a culture that rewards lying, when our body-knowing is disregarded as second class information at best because it is not clear and cannot therefore be controlled, when we are not even taught by our religions how to "dwell" in the truth of ourselves in the flesh and blood of our bodies, then we are thrown into the despair of living a lie. This is hell itself, for only in being real can we be in harmony with the rest of what is real around us.

Maybe I can better emphasize what I have been trying to say in this chapter by writing a few paragraphs in the form of an old-fashioned parable.

ONCE UPON A TIME, the people in a certain city heard that a very wise and holy man was coming to their town. Word got around and they were eager to see and hear him. They wanted to sit at his feet and learn from him because the reputation of his wisdom and holiness had long preceded his arrival. When word came that he was approaching the town gate, the people left their jobs and ran to greet him, escorting him with flowers and songs to the city square.

He sat on the steps of the great cathedral and the people sat down in front of him to be taught. Then he asked them if they would like to go on a pilgrimage to a very sacred place, a holy sanctuary where they would find God, would understand what life is about, would begin to feel the rapture of being alive, and would grow in freedom.

Of course, all the people immediately responded with enthusiasm saying, "Yes, we want you to lead us there."

The old man smiled and said, "Very well, I will then." But before the wise old man could say anything else, the crowd got up noisily and many of them rushed off to close their shops, prepare food and clothing for the journey, gather up their children and bring carts and horses into the square. Soon they were all back, and there was great excitement and animated talk as the people prepared to follow him.

But the wise old man just stayed there on the steps, sitting. The people became restless and disturbed, wondering what was going on, and asked the holy man when he would lead them to this sacred place where they would experience God and know in their bodies the meaning of life.

And the old man said, "Any time you are ready." And the crowd answered back, "We are ready now." Then the holy man said, "Good, sit down again and I will guide you to this place, for the path is INSIDE yourself. The doorway is the truth of yourself and you must let go into that truth in your body to walk through the door."

When the people heard that, they looked at one another and many became frightened and left the square.

When the wise man asked them to grow quiet, others grew restless and left. As he began to teach them how to sense the truth of themselves in their bodies and to let go into being in that truth, more and more slipped away until only a very few remained in the square.

Then the old man turned to the few remaining and said, "To enter the kingdom of heaven, it is easier for a camel to pass through the eye of a needle than it is for someone who refuses to walk the path of truth inside themselves."

* * * * *

So many events and circumstances try to guide us into walking the path of truth inside ourselves. I have often marveled at how even frenetic people, who never seem to pause for anything, will be drawn into an almost contemplative quietness as they watch a wild animal. Their awe and wonder, the stillness of their presence, feels like some deep longing and appetite is being nourished by the realness before them. The beauty of nature often calls out the same in us, because the wildflower or the gnarled oak, the soaring hawk, or the grazing antelope are congruently whole. They are simply being what they are meant to be—no deceptions, no game playing with reality, no out-of-touchness with the organic material that shapes them into what they are. Just to be a marigold or a pine tree or a rabbit connects them with the whole. I think our bodies instinctively know this, and that is what pulls us into nature, our gardens and our pets. We are drawn to realness like a magnet, because we too need to be real and connected to the whole. We are not made, anymore than nature around us, to be out of harmony with the natural world.

In fact, there is nothing more loveable than what is congruent and real. That is why babies are so attractive. They are not born into the world with all this programming that destroys their integrity. We so want to be that much "together" inside ourselves that we sometimes say when looking at a little child, "Oh, I would just like to gobble you up."

In Christianity, that is exactly what Eucharist is meant to help us realize is possible "in Christ"—i.e., people risking in faith owning whatever is real in their bodies and receiving empowerment to be community in this mutual vulnerability. To understand what "eating the Body of Christ" means, surely we must start with owning whatever is real in our body, which is, in fact, our carrying of the Whole Body of Christ as we have experienced it—wounded, "groaning" and not yet fully resurrected. That is why owning what is real is such a profound act of believing in a life-giving Higher Power, whether in the Christian context or not. Without it, owning something like despair, hopelessness or self-worthlessness feels like suicide.

We balk and draw back from ingesting (owning) what is real in our own bodies, because, as Jesus said, our faith is weak in not yet understanding who we really are. As Paul would put it: "membranes" of the crucified AND resurrected Body of the Whole Christ within which the gift of empowerment in mutual vulnerability "makes faith-sense." "Eating the Body of Christ" then is both owning together what is real in us as the Body of the Whole Christ and celebrating that around the altar. "Eating the Body of Christ" means allowing the gift of our real selves to be given us in the owning ritual, as much as the Mass and consecration/communion ritual we have inherited. They both need each other to give witness to and teach experientially the deeper and profound meaning of Eucharist. If we are to eat of this Body and never die, then we must start by not denying or rejecting whatever is real in this Body—our body. This is that final step toward healthy Christian as well as any sound community growth.

Eucharist "effecting what it signifies" is not only a theological truth, but a body-feel that anyone coming in contact with a life-giving relationship can sense. This, in fact, is the legacy of Jesus, who at the Last Supper reminded his followers that the Eucharist is the birthing process of a new kind of community of Real Presence, one in which it is no longer necessary to manipulate and control each other through dominance. Christians are meant to be a Real Presence, an openness to grace, and as such, a birthing process of wholeness. As Paul would put it, we can "glory in our infirmities" by risking being real and owning our wounds and limitations because we live "in Christ." Since the message IS the process and the process is the message, Christians must risk entering into that process (their mutual journey into wholeness). Only in and through that mutual process of wholeness is the message revealed. Change is possible ("thanks be to God in Jesus Christ"). There is an alternative. We do not have to live out the rest of our days stuck in the same place or manipulating and trying to control each other. There is hope. Tomorrow can be better.

No one nor any group of people, even if they call themselves "religious," can ever understand how the wounds of childhood, our limitations, weaknesses, and differences of all kinds, when owned together in the mutual vulnerability of Focusing become the medium of the message. They do not know until they let go of the hellish myth of dominance which so destroys life in the name of parenting, education, religion, spirituality, community and on and on.

There is an alternative. But not "out there," not as an unreal, abstract teaching, not as some ideas a theologian thought up. But more accurately, as the very life-force that animates our humanity and can be physically felt in our bodies as we struggle to discover meaning, continuity, integrity and connectedness among ourselves and with our planet. God's grace is not just another clever maneuver on the part of religion to perpetuate the myth of dominance. Rather, the body-openness and receiving of this grace is, in fact, the only antidote to the destructive power of dominance, especially in religions where so often a living contradiction exists with their teaching of a "gracious" Supreme Being.

When we lose our way in how we are meant to open our bodies for grace, instead substituting a spirituality of control, we dehumanize ourselves, our religions, and our whole culture. As Christians, we destroy the presence of Jesus, and our churches begin to feel increasingly unreal. We lose the depth and meaning of Eucharist to the extent that we lose ourselves. Then all we have left is empty and increasingly meaningless ritual, even for those presiding. Empowerment in mutual vulnerability by owning what is real together provides Christians with the means and the gut feel of hope that communities of grace are indeed possible—something many Christians I know have given up on in their marriages or religious communities.

What gives hope and promise to those of us who are part of a "Focusing companion" relationship is that we are experiencing the structure and support within which healthy communities of grace can be gifted to us. We no longer need to buy into any expression of religion based on the collective lie of "community incongruence" born out of a dominance spirituality and masquerading as religious. We have discovered experientially rather than theoretically or doctrinally what has always been central in Christianity—our radical dependence on God's grace for the journey of wholeness, personally and together.

As Marianne recently wrote me:

I want to share what happened last night at dinner. There was a pause in the conversation and out of the blue, totally unsolicited Lance said, "I can't tell you how relaxed I've been all day because of Focusing last night." Immediately, four pairs of ears perked up! "I think I know what it is that helps so much."

John asked, "What?" Lance replied, "Just holding whatever hurts or is blocked and not trying to change it."

Then, a conversation between Lance and the kids followed on how they try to do that, too. Elizabeth nodding and smiling, and David right in there as well. I was filled with awe at the rightness and spontaneity of it all.

I said to myself, "Oh, you of little faith," so many times you have been discouraged, especially when one of them would say, "This isn't working for me," or, "I'm getting nowhere, etc." So much has been percolating deep down inside below that surface, especially in Lance.

So many nights Lance and I have come together as Focusing Companions and we let our stuckness and old familiar places be how we were together. And the miracle of it has been that when we could risk that way of being together and not giving up because we were stuck, then another Presence was felt. Our brokenness became the channel for that Presence.

An image that fits our relationship is one of an old rope hanging on a tree with something very heavy tied to the end of it. All of a sudden, it starts to break. You know how it unravels gradually. Finally, there is just a strand or two left holding the heavy thing, and then, plop! The rope breaks and the heaviness crashes—all so naturally and without effort. There is "letting go," and then "room for gift," which can't be described in words. An old favorite saying of my Dad's comes to mind—"The map isn't the territory." That territory is, truly, the body-feel of grace.

* * * * *

I mentioned earlier this perennial struggle between a deep intuitive sense that to be whole we must trust in some higher power, risking owning what is real, versus that intense drive which impels us to hang on to the reins, manipulating and controlling whatever is incomplete or injured in us. We know this inner conflict all too well. Now there is a structure and a simple format within which the risk of letting go into what is real can be undertaken with the support of each other. At last the key issue of control, so paramount in healthy spirituality as well as sound mental health, is being directly addressed as the focuser and guide are being opened to the alternative—grace. As one husband, discovering this together with his wife, shared; "Owning what I feel in my body makes me also feel very vulnerable, and it's this vulnerability that diminishes my control." Cautiously, slowly, even reluctantly, this man is beginning in mid-life to literally feel his way into grace as an alternative to the myth of dominance. This is the only way in which any of us can know the hope to which we are called. This is a future worth living into, if we are willing to start by simply owning in our bodies what is real. This is why a young professional woman I know, a psychotherapist, decided through Focusing that she would bring a child into this world. Writing me not too long ago, after the birth of her daughter, she said, "If I can teach her how to be with what is real inside her, this will be the greatest gift I could ever give her for life."

The most important teacher in life is not some guru, even a venerable spiritual tradition, some outside role model, or a wise person, as valuable as these may be, but simply what is, when we discover how to own it. The new world we all long for waits upon our finding this new experience, and to our surprise and joy, discovering in it that what is real inside is not the enemy we imagined it to be.

Parents, grandparents and those of us who belong to the older generations in the human family will never be able to pass on the wisdom needed to help the younger generations grow beyond the limitations we passed on to them, unless we let our fears and those very limitations become our teacher. Those very limitations which we feel in our bodies can be our greatest teachers, not our dreaded adversaries.

To attempt some kind of reconciliation with our failures and guilt by simply saying, "We did our best,"—which is most likely true in itself—is a far cry from actually being reconciled with how we carry those feelings in our body so that they can become our wisdom and our strength. By owning and listening in a Focusing way to whatever we carry inside our body, it can change from a wounded, maybe even scary place we protect and defend or hide from, into our greatest strength. It can even become our teacher, our special inside place where better ways and new answers come.

No matter how old we are, no matter how many mistakes we have made, it is never too late to own what is real inside ourselves and let the wisdom in their hidden stories emerge into the open. Instead of the monsters we have usually made them out to be, they then become our greatest gift to the generations that follow us! A gift that is given, not so much in words, but in the body-feel others pick up when they are in our presence.

The younger generations already know our mistakes. They are suffering from them every day. They also know we are aware of these mistakes. So that when they cease to hear excuses from us, no longer feel defensiveness in our bodies, but instead feel physically our reconciliation and the inner quiet that grows with this "coming home" to what is real in us, then they are drawn by this experience into ferreting out what has happened. Maybe it simply will be in more closely scrutinizing how we now live. Maybe direct questions will be posed. Maybe our inner congruence will elicit trust rather than apprehension about blame, lectures, or fixing them, and then something of their real feelings will be shared.

However it happens, any steps in wholeness we make are so hungered for by all of us that this "holiness" draws like a magnet. It is our own body and its presence that is becoming a "real presence," a Eucharist, inviting wholeness in others. And when the time is right, it is in being "invitation" that we can share with them the wisdom we have learned that we did not pass on to them when they were younger. It is then we can teach them the pearl of great price we have found—viz., that the starting point for growth and change, no matter at what age, is simply in owning with care and openness each day what is real in our body. Then we carry it in a nurturing way until it is ready to tell its story. In short, we are sharing with them Focusing and ourselves as a focusing guide when they are ready to try it. There is an alternative!

Chapter 7

How Can We Risk Owning What Is Real In Our Bodies?

HE WAS AN OLD MAN OF 87 AND DYING, AS ONE SYSTEM AFTER another began to fail. I looked over at him asleep in his favorite chair. The urgency in my mother's voice was unmistakable as she asked me to gather the family and anoint my dad before leaving California. I agreed and said I would get back to her.

That night, reading through the standard ritual, so much felt missing. My dad had worked tirelessly all his life to provide for us. This was always his number one priority—to take care of his family. How must he feel now, knowing he was dying? What could we do to help? What did he need to share with us and we with him while he could still speak, hear, and understand us? What did we, as a family, need to do for ourselves and for our mother during these final weeks of his life? All these questions were not being addressed by that little black ritual book as I sat in my room alone that evening. I knew he would soon be gone. Now was the time for something, but I did not know what or where to turn for it. So I did what I always do in such circumstances. I focused on the body-feel of it all.

What emerged was a ritual all of us (mother, my sisters, grandchildren) could take part in, including my dad. In it we told him we were not afraid to let him know we knew he was dying. We told him how much he would be missed, and that we wanted him to know mother and his property would be cared for when he was gone. We shared with him that we were gathered together as a family to pray for his journey into new life. When he knew it was time to let go, we were OK with him doing that.

We could see the relief. Our love and prayers, we said, would always be with him for a peace-filled journey back to God. No coverup, no denial of our tears as we shared this. No pretending, but loving, honest communication. Next, each member of the family recalled some experience with him that had meant a lot—like a fishing trip, or the little red wagon made for me during the depression when we were too poor to buy the one I had seen in the Sear's catalogue. Then we knelt before him, one by one, as he put his hand on our head with the words: "I give you my blessing and ask God's blessing for your future life." In asking God's blessing on his own dying, he said, "I am sorry for any hurts that I may have done to you or anyone else, and I ask your forgiveness and God's forgiveness." We responded, "We forgive you and ask God to forgive you." Pete and I then gave him absolution, anointed him, read some Scripture, and celebrated the Eucharist as a family. We topped off the evening with a party of his favorite cake and ice cream.

Throughout the ceremony, he sat between Pete and me for help, but stayed alert, obviously delighted in being the center of attention while the family circled around. Even though he was hooked up to oxygen, every minute seemed precious to him as he held my hand and frequently squeezed it. At the end, I asked if there was anything that felt unfinished which he still might want to say. There was a long silence. Then he said, "How privileged I am to be surrounded by so much love that I can feel."

What he was feeling in his body then is what I try to help people give to the hurt and scared places inside themselves. I call this a "caring-feeling-presence." It is a presence that says to our own lonely or confused places inside: "You are not alone. I'm here and I care." It is a presence our body feels, like my dad could feel our presence inside himself. When we feel this, it makes it possible to *be in* our own fears, our confusion, our hurts, even our dying, instead of denying or running away from what is real inside us. Those scary places inside us need to have this presence communicated to them by our own body, because usually we have made them into the enemy or run from them. In caring, we start to build a kinship with them. Trust begins to develop. Then they hang around more easily and we carry them in a different way. No longer the enemy, we can wait, listen, own them in our body. Sooner or later they will start to tell us their story like a friend would. With that comes the processing and the change in feeling. This is Focusing. But often it cannot happen without a caring presence around stuck or painful places. These places need physically to feel from our own body-relationship to them, the openness and availability we are struggling to create.

We all know what a caring-body-presence is. When someone in the hospital is too medicated or weak for verbal talk, how instinctively we reach out with a hug or with our hand to say, "I care and am with you." We know our body has to communicate the message. When a toddler is frightened by the sudden lunge of a dog or a loud noise, once again we do not stop to explain about safety. Instead we immediately let our body do it by catching the child up in our arms and holding it close to us. Our body holds the scared infant differently than we hold a bag of groceries on the way to the car. Once again, we know our tone of voice, arms, hands, open and warm chest have to do the talking in this situation. The child needs to feel care and safety from our body. So too do those painful places inside us that we have rejected, neglected or disowned as enemy. They need to feel acceptance, openness, our availability and caring presence before they can speak and change in the way they feel. The tender squeeze of my Dad's gnarled and calloused hands as I guided him through our family good-bye that night reached deeper into me with his love than any words could ever have done. But we seem to need a lot of help to be able to do this for ourselves.

Perhaps the most important step is in breaking the pattern of how we react to pain in the first place. Almost all of us immediately push it away or numb it in some way. So as a Focusing guide, I begin by helping the focuser break this habit, repeating the following procedure over and over again as I guide. When they are new at Focusing, as they locate something that is between them and feeling really good, I will have them notice how it feels for a moment or two. Then I will do a little teaching and say: "As you are letting yourself feel this issue in your body, you are probably becoming aware that anything between you and feeling good is at the minimum annoying, if not downright confusing, hurting, scary or even terrifying. So your first step will be to change the way you interpret this body language. These feelings inside you are not the enemy, but your body telling you this whole feeling place needs special care. Therefore, you probably need to listen in another way to this message. You need to move beyond your old habits of denial, repression, neglect, anesthetizing or whatever you do. So let's begin experimenting with various ways you might try to change the old habit, until one of these suggestions or maybe a combination of them feels right for you.

"Here is one way of giving that place inside you some special care. See if you can be with it like you would try to be with someone you loved very much who was feeling the way you feel now. How would the teacher inside tell you to be present to that loved one so that your body can communicate: "I care and I'm here for you?" What happens to muscle tightness, to breathing, to all the chatter in the skull when we don't have to protect ourselves, or plan strategies, but can just be present to someone? How are you present when you know words are not going to work, but your body is going to have to carry the message? Take some time to create this same body climate, this caring atmosphere toward those feelings inside that are between you and feeling really good."

Sometimes when I am working with a person who has told me something about himself/herself, I will use a memory or an image from their past that carries a feeling of openness and presence. I recall a man in Chicago who had been sharing at meals how he missed the warm, spring days of Kentucky, his home state, as he battled the cold winds off Lake Michigan. Later in a session he was having a most difficult time creating a caring-body-presence around a terribly painful issue. So I asked him if he had had a swinging chair on the porch of his home when he was a kid in Kentucky. I took a gamble on the porch swing, given Kentucky's climate and his pre-TV, pre-air-conditioning youth. I was right. So I said, "See if you can put this whole issue next to you on the swing, maybe even put your arm around it and just rock there with it on a lazy, warm afternoon at home, noticing how that feels in your body." This image finally opened the door for him. In this nonthreatening climate, he was able to draw close enough really to hold his painful feelings. With this caring presence, he could remain long enough without running away so they could begin to tell their story. Afterwards, he described how appropriate that image had been for him, because as a child he often sat with his feelings on that swing. He described how he could feel, even smell what it was like to be there again, rocking on the porch with his present fears; how much affection he felt for that porch and swing; how the body-feel of it now helped him be that same way with his pain.

At this point, you the reader might want to pause and ask yourself: "What is my usual pattern of relating to irritating, hurting, scary or overwhelming feelings—anything that is between me and feeling good?" Once you know more about your own patterns, you might want to try some of the further suggestions I will make in this chapter if you feel a need to grow beyond old disowning ways of escape.

Whenever I am working with someone over a period of time or with a group for a week, I will ask them to recall some situation, some relationship, or some special place like the porch swing—maybe a vacation spot, tree house, grandma's lap, the corner of a room where they played with a doll or pet—anything where they have felt affection.

I usually remind them that by "affection" I mean our availability to let someone or something get inside us and penetrate our walls and barriers. If they can recall such a relationship, I then ask them to notice how their body feels. What are the body signals, the body language that their brain might translate as "affection?" Often they will describe muscles feeling loose and relaxed; a warm feeling, especially around their heart; more open breathing; not having to perform or wear armor (which makes them feel relaxed); the feel of all their pores open, etc. People frequently say that they "love" the feel of being with that person, doll, pet, or in such and such a garden or room.

Next, I ask them to notice when they are back in this relationship what their planning, worrying, manipulating, thinking mind is doing at that time. Usually they will say something similar to the response one woman gave: "My habitually busy head feels like it's out to lunch."

After this, I ask them to take the time carefully to note what their inside teacher is pointing out for them. I encourage them to pick up the body-feel of affection as they would pick up the body feel for typing, swimming, golf or anything else where they needed to learn from their body in order to reduplicate it again. Then we return to something between them and feeling good to see whether they can recall the body feel of affection and try to be that same affectionate way with this negative issue.

Often at this point, if they are having trouble finding a memory or image from their past that effectively stirs up affection, I will suggest some images to which most people can respond with caring. For example, I invite them to hold their painful feelings like they would hold a hurting child in their arms, maybe rocking it, gently caressing it, even suckling it. I recall a sister who had never worked with small children and who, of course, had never had children of her own. She realized, however, that injured animals and birds called forth from her those same nurturing, caring feelings. So she moved into holding her hurting and sad feelings in the palm of her hand, stroking them as she would a little bird with a broken wing. Soon the words came, "I've needed this for a long time. Stay with me." It was such a graced moment for both of us, listening as that neglected place inside continued to guide her. On another occasion a married woman, drowning in feelings of humiliation, anger, shattered self-esteem, and confusion because of her husband's flaunted infidelity among their friends and professional colleagues, finally found a way gently to hold and not run from this pain. Listening as she spoke, I suddenly recalled her beautiful singing voice and suggested that she try gathering all those feelings in her arms and then sing them a lullaby. Finally, the rejection could be reversed as this nurturing body-climate enabled her to own her rage and pain long enough that it could begin telling its story.

Imagery that puts us in touch with a body-attitude of caring, when used with feelings we usually push away, can be a powerful assist for letting go into how the whole thing really feels in our body. Some people have found that the image of holding and stroking a beloved pet can create this openness. Sometimes an image of one of their children or grandchildren when that child was little—often connected with a very concrete past experience of warmth and closeness—triggers the body atmosphere needed to own the negative feelings.

The point of creating a caring-feeling-presence is not to anesthetize it or play Pollyanna, but to create an open enough body climate within which negative feelings can be owned and not disowned inside us. In Focusing terms, this presence permits the focuser actually to hold the felt sense in his or her body long enough for it to symbolize itself and shift. This is much more than just a mental attitude, but a body presence as well, which is why I use the word "affection."

Affection is the body's way of surrendering, of letting go, of being vulnerable and open. Affection disposes our body, as well as our mind, to be changed. In affection there is an opening up to be penetrated by the object of our affection. For example, we allow the other to bring tears to our eyes, caring to our touch, warmth to our embrace, gentleness to our voice, patience to our presence. We do not put up barriers to being touched, moved, entered into by the other. There is a letting go in responding with our body and our feelings, not just our mind. In this there is vulnerability, which is why nurturing our capacity for affection is so important in growing in openness to grace.

I smiled the other day, sitting on the porch, as our cat reminded me of this. Frankly, I've never been attracted to cats, but this one wandered into our lives from the wild. Looking out my office window each day, I could see it stalking the birds around our feeder and bath. Partly to save the birds, as well as feed this poor emaciated thing, I started to put out food. The cat was very wild and would never let itself be seen when I worked in the garden, but the food would disappear each night. This went on for weeks. Finally the cat began to appear at a great distance, hissing at me as I went into "its" feeding territory to replenish the food. Slowly, day by day, it came closer and closer until I could see it was a tom who stood only feet from me while I put out his water and dinner. Then one day, he brushed against my leg and I was a goner.

What brought the smile, as this cat jumped up on my lap, was the realization of what we had been through together as both of us grew closer and closer. My body as well as my head knew that this cat had gotten through to me. I know I will forever have a more open spot in my heart for cats (and maybe a lot of other things) as a result of the affection "Hiss" nurtured in me.

Our capacity for affection then is the key in learning how to dispose our body for grace, for the gift of healing change that needs to be given in precisely those areas where we would never spontaneously feel affection or even consider that it had a role. Experiences have hurt and hardened us. Experiences that we fear to feel again because they have shamed, confused, humiliated or wounded us so painfully. Often these are childhood experiences, if we are even aware of them, that now as adults we would consider silly or inconsequential. Yet, as children, they did not feel that way and something hardened inside us.

Today, as adults, we would never dream that "affection" toward such experiences would be the precious key opening them for the healing and change our body still longs for. Why? Because a caring-feeling-presence, which always embodies some degree of affection, is the only way we change our body's attitude toward this experience. It is the only way in which we begin bodily to own and hold this part of ourselves, rather than closing it off. Until that happens, it cannot change.

Affection, which is literally at the heart of a caring-body-presence, postures us in a more open, unselfish, "for-the-other" stance. We are there more as gift to the other, rather than fixer or manipulator. We let ourselves feel value, respect, awe, tenderness, openness, uniqueness, beauty—whatever gets inside us—as we contemplate the other. This transforms the controlling behaviors, drawing them off center stage. We are much more inclined simply to let ourselves and the other just *be*. However, people often confuse affection with their feelings toward a child, spouse, friend, etc., when they need that person to fulfill unsatisfied goals and needs in themselves. Real affection does not control and manipulate for personal aggrandizement, and that is how you can tell the two apart. Real affection involves a letting go of manipulation, together with an availability and vulnerability in our body to being changed by the other, *as that other is right now*. Thus, being in relationship with affection is always growth-producing, healing, expanding and supportive of wholeness (often for all involved) because it is our body's way of inviting grace.

Having affection toward someone or something *tones* our way of being with the other. That is why nurturing and learning from our own capacity for affection is so vital in creating a caring-feeling-presence toward the feelings we hold at arm's length. With affection, we are far more able simply to be quiet, just to be with the object of our affection, rather than needing to do something or move on. This is crucial when disposing ourselves for grace. The fixing mode is restless and itching to get on with it. Affection quiets us down and eases us into waiting and presence. In Focusing, this is essential for carrying the felt sense of something until it is ready to speak on its own schedule. The allowing for grace to happen is the critical factor whenever a step toward wholeness (holiness) is the issue. Thus, human/spiritual maturation really depends upon how we carry our body feelings.

Caring-feeling-presence is what allows us bodily to hold, without destructive tension, the issues still needing to tell their story. This is not to say that we will not feel pain during such holding. But it is not the kind of terror and exhausting, debilitating tension that we feel when all our fight-or-flight apparatus is revved up for battle or escape. This war syndrome is hazardous to our health in every way. The alternative, even though it includes unfinished pain, feels like we are on the path home. There is anticipation and excitement in being on the right track.

Caring-feeling-presence is an umbrella term I use to describe a wide range of body approaches which help us become reconciled with feelings that we have made into our enemy. It is the most effective approach of which I know to restore our sacred body covenant. This covenant with which human life blesses us has provided us with a body and its own language—our feelings. Honoring this covenant is the antithesis of those disowning habits which our addictive culture programs into us.

We have been taught in a thousand subtle ways that pain is the enemy, as is the healthy tension of any challenge to grow. By deadening this pain, we separate ourselves from the feel of our own unique spirit struggling to be born and express itself through our body. Separated from the body-feel of this life cycle of dying and being reborn, which is our own emerging spirit, we become hooked on the painkillers of canned entertainment, shopping, drugs, or other escapes. How easy it is then to be manipulated and led from the outside rather than from the body-feel of our own spirit. It is the rare person today who even has any knowledge (in the Biblical sense of knowing by being "bodily in") about what living out of the truth of one's own spirit means.

No wonder that our two most formative institutions, school and church, confuse "information" with this process. They both substitute more and more techniques for control in place of nurturing the child's absolutely necessary body-feel for tension and pain as an exciting and fertile ground wherein each of us finds our own spirit. The kind of skill training and information that our culture emphasizes has its place. But it is essentially a more refined way of enabling us better to manipulate our environment and one another. It is potentially lethal if not balanced by an equal effort directed toward nurturing our children's discovery of spirit in their bodies and how we must live guided by the body-feel of that spirit. If we and our children do not live out of a truthfulness to our own unique spirit, the pain of this self-alienation will continue to destroy our relationships.

The lethal cultural value of disowning the very process of spirit-growth in our body cannot be broken unless we use some embodied way of helping people feel not only reverence and awe but affection in their body for the *whole process* of spirit-birthing. This includes holding with affection the pain of the tension (as I have described it in the last chapter), as well as the new life that eventually is born. Restoring our covenant with the whole body-process of spirit-life is the only way in which the Spirit in the Whole Body can guide us as a human family into living with care and in peace on this earth.

When spirit-life in our body is maintained intact, we immediately share a common bond through our bodies as they guide us toward solutions and lifestyles that will not destroy us and our environment. But the life-cycle of frequent death and resurrection, the womb of our human spirit's birthing process, must be kept alive. Our culture, supported by much in religion, has baptized its abortion. Until we find a way not to abort our own body's feelings, they cannot be born to new life. Affection toward the feelings we have made into the foe is our body's way of inviting the healing grace that reconciles and forgives. In this sense, affection is the human body's way to be prayer, to be an embodied connection to God. In this movement, we continue the Incarnation and the gift of the Spirit within our own bodies.

There is a kind of ageless wisdom in all this that comes through in stories and examples we all know. I recall hearing once of a grandmother who came to visit her sick little grandson. The little boy had just received a puppy for his birthday and wanted it on the bed with him during his recuperation. His mother said no, because the puppy was not yet housebroken and would do "puppy things" on the bed. But the old grandmother insisted that the boy was right, because, as she told the mother, "He loves that puppy and will get well sooner if he can hold it near him." She instinctively knew that the affection stirred by the puppy in her grandson's body would speed up the healing process. Holding the puppy with affection, he would more likely hold his own pained body with affection and the recovery would be enhanced.

Much like the story I have just recounted, I frequently inquire of adults who are having difficulty befriending a hurting place whether they had a special doll or teddy bear as a child. If they say yes, I probe a bit more as to what feelings come when they recall this childhood companion. If I detect "affection" there, then I suggest they try to hold, cuddle up to, rock, or put their arms around their painful or frightening feelings in the same way they used to care for their doll. Maybe I tell them how I used to have a teddy bear that I loved so much I wore all the fur off his little body. My mother then had to come to the rescue by sewing him overalls and a shirt to keep me from wearing through to the stuffing. As an adult searching for practical ways to hold affectionately my scary feelings, I rediscovered how I still carried much affection for that bear. Memories and the image of him stirred up such an availability in my body, especially when I could hold him "snuggly close" at night. So now, if I am going to bed with something that is bothering me—perhaps I have been with it in a Focusing way during the day, but it is still unfinished—I will put it next to me on the pillow like my old bear and, with arms around it, fall off to sleep "with affection." Inevitably, I will suddenly awaken in the middle of the night with an answer. Something will connect in my sleep and I will wake up knowing "That's it," or "That's what I need to do," or "That is what I need to write in the place where I'm stuck." In fact, I use this so often now that I almost welcome stuck places inside myself because when letting go into them in this affectionate way, what always arrives is so exciting.

I must admit that perched near my desk sits a menagerie of furry little critters which, over the years, I used to tell myself were bought as birthday presents for nieces and nephews (now in their 20s and 30s). Somehow they never got beyond my desk. I think now I know why. But the old bear is still the best. Little did the gifted baritone who left the stage of the Metropolitan Opera in New York to come west and invest in the gold mines realize what a real treasure he was bringing when he put that teddy bear in my arms.

Now, to continue with a few more concrete suggestions. If you are guiding someone in Focusing and you don't already know what it is they are working on, then as they finish step 3, I have found it very helpful to ask: "Is this something that is between you and feeling good or is it something else?" If they respond that it is something between them and feeling good, then I propose that before they go any further, they might want to create a caring-feeling-presence around this whole issue—one that feels right for them.

I usually suggest several possibilities for how they might form such a feeling-climate, using what seems appropriate to me in terms of anything they may have shared or that I have observed is their degree of fear. In other words, I tailor my suggestions in a way that feels like it might be helpful, given what I can pick up of their situation and feelings.

For example, I listen more carefully now when someone whom I will lead in Focusing is sharing. I try to notice where I detect affection in their life. Offhand remarks, like a grandmother at lunch talking about looking forward to holding her grandson for the first time; or a young father proudly relating to the group before a session a recent achievement of his little boy; or the older lady in her introduction to the group expressing concern about leaving her cat for the weekend. All these hints of affection I note and may make reference to if it seems appropriate for the person to spend some time in a caring-feeling way with something difficult they are later Focusing on. They then have a familiar experience of affection, a concrete body-feel to work with as they give themselves time to discover how they can be with this scary or hurting felt-sense in a way that does not reject or try to fix it.

I used to suggest the word "friendly" when inviting someone to consider a caring presence. Now, when I sense fear, shame, deep hurt, holding back, etc., I will use words like: "Would it be OK to spend a little time now with this place, letting it know that you are trying to be more open to it . . . (or) not trying to fix it . . . (or) not push it away, but just listening so it can tell you something if it wants to?" Often I use phrases like: "If it feels right, see if you can be with this whole thing in a way that it can feel you are at least trying to be caring . . . (or) respectful . . . (or) gentle . . . (or) patient," etc.

For one person recently, all these suggestions were, in her words, "simply out of the question," she so hated and rejected what she felt inside. As a last resort, I remembered her telling the group she worked in the justice system in a courtroom. Therefore, I asked if she could be with the whole thing in a way that allowed it a fair hearing and a chance to say what it had a right to say. This turned the whole thing around, because that attitude felt on-target to her. So, before going any further, I encouraged her to take the time, discovering as best she could the body attitude toward what she was Focusing on that let it know she respected its day in the courtroom. This then gave her the setting inside herself within which, for the first time, she could own how it all felt in her body. She finally could be with it bodily, instead of rejecting it—the old pattern. The felt-sense gradually emerged as she was with it "in a fair hearing way," allowing several symbols to connect and felt shifts to move her issue forward.

The key, however, was in helping her find the unique way that she needed in order to break the pattern of bodily disowning and rejecting what she was trying to focus on. Once we found the special caring way that allowed her to risk actually owning the felt-sense of this despised issue in her body, the story was eager and ready to unfold. Indeed, it took the stand and had a lot to say. The tears of relief gave clear evidence of long overdue testimony!

What many of us are finding today is that if the caring-feeling-presence is created before beginning step 4, it fashions a different inner climate that often bypasses the panic, the old set patterns of rejection, the habitual defenses, etc., from locking into place and blocking the body owning of what is there— which is, of course, the heart of Focusing. Doing this, we find, is far more effective and efficient than just waiting for the focuser to tell you later on that he or she is stuck. By then the barriers are usually firmly in place, the old walls have come down, the process is blocked, the focuser's and your energy have been drained, discouragement and frustration may have clouded the picture, as well as precious time for both of you has elapsed.

Owning negative feelings in our body is where we usually get blocked. Instead, we fall back into analyzing, trying to fix them, rejecting them with our old patterns of defense, controlling them, scolding them, denying them and on and on. Our old habits take over. Therefore, before going into step 4, if the issue is uncomfortable to hold, I suggest taking time to discover how your body can be with this issue in some caring-feeling way. You will find that very often this breaks the old pattern, allowing you to move into the crux of Focusing—bodily owning the whole feel of it.

One of the most helpful bits of wisdom Carl Rogers taught me years ago was to promise a negative feeling which surfaces when you are in the middle of something and cannot attend to it that you will come back to it later. This helps you to be more in touch and not ignore what you are feeling, as well as create an attitude of respect and kinship with it.

Another suggestion I often make, which creates a non-adversarial climate, is to ask a hurting, scared feeling—perhaps, one that feels stuck—questions like these: "How are you trying to help me?" Or, "How do you need me to hold you so you can speak to me?" A maturing focuser, as well as a wise guide, are always pointing the one Focusing toward the teacher inside. Thus a question like this is sometimes useful: "How do you want me to be with you so you can be my teacher?"

Another way of helping you realize what we are doing in creating a caring-feeling-presence is to refer to one of the most important findings Eugene Gendlin discovered in his research. This broad, underlying principle can guide you in understanding how feelings unfold, as well as how the Focusing process actually works. He wrote: "Every 'bad' feeling is potential energy toward a more right way of being if you give it space to move toward its rightness."[1]

What a caring-feeling-presence does is create the nurturing climate—Gendlin's "space"—so the "bad" feelings can "move toward their rightness." It engenders an inside atmosphere around the feelings which permits the "potential energy" there to be released toward a "rightness" in the body.

The above simple and direct statement of Gendlin's emerged from a long history of clinical observations and experimentation begun by his teacher, Carl Rogers, and carried further by Gene himself. Both found that negative feelings are not some sort of enemy to be conquered and eliminated. Rather, they contain special indicators of the unique direction for growth within each person. Both Rogers and Gendlin realized that *congruence* with one's own feelings was crucial for successful change and growth. By congruence we mean being able consciously to feel our feelings physiologically and allow them to symbolize themselves accurately. For Gendlin, Focusing is an effective way to become congruent by remaining in touch with the body's direction toward wholeness. He wrote:

> The very existence of bad feelings within you is evidence that your body knows what is wrong and what is right. It must know what it would be like to feel perfect, or it could not evoke a sense of wrong. The bad feeling is the body knowing and pushing toward what good would be. The feelings of "bad" or "wrong" inside you are, in effect, your body's measurement of the distance between "perfect" and the way it actually feels. It knows the direction. It knows this just as surely as you know which way to move a crooked picture. If the crookedness is pronounced enough for you to notice it at all, there is absolutely no chance that you will move the picture in the wrong direction and make it still more crooked while mistaking that for straight. The sense of what is wrong carries with it, inseparably, a sense of the direction toward what is right.[2]

For Gendlin, when difficult feelings are a problem, the principal resource and starting point for change is the felt-sense of what is wrong. *It is never some ideal "opposite" of the painful way in which you find yourself, as our religious and cultural conditioning so often suggest.*

There is an erroneous assumption in any approach to change which bypasses a congruent presence to difficult feelings and instead concentrates attention upon some imagined ideal from which one seeks to draw strength or substitute in place of whatever troubles us. Such effort invariably results in a lack of "congruence"—the not owning of what is real in ourselves.

Such out-of-touchness is the psychological underpinning for most addictive behavior. Addictive behavior is an incongruent person's substitute for genuine presence to his or her feelings. When culture or religion lead you away from your actual feelings by substituting something else in their place, that culture or religion are already innately addictive in themselves and will foster addictive behavior in their followers.

Caring-Feeling-Presence Changes Awareness

In guiding myself and others into a caring-feeling-presence within our bodies, I have noticed that the quality of our consciousness changes. We become less impatient, less judgmental about what we feel, because every feeling is valuable. We do not need to hurry to get someplace because we are already there. A gentleness and patience with our own feelings grow. They become less unwelcome intruders and more like honored messengers. We can let go of needing to control so much with our minds. There is not that frantic striving, so characteristic of people put through our educational system, to get a handle on things by better understanding them. There is a letting go of much of this clutter, and a willingness to enjoy simply being in the consciousness of our bodies, allowing much of the frenetic activity of the mind to recede into the background. Living more in the body unclutters and simplifies life, because by surrendering to what is real inside us, even the pain, we move into the rhythm of the growth tension we carry in our feelings.

The feelings of pain can be sensed as necessary and as an intrinsic and normal ingredient of the whole dying and resurrecting cycle of growth and new life. In fact, just by doing it we learn (know from being "in it") that pain is a necessary part of the process. An awareness grows as we make friends with the body-feel of the so-called "dark side" of this movement that allows us to relax more into simply what is. Something in our bones begins to tell us not to run from the scary feelings inside, not to fall into the trap of again making them an adversary. In finding our own way to befriend them, something deep inside allows us to rely less and less on the old script that prescribed our role with all the "shoulds."

Learning to hold with affection what it truly feels like to own your humanity (which seldom measures up to all the "shoulds") gives birth in us to a consciousness much more powerful than mastery of the techniques of control or living up to the "shoulds!" When we do not understand and feel anxious, then our own special way of holding these feelings with care can begin letting go into how the whole thing feels inside us. Something now feels right in just waiting like that until they guide us. When we have no answers and that frightens us, we do not have to search frantically outside ourselves for the meaning or numb the pain of not knowing. Increasingly, it feels right and normal just to own it all gently with no pushing, no blocking, no blaming, no manipulating until it is ready to tell its story. A learning deep in the tissues of our body now tells us that. The more we let go of trying and the more we cultivate a caring presence to whatever is real, the more open and receptive to the gift of the next step our body becomes. Experience has taught us that in time, the answers are always given, if we stay in our body this way.

Other Suggestions

Persevering and creating a climate that gives us access to the stories hidden behind the body armor and walls we create to protect our hurts is what caring-feeling-presence is about. Sometimes placing our own hand in a caring way on the pain as we notice where we carry it in our body gives concreteness to the body-feel of presence there. To caress or pat lovingly and tenderly with your own hands where you feel the tension in your body augments the caring presence because it conveys with touch that you are really trying to be there. This body gesture enriches very tangibly the nurturing atmosphere you are trying to create around these feelings.

Sometimes words from a song, a poem or Scripture, which carry a body-feel of openness or caring, help in developing this body-presence. This is especially true if you get to know your pattern of trying to fix the feelings you don't like in yourself. Choosing a phrase or a word that is just the opposite of the way you treat yourself, like patient, gentle, tender, soft, open, kind, etc., can help "tone" the inner climate. One person told me that letting a certain song replay itself again and again always created an open and available body feeling inside. "Some music closes me or distracts me from what I'm feeling inside, while other music and sometimes certain lyrics help me to be present to whatever is there," she said.

But in all of these, when timing and certain conditions are right, the most effective breakthroughs I have personally experienced, as well as seen in others, have come through what our group is developing and calling, "Focusing massage."

Focusing Massage as Caring-Feeling-Presence

Gradually, we are finding qualified massage therapists open to allowing the person receiving the massage to guide them, rather than the therapist putting the person through a certain technique or system. This is difficult for many people, both therapists as well as clients, because they are only familiar with one model—the present medical one in which the patient goes to the doctor to be "fixed." But once we find therapists who are willing both to learn and live Focusing, another option opens up in the way they relate to their clients. Then, if the client has a natural instinct for Focusing or is a Focuser and is locating "issues in their tissues" that are between them and feeling good, the two can journey together in massage in a very different way. The massage therapist can be told what part of the body needs attention and then both can be deeply present to where those feelings are carried in the body. A Focusing massage helps both client and therapist to be more present in an open, listening way to the story the focuser's body wants to tell. It is an in-depth way of experiencing support to stay with and allow a bodily-felt issue to move forward.

My own personal experience and the conclusion I would have to draw from working with hundreds of people is that often we carry in our bodies what I call "habit-protected places." We have developed the habit of hiding them from everyday consciousness. These can become not only accessible through body work such as massage, but when the client is taught Focusing as a way of being with themselves and listening to the story in their body, then they also know how to process what they discover.

This is extremely important, because only rarely do both client and the person doing body work understand the process of congruence and how to facilitate it, which is Focusing. Focusing Massage provides an effective, healing presence to the story of our lives which we carry deep in the tissues of our body. When the therapist lives an authentic Focusing life and is not there to "fix" the client, but to accompany him/her on a deep sacred journey, then the feel of the massaging hands do not say: "I'm here to make you well, to fix you or to take your pain away." Instead, they say: "I'm here, I care, and I'm with you if you want to risk being here, too." This attitude promotes spiritual, psychological, and physical health.

When both client and massage therapist can be present in a non-fixing, Focusing way to something the body wants to say, this special "allowing" relationship becomes a profound invocation for the empowerment of God's grace. Healing and the forward movement of that person's life under such circumstances can be extraordinary.

As one of our massage therapists says when quoting her teacher, "Often the body speaks that which the mind refuses to utter."

Teaching Children Caring-Feeling-Presence

Finally, in all the different areas where exploration is going forward throughout the Bio-Spiritual Movement, none stir so much hope and excitement as the positive response which children express when learning to care for their feelings. Their spontaneous and immediate attraction, the relief they feel when adults not only approve but teach them how to nurture and listen to their feelings, gives us energy and courage to reach out to them more effectively.

One little girl's creative way of doing this is to ask her uncomfortable feelings "if they will stay and play with her." "Being with the feelings like I would be with a new kid at school," was a boy's way of creating the body-feel, because he could remember how gentle and kind he needed to be with a frightened immigrant child as he showed him around on the first day of school.

One of our group, Victoria Kumor, a 5th-grade teacher in Denver, has found that most children easily bypass the inventory and go directly into what has a feeling priority in their body. Therefore, her efforts have been spent in teaching the

Caring-Feeling-Presence, using posters that convey a gentle, caring body-feel. For example, a child tenderly caressing a chick; a puppy carried in a boy's pocket, nestled warmly against him; a nose-to-nose encounter with a child and kitten. Miss Kumor will also use the opportunity in writing class to have the children search for words that they feel convey a caring-body-presence. Then when the time is right, she dresses up in a mouse costume and role-plays, Focusing on how she feels about her best friend moving away. The Focusing guide is a puppet on her arm called, "My Friend." What this teacher found is that children easily put themselves into Miss Mouse's place and the puppet guides them into their own feelings. "My Friend," the Focusing guide, is so attractive to the children and they feel so safe in this atmosphere that even in the large class, Focusing shifts take place. One little boy who was a constant problem in class asked the puppet if he could come up and give him a hug and his friendship bracelet.

Of course "My Friend" said yes, and the teacher wrote me that when he was hugging the puppet he told "My Friend," "It's so good to have someone listen to my feelings." This child, along with several other problem children expressed warmth and friendliness with the puppet never before observed by the teacher toward anyone. She wrote that something was freed up in them and their classroom behavior improved considerably. Remembering that these children are at their classroom desks without any personal one-to-one guidance, feedback like the following was common: "My Friend helped me to feel a lot better inside about my dog that died." "My Friend told us how to take care of our feelings." "My Friend showed us how to help each other."

These children have brought new energy and life into their teacher and their classroom, asking for "My Friend" to visit them every week so they can "take care of their hurting feelings."

Final Reflections

There is a strange paradox for most of us as we get used to creating a caring-feeling-presence around feelings that before we would have mustered all our forces to push away. We discover power in gentleness, but not in the manner or with the characteristics we generally associate with power. Here, there is no pressured, intrusive, forcing, manipulating, driving. This is not an approach that will break down blockages, pierce through the armor, powerful enough to muscle its way right in and fix all that needs fixing.

Instead, gradually what we find is that the gentleness of this presence is far more powerful than any driving attack we could ever put together. The power lies not in what we do, but in what we do not do; not in the more perfect person we try to create, but in a coming home to the person we really are; not in the fixing of our feelings, but in an open invitation which our body becomes when we let go of fixing ourselves; not in all the strategies of control that we assume will move us toward our goal, but in the vulnerability of letting go of such control. Then, the empowerment just happens. And it dawns on us eventually that indeed this gentle, caring way of treating the adversaries we create inside ourselves is the path home. To journey on that path is to hold with loving and open arms the truth of ourselves. Those open arms embrace not only what is real, but cry out as a prayer never left unanswered. Living that is power.

Millions hunger to live in that power, hoping for peace. There is a direct relationship between this power and the way we treat ourselves, each other and the environment. The worldwide cooperation needed to effectively address environmental issues will not happen without a global spirituality that teaches us, irrespective of religious traditions and cultures, how to take care of our own inner ecology. Effective "outside" environmental care flows out of effective "inner" environmental care. There is really no separation, but an interdependence and interrelatedness that demand we live a caring, inner ecology of growing wholeness within ourselves to nurture the wholeness of the planet. This is what caring-feeling-presence is ultimately all about.

People who remain at war with part of themselves will inevitably spread wars around them. War is not just bombs and guns. The most direct, practical way for human beings to assist the process of planetary wholeness is by learning how to be reconciled with the enemies they carry inside themselves. We, who are now the older generation, can develop through caring-feeling-presence in ourselves a spirituality of global care and reconciliation as our gift to the planet and to the generations that follow us. By living and modeling a nurturing body-spirituality ourselves, we will encourage younger people to discover an environmental spirituality that begins by honoring and respecting their own bodies as integral to the process of learning to respect the planet. Caring-feeling-presence gifts people with self-esteem and connects their hunger to experience the Sacred with the way they treat themselves. The effect of this on youngsters literally would be earthshaking, if we adults in the family, church and school would connect this process of discovering our own precious spirit with what we prize as spiritual and educational.

If children could experience that gently owning in their bodies whatever is real was honored and cherished by adults because this truthfulness and vulnerability connected us to each other and a Higher Power, then a caring, unifying, environmental spirituality could be born. When spiritual values are communicated in and through a process of human wholeness experienced within the common Body/body we all share, then cultural, ethnic and religious diversity are no obstacle to the emergence of a nurturing global spirituality. When people with diverse backgrounds realize that such spirituality is environmentally healthy, they will simultaneously realize that it is in no way a betrayal of whatever is healthy in their own spiritual tradition.

I believe millions of people are ready for this. People raised and nurtured within the traditional framework of religion are hungry to enrich their spirituality with a broader vision of how to treat themselves, other people and the environment they live in so they do not destroy it and at the same time find the Sacred within it.

What distinguishes our approach from others articulating a global spirituality is that together our starting point is always in owning *bodily* whatever is real, then developing our cooperative projects and policies out of that body/Body experience. This simple, practical, teachable method, which we call "Bio-Spirituality through Focusing," is a process easily adapted for children and for widely diverse cultures. Focusing provides us with the concrete steps and experience of change as the basis for healthier ways of relating to ourselves and our environment. Rather than just discussing ideas or theories about the need for change, Focusing helps people process the way they actually carry their fears, guilt, anger, loneliness or frustration in their bodies. Such feelings are the underlying engine of de-structiveness that must first be addressed if any of us are to *sense* (not just think) alternatives to the way we now do things. Without an ability to own and be drawn inside the untold story within our potentially destructive feelings, then fear and our need for security will continue to dominate human life and re-lationships on this planet.

I believe growing numbers of people all over the globe are poised and ready to take a momentous step beyond what Mar-shall McLuhan counseled us to do in the 50s and 60s. Then he used to say that we must re-enter the tribal night, but this time with our eyes open, which, of course most people interpreted as open-mindedness or not being naive. I think we now know how to enter that tribal night with our *bodies open*. This is a precision and an evolution of extraordinary significance.

Finally, if we choose, we can embrace a body-spirituality that opens our "inward eyes to be illumined, so that (we) may know (in our bodies) what is the hope to which (we are called) . . . and how vast the resources of power open to (those) who trust."[3]

Chapter 8

What Holds the Myth in Place?

by
Peter A. Campbell

THE MYTH OF DOMINANCE CLEARLY PENETRATES DEEP INTO
our bodies—not merely our surface feelings or emotions. How
does it maintain such a stranglehold within us? What is the secret
of such sorcery? How does it work its spell?

In an earlier chapter, Ed wrote about the significance of
what Gendlin describes as the *"felt sense."* Experiencing felt
sense is important because in this book Ed is doing more than
merely analyzing a problem. He is not just asking *why* dominance controls so much in human life. He is going one step
further, probing into the actual mechanics of *how.* How does
this myth restrain human potential? How does it curb the
body-life of Spirit? How can we actually change?

Not Why? but How? The answer to "Why?" merely
generates more abstract analysis. Such speculation may be cor-
rect or incorrect. But, even when accurate, it still does not help
us to become more whole, to deepen our identity. Analysis affects our thinking and, to some extent, our feeling or emotion.
It rarely touches the body's felt sense of an issue—and that's
where change and embodied transformation in the experience
of who we are can occur! The actual process of moving toward
wholeness is radically different from speculative analysis about
why we are the way we are. "Felt sense" is a key to the actual
process of change—not more understanding.

But there is one more piece to the puzzle. One further
inhibiting structure that gets in the way of growth toward
wholeness and maturing in the body-life of spirit. In this chapter, I want to describe another discovery of Gendlin's, one as

significant as the felt sense. He has located the psychological key that unlocks one of the oldest questions of humankind: "Why is it, even when we know that some behavior is destructive and don't want to do it, that we go right on repeating it over and over again?" St. Paul put it more eloquently: "For I do not do the good I want, but I do the evil I do not want . . . miserable one that I am! Who will deliver me from this mortal body?"[1]

Gendlin found that each of us has our own unique and highly developed systems of dominance right inside ourselves. These are structured ways of remaining out of touch with hurting feelings and the vital felt senses associated with them. These sophisticated ways of numbing and distracting help us to understand why relationships of dominance are an inevitable outcome of the way in which we treat ourselves. Gendlin has named these largely unrecognized strategems *"process-skipping structures."*

What is *"Process-Skipping"*?

"Process-skipping"[2] is something we all do in order to avoid or "not deal with" difficult feelings—emotions that in actual fact are our most readily-available doorways into the felt sense. Remember, our inner resource for change lies in the vague, fuzzy felt sense—what Ed describes as the MORE of our story.

Process-skipping is the psychological mechanism that holds systems and relationships of dominance and co-dependence in place by keeping people out of touch with how their bodies actually carry these systems and relationships. We become addicted to whatever numbs or distracts us from these painful feelings. This locks in our stuckness and unfreedom, blocking any change.

Process-skipping may well be the psychological key that locks denial in place. At this writing, Eugene Gendlin's work has barely been discovered by those in the field of addiction. But addictive behavior and denial are the result of imposing systems and relationships of dominance upon ourselves and others in order to gain control. The bottom line for an addictive person is control. Process-skipping is the mechanism or patterned structure we fall into, or choose, as a way to numb or distract ourselves from whatever hurts.

Rather than trying to describe process-skipping in a technical fashion, let me share one of my own process-skipping structures as an easier way of illustrating this addictive psychological behavior.

Nineteen years ago, it became clear that my mother needed to be moved from her apartment into some sort of care facility. I was, fortunately, able to find one that fit our budget, and mother has certainly been well cared for ever since. However, the personal inner struggle triggered by that experience led me on a journey through unowned aspects of my experience that at the time I scarcely knew existed.

When I walked out of the retirement center, I felt bad. But the "bad" was nothing compared to the guilt that surfaced two or three weeks later. Finally, I could not take it any more and went to visit my mother. The guilt ceased for a time. But soon would come a phone call or anniversary and the familiar pattern repeated itself. Guilt inevitably returned. Fairly soon, a predictible sequence became evident, not to me, but to those who knew me. Something would trigger feelings of guilt about my mother being alone in the retirement center and my response, in order to alleviate the guilt, would be to visit her.

I never took time to sit with my guilt, to wonder about or listen to it. I simply reacted. GUILT—go visit mother. In fact, I soon became addicted to visiting mother as a way to handle my guilt. Some people use work, alcohol, or drugs to deaden such feelings. Others have such an overpowering need to please that they fall into all kinds of addictive behaviors as a way to ease inner pain, insecurity, and confusion.

Gendlin makes it clear that the direction toward a felt sense is always *into and through* the feeling, never away from it. Yet, for me, every time I felt guilt, I moved in the opposite direction, trying to "deal with it" by visiting my mother. I skipped right past the point of entry into my own process. I quite literally became addicted to visiting my mother as a way of controlling the feeling of guilt. I substituted this activity in place of entering through the emotion into the felt sense of it all and allowing my untold story to unfold.

Right at the threshold of guilt, I took a direction that made some form of addiction inevitable. I substituted visiting my mother in place of being in touch with how my body carried the uncomfortable feelings that no one had ever taught me to be with when I was a child. Psychological addiction involves a substitution of one behavior, feeling, or attitude in place of another, rather than becoming congruent with and *processing* what is real, thereby allowing it to unfold and tell its story so the body-feel of it can be carried in a different way.

People make this same tragic choice every day of their lives in situations far more complex than the simple example I am sharing. But the psychological process remains the same. We seek to control the bad feeling, to make it go away, or substitute something better in its place. In the course of doing this, however, we fall prey to the very psychological mechanism of escape that we have stumbled into or perhaps deliberately chosen. It soon becomes our jailer, locking an addictive pattern in place. We become its slave.

Every time I came up to the doorway of guilt and could feel those unpleasant stirrings in my body, I was whisked away to a temporary soothing of these feelings (through a visit to my mother) and the doorway to permanent change remained tightly closed. The untouched treasure in my body's way of carrying guilt remained nothing more than untapped, hidden wealth. Such potential lies in all of us. It is available right at the point where addictive confusion leads so many of us away from our bodies.

We can now put a label on that pattern. It is "a Process-Skipping Structure." The label, of course, can never help us to change. But the understanding it brings can alert us about where to look in experience for our own process-skipping structures, and then use Focusing to grow beyond the pattern.

Psychological addiction develops because people have feelings they do not like, and they do not know how to be with those feelings in a way that allows them to change. A process-skipping structure, like visiting my mother, is substituted in place of the body-process of real change—and the substitute soon becomes our prison. That is why the preceding chapters in this book are so important. They offer a real alternative to this dead-ended pattern.

Process-skipping structures are not just obvious things like drugs and alcohol, sex, work, or pleasing other people. Prayer, meditation, volunteer work, anything that can be substituted for a congruent owning of what is real inside me contains the negative potential for contributing to a process-skipping pattern of addiction.

Focusing teaches us a special way to be *"in"* our guilt, or whatever other feelings need to be heard, without trying to fix any of them. The fourth step in the Focusing process allows time just to be quiet in how something actually feels in my body, right now—how it is carried within the sensations, emotions and body-felt sense that lie beneath every aspect of awareness.

If we remain with this nonverbal resonance in our bodies long enough, without trying to force the mind's meaning upon it, sooner or later it will speak and symbolize itself—often in surprising ways. A word will come, an image, a memory will bubble to the surface, perhaps tears or a delighted giggle at some felt humor in the seriousness of it all. And when the connection is made, when the symbol fits, something inside says, "Yes," and lets go in our body. From that point forward, your felt carrying of that issue is never again the same. You may still need to take further steps. Other aspects of the issue may yet remain to be heard. But your body has been blessed with some kind of loosening. The ice has thawed and cracked a little. The floes break up and begin to float once more. Movement starts to happen, meaning begins to unfold.

What becomes so painful for each of us is when the feeling of being blocked always remains the same. That is where burnout and breakdown occur. But if there is some sense in the body that movement, any movement in the feeling of an issue has happened, then hope rises anew. It is amazing how much "unfinished stuff" one can live with when we sense it is "on the way."

I certainly know I felt this in my own guilt. When I finally took time to create a caring presence around this negative feeling and not just react in an addictive way, my incomplete story began to unfold. There was deep anger and resentment over unfinished issues in childhood—separation because of war and illness over which my parents had no control. But I still felt these absences and the pain of them. The resentments were deep inside, still carried in a body way. My mind had arrived at its own adult peace and understanding. But my body was still seven years old.

How little we understand the process of human whole-ness. Our mind seeks *solutions*. It wants answers, information, facts. Our bodies, on the other hand, seek *resolution* in the way they carry painful or even joyful experiences. If there is no res-olution, then we go to our graves tense and dissatisfied.

Focusing provides a simple, practical way in which to be gifted with our own body resolution. That is what makes this process so different. The goal is not analysis—acquiring more information, finding out what is wrong with us, or simply get-ting in touch with feelings. All such busyness still leaves us with the troublesome question: "Then what?" Focusing teaches us how to be with the feelings and felt sense in a way that allows them to change so our bodies may carry these experien-ces in a forward-moving way.

I was taught a vivid lesson about this one evening when I went for a quiet stroll and noticed a small, stuffed ball lying next to the road. Picking it up, I continued my walk, idly toss-ing and catching the ball. I was struck by how rarely I had taken time for this simple pleasure since boyhood.

Frequently, my toss was off and I would need to run a bit to catch the ball. It was then that I became very aware of something—a consistent pattern. As I tossed the ball and it fell back toward me, I would follow until it was about a foot from my hand and then, suddenly, my eyes would veer away in the last split second before the ball actually came into my grasp. "Keep your eye on the ball." The words came back from grammar school baseball experiences—but this time I really heard them. For the next several moments, I was very con-scious of disciplining myself to watch the ball all the way into my hand. I could sense a different body feel in the experience. When my eyes veered away, there was a feel of flinching—an avoidance. But when I followed the ball all the way into my hand, I noticed a kind of newness, something fresh, like I had never done this before.

Then I fell into one of those precious moments of reverie where things began falling together, and my experience took on a meaning far more significant than what appeared in this idle pastime. Not only did it reveal a great deal about myself, it offered a fresh perspective on my life's work.

Most people know that they *have* feelings. *What they do not know is how to follow those feelings all the way into the body whenever they need to change.* Like my eyes following the ball, most of us veer off at the last moment, rarely experiencing the newness of what it is like when such feelings can change and unfold from the inside.

"Focusing" is a simple, easily-learned process that can help you follow a feeling all the way into your body. It is a potential key to unlock even the most stubborn patterns of psychological addiction. Then we can freely listen to our own spirit as our story unfolds from inside. Such freedom threatens every relationship and system of dominance that attempts to manipulate and control us from the outside. Process-skipping holds these systems in place because we are not free enough on the inside to be true to our own spirit.

The difference Focusing made for me was striking. When compulsively visiting the retirement center, I was invariably there to get the monkey of guilt off my back. I fulfilled a duty. But I was rarely present to my mother with that deeper communication and sharing wherein there is true companionship. I am sure mother felt this in some way. But, as I have taken time and begun allowing guilt to unfold, I find that mother and I are becoming friends. We share a great deal, have much in common, and are blessed with a similar sense of humor. It is a wonderful gift, finally, to discover your parent as a friend.

The Emerging World of "Felt Sense"

Many years ago, people routinely died of something called "consumption." It was an ominous word covering what we now know could have been anything from cancer to tuberculosis. Given the limited knowledge at that time, one word was used to cover a multitude of maladies.

We face much the same situation today with our very limited traditional distinction between "thinking" and "emotion." "Emotion" is a word much like "consumption." It is a generic title for the teeming world of body-knowing which we have only recently begun to understand. The average person can differentiate physical sensations like sweaty palms, dizziness and palpitations from emotions like anger, loneliness and love. But that is about as far as our everyday ability to differentiate goes. At least it was until Eugene Gendlin came along to open for us the world of "felt sense."

A felt sense is not just an emotion. Fear, anger, joy, sadness—these are emotions. A felt sense is different, it is global and fuzzy. It includes more than the emotion—many things, most of them not clearly known. It is a *bodily* quality, like heavy, sticky, jumpy, fluttery, tight. At first it has no fitting label . . .

Let me show the difference between an emotion and a felt sense. Anger is an emotion. When you are angry, you recognize that. No puzzle, nothing vague, you're mad. But if you relax a little, you can sense: "There is more involved in the whole thing." For example, you may sense a breathless, hurried quality, a sense that you'd like to stay mad—you don't want to stop and see that you're a little wrong. *That* uneasy quality has no name of its own. Where would you find that? Under the anger, in it, around it, at the edge of the anger. But words like "edge" do not describe it literally . . .

You can sense that it has a life of its own if you try to talk yourself out of it. It will resist. If you say something about it, and then attend back to the felt sense, you can sense that what you said is wrong. Yet you don't know what would be right to say. You cannot control when it opens. Something comes directly from it when it opens. Or perhaps you accidentally thought something right, and it opens in response.

A felt sense is unmistakably meaningful, and yet we don't know what it is. In contrast we know the emotions when we have them.[3]

Eugene Gendlin has probed further into the world of body-knowing and helped us realize that within every emotion is a broader kind of body-sense which he named the felt sense. We generally do not have easily-available words or concepts to describe this little-recognized aspect of body knowing. It is more like your body sense of "all about this relationship" without going into specifics and details. If you stop for a moment to reflect upon the experience of someone you love, you may notice that your body-sense of them can be both warm and cuddly as well as irritated and annoyed. Your body knowing of someone you love is quite complex. Attention may be focused on the current emotion of the moment. But at the same time, your body simultaneously holds all your other dimensions of "feltness" about this relationship.

Why is this important? Well, just as it is useful to know whether someone has tuberculosis or cancer so, too, it helps to locate and understand what is going on inside us in our body knowing. This is especially true because what Gendlin discovered is that feelings are able to change inside the person to the extent that a person can be in touch with *more than* the emotion—that is, the felt sense. *The potential for change and growth lies in the felt sense, not in the emotion!* If all you do is feel and re-feel your emotions, you just go in circles or wallow in them. Merely feeling a painful emotion over and over again provides absolutely no assurance that it will ever change into something better.

Being able to be in touch with a felt sense in a way that allows it to unfold and tell its story is the key to any lasting, forward movement in the emotions connected with it. Gendlin deserves great credit for uncovering the felt sense. But, equally important, he also found that we have our own unique and highly developed ways of remaining out of touch with this vital felt sense.

Process-skipping structures and the felt sense together provide a psychological framework for evaluating many of the so-called "spiritual" practices that foster addiction within religion.

Bio-Spirituality—"body" spirituality—is not some modern ideology or dogma. Neither is it a New Age practice or system of thought. It is simply being on the inside of how our bodies carry what we already know about the meaning of life and death, love, hope, believing and God. It is being on the inside of life itself, your life! Spirit waits to be born as gifted inspiration, movement, and resolution within our body. Bio-Spirituality is the story of how each of us grows beyond the myth of dominance into a life of grace together.

Spiritualities of Control and the Denial of Grace

But there are other spiritualities, best described as *spiritualities of control*—spiritualities that, in fact, can become part of our arsenal of process-skipping devices. They protect us against change and, therefore, become a piece of the system that firmly locks dominative relationships in place. Here, the goal is not process but *containment*, the polar opposite of grace and spirit.

Let us consider an example of what at first might appear as an effective prayer for healing anger and bitterness over past hurt. We will point out the negative, process-skipping, addictive potential in this prayer. Then, we will take time to reflect on how that prayer might have been offered and experienced in a way that could lead toward inner wholeness rather than repression or neglect of whatever is real in our body.

The prayer in question appears in a book by Eddie Ensley, *Prayer That Heals Our Emotions.*[4] Ensley quotes from Anthony DeMello's book *Sadhana,*[5] and begins by having you relax and recall scenes from your past where you were hurt by someone. He invites you to imagine taking the offending person by the hand and telling him or her that you forgive them. The exercise continues as follows:

Each time you use this prayer experience, you can imagine different scenes and different people.

As some of the people pass before your mind's eye, you will feel uncomfortable telling them, "I forgive you." The hurts are held so deeply that it is difficult for you to let go of them. Father Anthony DeMello, in his . . . book, *Sadhana,* . . . suggests the following way of letting go of deep hurt and unforgiveness.

"First, imagine that you see Jesus Christ on the cross. Take whatever time you might need to have a sense of Him on the cross.

"Now turn to the scene of pain where you are hurt and stay with that scene for a while. Keep alternating between the picture of Jesus on the cross and the scene of your hurt. Soon you will find your resentment slipping away from you, and a feeling of peace and joy will sweep over you. *A feeling of lightheartedness will overcome you as the image of Our Lord on the cross enables you to let go of imbedded hurt."* (emphasis ours)[6]

I am uncomfortable with this prayer exercise for three reasons. First, I always become ill-at-ease when someone describes a practice and then tells me in advance how I am going to feel after I have performed it. Second, this particular exercise has the negative potential of shaming with guilt. "Jesus died on the cross for you as well as for the one who did you wrong—and you still won't forgive this person?" But even more negligent and misleading, in my view, is that absolutely no attempt is made to enter into, to own, and to process one's anger. Instead, feelings of compassion and love for Jesus on the cross are deliberately cultivated in order to override and subdue, to smooth and soothe away the negative emotion of anger.

In short, feelings of compassion and love are *substituted* in place of feelings of anger. The anger is in no way owned. The deeper, felt sense is neither heard nor allowed to express itself. Unprocessed anger is pushed down for a time—only to re-emerge whenever another occasion arises that provokes the memory of all such unfinished business.

Whenever this occurs, as inevitably it must, the prayer exercise and feelings of compassion for Jesus on the cross will need to be used once more in order to control this troublesome resurgence. Soon, a predictable and addictive scenario of process-skipping prayer will repeat itself, just like visiting my mother to exorcise the demon of guilt. The bottom line in all this is that the anger will never change. It will just go on repeating itself over and over again until, finally, it is owned and the body's felt sense is allowed to unfold.

Having said all this, what might have been a healthy way to present such prayer—one that could preserve a familiar and cherished prayer form, while at the same time incorporating sound common sense that would keep us in touch with the truth of ourselves?

If Jesus could be a presence accompanying the person as he or she walks into and owns their real feelings, "I'm angry!"; if Jesus were an enabling support who encourages the person not to run from but actually to enter into their own inner Golgotha, then this could be a prayer that helps them toward wholeness.

In the one instance, Jesus takes the one praying away from anger, substituting in its place feelings of compassion and love. Nothing gets processed. The person is being "set up" for addictive prayer. In the other experience, he/she draws upon a resource (Jesus) strengthening his/her resolve to enter the dark and frightening body feelings wherein lies the potential for gifted healing.

Eugene Gendlin could not have said it more eloquently and simply: "Every 'bad' feeling is potential energy toward a more right way of being if you give it space to move toward its rightness."[7] The surprise of grace waits at the core of what I run from and avoid inside myself. The body-life of Spirit yearns to unfold within the as-yet-unheard story of my anger and the hurt that sustains it. The prayer addict misses all of this. *An overriding need for control closes down openness to grace!* Such persons become as psychologically addicted to using Jesus on the cross to manipulate their anger as others might use work, drugs or alcohol as a means of escape. Many Christians need to grow beyond their addiction to Jesus into personal and community wholeness "in Christ."

I know this will be difficult for some to accept, because they view prayer as a good and drugs as bad. But we have been too uncritical in the area of religion and religious practice. The same negative potential for escape is here, perhaps even more so, because it is socially acceptable to pray, whereas it is frowned upon to become a drug addict.

But is the prayer addict any better off, or any less destructive in passing on an addictive pattern of escape to the next generation? We need more public awareness and discussion of the latent addictive power that lies in religion when it is abused by persons whose need for escape is so great that they will use anything to control feelings.

The starting point for any change in how we feel inside is not prayer, or Jesus, or religion, or New Age practices, or anything *outside* us. It is being in touch, being congruent with, owning what is real "inside." I am angry! I feel guilty! I'm lonely! Then, in prayer, if Jesus can be a resource who enables me to sit down with and listen to the story in my body—feelings of rage, guilt, or loneliness; if Jesus can be a presence that helps me not to escape from or process-skip around the truth of myself—then that will be a prayer opening me to the gift of healing and guiding me home to wholeness.

Any religious exercise, any form of meditation, any "growth" practice that takes me away from whatever is real in my body and substitutes, instead, some more acceptable feeling in place of what is actually there—that practice is an exercise in process-skipping. It feeds a relationship of dominance and, if engaged in for any length of time, will inevitably become addictive. "I can't make it through the day without meditating." How often have I heard that phrase and wondered what was really going on in that person's life.

The negative potential of process-skipping, as I have just described it in a contemporary prayer exercise, is even more uncritically advocated by a clinical psychologist, Dr. Tony Kreuch, in an article in the *Journal of Christian Healing* titled: *"Dealing With Anger: A Christian Response."*[8] The title itself is a tip-off that what we are reading is a well-articulated presentation on the spirituality of control. Despite a cursory nod in the direction of even-handedness, where he acknowledges the need to accept and communicate feelings, their actual transformation comes straight out of an exercise in Pavlovian conditioning.

In this article, as in the prayer exercise of Eddie Ensley, the reference is to transforming prolonged, deep, and unresolved anger. According to Kreuch, such anger ". . . can be overcome without great difficulty if therapeutic application is made."[9]

The direction of therapy involves:

. . . emotions being changed into responses that are incompatible with destructive, unresolved anger—a perspective consistent with psychological theory and the scriptures . . . . We bring about this transformed or incompatible response primarily through prayer in the context of physical and mental calmness.[10]

After being taught basic relaxation techniques, such as deep breathing, imagery, etc., the angry person:

. . . . is helped to imagine the individual he has been with *while* he is in a condition of physical and mental relaxation. This is consistent with the psychological principle of counterconditioning (Wolpe 1958, 1973). The theoretical presumption behind counterconditioning is that two incompatible emotional responses cannot coexist. As the individual becomes more practiced at imagining the individual with whom she is angry during these conditions of relaxation, her anger toward the individual will tend to diminish. In a word, the psychological response of anger has been *transformed* into another, healthier response. This response, which may include any combination of the fruits of the Spirit mentioned by Paul in Galatians 5, reinforces the final step in overcoming and resolving the anger before it becomes destructive . . .

. . . the response of anger is transformed through the process of learning new emotional and cognitive responses
that are incompatible with the response of anger. Through
this process the individual literally becomes new. She no
longer identifies herself as an angry person. She becomes a
peaceful person able to acknowledge, accept, communicate,
and transform her anger.[11]

I confess to being at a loss as to how Dr. Kreuch can link
counterconditioning and the fruits of the Spirit in the same
breath. Grace is never the product of any effort at control.
Counterconditioning aborts any interior process and, instead,
substitutes calming relaxation in place of the incompatible
emotional response of anger. It is no different from substituting love and compassion for Jesus in place of the anger. The
effect is the same. The process of human wholeness is skipped.
The underlying feeling remains the same. So long as a process-
skipping mechanism is employed, the anger may remain under
control. But the cost will be high—*an addictive person, prone to
addictive solutions with no body feel or openness to grace, alienated
from the body life of Spirit, and lacking congruence with the process
of self-identity.*

Behavior modification, no matter how clothed, still stands
out as just another form of dominance. The real alternative of
grace is missing—and that is the point of this book! Focusing
positions us at very special doorways into our body knowing,
unfinished places where we are invited to take a further step
into Spirit and wholeness. Many growth practices and systems
try to help us be in touch with our true feelings. But they do
not always teach us how to hold or be in those feelings in a
way that allows them to change. The goal in Focusing is not
detached observation but process. It is not the substitution of
one feeling in place of another, but forward movement in the
body-carrying of what lies inside us.

Five Criteria for Evaluating Spiritual and Growth Practices

Before closing, I would like to share five criteria for
evaluating spiritual/growth practices. These are not offered as
an exhaustive summary of such criteria. They do, however,
provide some direction for making sense out of the many New
Age exercises and other so-called "spiritual" techniques that

abound in our time. The criteria are also good for taking a closer look at some older spiritual exercises with which we are more familiar.

(1) Does the practice support you in owning your feelings, or does it merely make you aware of emotions without helping them to be in process?

(2) Does the practice keep you in touch with your own feelings in a way that allows them to unfold, or does it try to *substitute* other, more acceptable feelings in place of those that are troublesome?

(3) Is the practice one that actually facilitates change in the feeling of some issue in your body, or does it merely provide you with information that affects your ideas and thinking about that issue?

(4) Is the practice one that achieves its effect in you through self-engineering and control or through self-surrender in openness to a process of grace?

(5) When using a practice to grow beyond stuck feelings, is the level of positive change that occurs in the way an issue feels in your body something that endures after the exercise, or must you keep repeating the practice in order to maintain the level of change that happens?

* * * * *

I have read superb analyses of the dysfunctional state of church, family and our nation. I appreciate the incisive way in which brilliant minds have dissected the foibles and pathologies of our age. But I am always left with a question. The analysis of what is wrong and an outlining of goals for the future *are never the same as the process of actually moving forward!* The more brilliant such analysis, the more confusion it actually creates. The accuracy of contemporary critics often leaves an impression that the analysis itself is the solution. But it is only a signpost along the way, hopefully pointing out some sort of direction. Reading the signpost and journeying toward one's destination are two very different experiences. The worst mistake of all is to imagine one has arrived at the goal merely by climbing the signpost.

People today yearn for intimacy and graced community. Old systems of dominance and patriarchy are breaking down with regularity across the entire globe. We seek a fresh way of being together and will never find it until we discover a new way of moving beyond the myth of dominance with/in ourselves.

In the next chapter a couple, married for some 20 years, describe their journey beyond the myth through Focusing.

Chapter 9

Empowerment in Mutual Vulnerability: A Couple Become Focusing Companions

by
Marianne and Lance Thompson

HOW DO TWO PEOPLE FROM DIFFERENT BACKGROUNDS AND with many conflicting interests develop an inner freedom enabling them to journey inside each other in a non-controlling way? Is there hope that this can happen between people who want to grow together while at the same time realizing that there is much that feels blocked between them? As we answer with our own resounding "yes" to these questions, we invite you to share in what we have learned.

Marianne: I was first introduced to Focusing over 12 years ago during a Focusing and Spirituality workshop. Although immediately drawn to the realness of the process, I felt myself hanging back, wondering whether I was willing to face the hurting, wounded, stuck places inside myself that needed to be heard. Could I make the commitment to myself that I knew was necessary to become more whole?

As I began to get in touch with my own brokenness and began to sense the inner freedom this brought, I felt a strong desire to share this with our three children who were seven, five, and three years old at the time. I knew what a tremendous gift it would be if I could pass this on to them while they were still young. I was intrigued by the possibilities of what life would be like for them if they could be taught such a precious tool early in their lives. (I have written about this early teaching of Focusing to our children in "Teaching Children to

Focus."[1]) What would it be like for them right from the start to own what was real in themselves, rather than going through life haphazardly connecting to the stories beneath their joys, fears, rejections, anticipations, etc.?

And so, I began to teach them Focusing, experiencing a realness and closeness to them that felt so right to me. I learned a way to be a mother that allowed them the discovery of being and valuing themselves. A freedom began to grow in me that said, "I don't need to make everything all OK for them. They do not need to be fixed." The children and I continued to Focus and grow together as the years quickly passed. However, as time went by another awareness surfaced in me. This one did not carry with it the excited anticipation of the first. There was more hanging back as I sensed I was both frightened yet hope-filled at the prospect of perhaps Lance learning to Focus. While the children and I were growing in this journey together, Lance was on the outside. I became more and more uncomfortable with a gap that was developing between us.

But it was not until I was writing one day and felt a stuck place inside me that I realized I was carrying my relationship with Lance in a way that felt exactly like this stuck place. This new awareness gave me courage to be with how this whole thing felt, and then to share this with Lance.

I remember saying to myself that I could be with anything except my feelings about our marriage. Would facing this be the end? I wondered. My personal struggle toward wholeness made me keenly aware of a growing gap between us. I had been very dissatisfied with Lance's lack of presence to me and our family. I yearned for someone who could walk inside with me, who would help me risk going into my own scary places. Being in an intimate relationship this way seemed to be the only option we had for growing together. I asked myself, what is a marriage all about if not for this? My search for meaning, for God, for wholeness seemed blocked. What was I to do?

It all seemed so hopeless, and I was scared that our marriage would fall apart. The painful owning of such brokenness, as I really carried it inside me, opened a new sense of freedom, which then gave me the courage to talk to Lance from this inside place.

Lance: I did not realize how important this was to Marianne. I was not very aware of my lack of presence and how it was affecting my relationship to her and the children. I felt surprised and hurt that she felt a closeness was missing in our relationship. I was reluctant to face her concerns. Yet I knew vaguely that things were not right between us. I was somewhat more aware that my own inner life seemed in turmoil. Because of my love for Marianne and our commitment to each other, I decided to try Focusing with her. And so, more than three years ago, we began Focusing together.

Marianne: While I felt freed up from the need to fix the children, I sensed somewhere inside that this was different with Lance. As I was more honest with myself I realized there were things in Lance I could not accept, qualities in him that grated on me, that seemed to interfere with my desire for the two of us to grow closer together. I even thought this might be a stumbling block to any future growth. How could I be open to myself as I really felt about him, then be this same way with Lance? Some sentences from the book, *Living in Sin* by John Shelby Spong, touched a deep truth in me. "The desire to possess godlike powers over another is a manifestation of the hardening of the heart of vulnerability. It is interesting to note that the climax of the Christian story is in the affirmation not of power, but of powerlessness, which is nothing other than the willingness to be vulnerable. How else can one read the story of the cross?" So, I knew that the answer for us lay in our willingness to risk mutual vulnerability in journeying inside with one another.

I found myself poorly prepared for my part in this whole decision to begin Focusing together. I did not bargain on the need to let go of wanting to "fix him" over and over again that proved to be so vital if Lance was to own the truth of himself. As I still continue to sit with Lance in a Focusing way, gradually I am learning to hold gently in myself whatever is real in him as he begins to Focus. This allows me to grow in the inner freedom of not getting trapped or caught up in my own agenda. I needed to let go of a whole variety of things in myself: wanting him to succeed so he would not feel like a failure, wanting him to have a good experience of Focusing so he would continue with it, even thinking that I knew what was best for him to Focus on. Just the time and energy it took on my part to be present and open to Lance was filled with meaning. It was a gift that allowed me to be open to how all of that felt in me as well. In this way the pull of having to fix everything, to make it all better, or even the feel of having to make something happen is broken. All of this manipulating loses its hold on me whenever I can own how it feels inside. It is this freedom in me that somehow gives Lance the space to allow what is in him to surface and be owned.

Lance: I notice a tangible difference in both of us when she can be with me like this. Her quality of presence is different. She shows a calmness as I quiet down and am able to be more gentle with myself for longer periods of time. Letting go of her need to control lets me know that it's O.K. to be with anything. I won't self-destruct just because it feels so hurtful, shameful or guilty inside. A trust in our bodies' wisdom to lead us toward wholeness begins to develop. A kind of softening begins to happen.

Marianne: It is like we are both enveloped in another kind of Presence that is gently allowing us to be with one another with all our pores open. *Our vulnerability then becomes our gift to one another!* It feels very much like two people walking together as one in the Presence of so much More.

As we have been Focusing together over the months, certain learnings have become our guidelines. We so often destroy ourselves, each other and our relationships by trying to control, manipulate and fix each other. Certain guidelines help guard against such destructive behavior. As our bodies physically change in the way we carry the other person, this is communicated in the body-message of acceptance of the other. As long as either of us feels in his or her body a non-acceptance of the other as he or she is now—regardless of our best mental intentions—something will remain stuck between us. Each of us can feel non-acceptance if it lies within the other's body. We both needed to be healed, through the graces of Focusing, of our need to fix and control each other in order to feel good about ourselves. On this journey, we have found the following learnings important.

1. Prizing our own brokenness: Unconditional acceptance as invitation to journey inside.

As I reflect back over our months of Focusing together, what stands out for me as the essential ingredient in this way of growing intimately is allowing myself to own how I really feel about Lance and our relationship. It seems to me that in most relationships we are always trying to change the other, endlessly pointing out how he or she should be. It is as if we say it often enough, that person should be able to change to our liking. Our explanation and analysis of the situation may be completely on target. We may in fact know how this other person could be more productive, more of a success at work, more present. But the essential ingredient needed for inner growth is missing in all of this! What needs to be faced is how our very valid, often accurate insights and needs blind us to how we need to be with these vested interests in ourselves as we relate to the limitations of those we love the most. How can I be open and help the other risk going into what is unfinished and feared? That is the key that most of us miss as we struggle to grow together. The heart of self-renewal is being on the inside, where everything seems to be connected. It feels like we are being led along by a movement that is not of our own making, a movement in which a new identity is developing in our marriage.

It seems so natural for most of us to try running from or eliminating what we dislike, cannot accept, or do not understand in ourselves by having power over it. How many times have we all heard, "If I could just figure this out," or, "If I could just understand the other person," or, "If we could just talk this out, it would get better." Or for those of us who have been Focusing, another very subtle attitude of control can creep in that goes something like this: "I'll just sit with this today so that it will feel better and leave me alone." All are forms of control that we use to make ourselves feel better.

As Lance and I have Focused together, we have learned to prize our own weaknesses. Whether it was Lance's stubborn tenacity, at times refusing to Focus, or my attempt to convince him to Focus, we both knew we would have to let go into those areas of brokenness in ourselves. Prizing these places gives the other the freedom to own and accept them. These fears, or controlling places, then become doorways, not obstacles to change.

One afternoon when we were first trying to Focus, I realized the discomfort I was feeling came from the fact that Lance had not asked me to sit with him for weeks. I knew that the regular owning of what is real in me as well as in him was vital if we were to continue to be gifted in our mutual openness and vulnerability to each other. I brought this up and said, "You know, Lance, if we're going to continue growing together as a couple we'll *have* to keep going with our Focusing together." Pow! Even as I said it, I felt the control in my body as muscles tightened. The look on his face told me he felt it, too. Lance was quiet for several minutes and said, "Marianne, if I'm going to grow, it's not going to be because you tell me I have to. It's because I want to, and you are never going to force me." I quietly took that in and said, "You're right." We both felt in our bodies I had slipped back again into the old model of *me* trying to *make* something happen. It is hard to let go of being in the driver's seat! If *we* want to grow, it is imperative that *we* do! There was a felt-sense of rightness in me to just let that be. Maybe we would decide not to continue with Focusing. I would just have to wait and be with how that felt inside myself. There was a kind of deep trust that in spite of myself I knew this would work out.

Two days later, while sharing small talk in bed, Lance said, "Marianne, you know I searched the world for you 18 years ago. I traveled through Europe, Greece, Israel, spent two years working in Peru, all the while looking for someone I wanted to spend the rest of my life with. I'd be a fool not to continue with Focusing. I'd have so much to lose if I stopped now." He continued, "I now see that my search for you had to do with my need to break through my own blockages and walls. I sense my own need to Focus."

Holding our woundedness with an open, caring, waiting attitude has taught me that strength comes when we can drop the reins together and trust the body's innate wisdom to lead toward life. Empowerment happens when every attempt to maintain security fails, when we can allow ourselves to surrender into the uncertainty, fear, and confusion. *When this letting go feels like we're going to drown, then we are positioned to grow.*

Gradually, we learn to prize and trust our own brokenness as a doorway into the greater Mystery. As grace begins to guide us, we know in our bones how it feels to be empowered in mutual vulnerability. Being with each other, all pores open, becomes our gift to each other. A strength develops in us when we can own our incompleteness. We then touch another kind of power, a power always waiting to be tapped, when through owning this brokenness we become strong.

2. *Risking mutual vulnerability as Focusing Companions leads to empowerment.*

Addictive relationships, poor self-image, a negative attitude toward ourselves invariably lead to the need for control and codependent behaviors. Our bodies already know the direction toward healing and wholeness. There is a wisdom already in place far more profound than anything our minds can think.

Marianne: After months of sitting with Lance as he Focused, I realized something felt missing. It felt like I was seeing only half the picture. We could Focus alone, I could sit with him, but until we risked being *mutually* vulnerable by both of us Focusing and guiding in the same session, we seemed stuck on one level.

Being vulnerable together is the single most important aspect of our Focusing. It has literally plunged us into a deep awareness. A whole new tangible sense emerges between us, an awareness that our relationship is so much more than Lance and I separately. Our relationship has become an invitation to divine Presence and healing. There is nothing in us that cannot be opened up to grace. *What I realize I really value is not if Lance fits into my script for him at all, but that we can be truly vulnerable together.* That way of being together brings an intense freedom, a lightness and an OKness that is indescribable! What totally boggles our minds is that externals may not in fact change, that sometimes things may even get worse, but there is so much hope, new life, new affection for each other when we can be vulnerable together. It changes the feel of everything. The closest we can come to describing this is to say it feels inside like it did when we were newly in love. It is fresh, soft, exciting and hope-filled: *Our minds could not comprehend what was waiting for us on the other side of control!* It almost seems as if our rational minds are not made to imagine what grace feels like in our bodies! I suspect it would be hard to convince anyone of this in words. It is a reality, a gift that needs to be experienced before it can be understood. And my sense is many heartaches and divorces could be avoided if we could learn to build our lives and relationships on another model, a model of Focusing in mutual vulnerability. The primary spiritual as well as psychological and community value is what happens between us in relationship when both have a chance to lead and be led. The empowerment is given *in the relationship* of mutual vulnerability.

My willingness to be vulnerable seems to break through Lance's resistance as he starts to Focus. His words to me one evening as I had finished Focusing were, "As you Focused tonight, you seemed to draw me right into yourself." The impact of his words felt so spiritual and so sexual to me. It is as if right within my own vulnerability lies the key to intimacy. A trust builds in him when he can be drawn into me like this, and then not only does he have the courage to let go into his own resistances, but he also touches the key to greater intimacy between us. *Owning his walls breaks down the walls between us.* Then we literally become one body. We become one body in the greater Body. When we physically come together like this, another felt-sense grows between us, the sense of giftedness breaks through. There is MORE than the two of us! This MORE between us then becomes our gift to the Larger Body.

3. Having a regular routine for Focusing together.

Without a commitment from both of us to a regular time for Focusing, we found we could come up with a million excuses to skip just this one time. A regular time together seems vital so a basis of trust in the process can begin to grow, not only in us individually but also between us. Without a regular time set aside, I know our natural resistance to Focusing would have won out. Three times a week felt right for us.

4. The starting point is owning what is real.

If I can always be true to what is real inside myself, I already have a sure-footed guide. A bodily wisdom is already in place, drawing me ever closer toward wholeness/holiness. We all are so programmed into thinking that if we take a chance and own what is real inside, it will annihilate us; that somehow if we face how we really feel about ourselves, our sexuality, about those we love, we will be destroyed. Fear comes from expectations that if I let go into how I really feel, I will have no control over the outcome. Moreover, we usually fear not having control over the other's Focusing. It is fear that needs to be gently owned over and over until it is ready to tell its story.

Marianne: In marriage where our relationship is the primary value, I thought as we grew older that risking how I really felt would be the beginning of the end. How can owning what is real in me bring greater wholeness and freedom?

One evening while Lance was Focusing with me, I was staying with a particularly heavy feeling in my chest. I sensed it was something about our relationship and I had to first stay with the fear of this being too much to handle. The words that surfaced, "Lance feels so heavy to me," brought a surprised relief. I'm still somewhat surprised that the content of our stories never blows us away. I sense the fear comes from being out of touch with the meaning beneath the heaviness and not from the story itself! The owning of what's real and the sharing after Focusing bring a tremendous openness between couples because at some level both know when they are living a lie! When something feels stuck or unspoken or denied between us, it comes as a relief to recognize and own it.

5. *Learning the Art of Waiting.*

Marianne: Learning to wait with an alert awareness when "nothing" seems to be happening inside has come to be very important for me. The ability to be soft, gentle and caring with my hurt seems to create the right climate more than anything else. When I have invested so much time and energy and little seems to happen, I have learned the importance of the "back burner approach" with my unfinishedness. So much of our life story is always unfinished. This kind of patient waiting with ourselves prepares the soil so beautifully for the next step.

Lance: So often as I begin to Focus, I find myself coming up against a wall of resistance. In my Focusing I can feel wanting to let go, yet I also have a strong resistance of not wanting to let go. Sometimes a feeling of playing a game, a head trip comes up which tells me I am not willing to let go. At other times my critic, my wanting to be hard on myself, comes forward just as I want to be gentle with my feelings. It is a familiar pattern. I seem to cancel the whole process by taking on too much. Then I come up against a hard wall where everything seems impossible, and the harder I push against this wall, the harder the wall becomes. It is like I am giving that wall additional strength and energy. My first reaction is to run! I have learned to make a space for this resistance, sit next to it, go camping with it, promise it I will come back to it during the day.

I can feel the gradual chipping away of an old pattern in me. During one Focusing experience, I came up against the familiar thick wall. My body felt tight around the issue of control. As I took time to own what playing games and clinging to control felt like, the words "I feel so weary hanging in like this" eased the tightness a bit. As Marianne and I were reflecting back on this experience, it moved again as I said, "The owning of what I feel in me makes me very vulnerable, and it's the vulnerability that diminishes my control." Marianne said the look on my face was one of a trusting child. I could not believe it. I have always said if I could just let go of this damned control, I would. But that has never worked. This time I let go by surprise!

Marianne: It is so necessary to check in during the day to be gently with the feel of an issue. Being with ourselves this way prepares the inner soil for growth when the time is ripe. Creating this kind of atmosphere with ourselves day in and day out is the key, we have found, to nurturing further growth. My hands are tied *and* I have to sit and wait. I cannot *do* anything *myself*. Then this quiet waiting somehow creates a different inner climate. A deep knowing is tapped, a knowing that bypasses the usual frantic needing to have results, to manipulate ourselves and others in order to feel good about ourselves or in order to fit everything into our script for each other. *There is a kind of knowing that somehow this waiting place is pregnant with grace. It is precisely in that waiting place that we have to be with each other, no strings attached.*

6. Owning our fears as a way to grow spiritually.

Marianne: As I was owning a particularly heavy, frightening place inside myself one morning, the image of an old turtle fit exactly how I was feeling. I could feel the heavy shell on my shoulders weighing me down so that I could hardly walk. My nose was only a few inches from the ground. Only my head and neck were out for air. Heavy legs added to the heaviness I already felt in my shoulders. I was dealing with the issue of my own mortality. Waiting for reports of blood tests from a recent visit to an oncologist always seems to plunge me into the heart of my control versus letting go. The words "I really can't hold myself up," came. I always feel there will be a reccurrence of cancer, even after more than three years of a clean bill of health. I know it is one of the last really big issues I have ignored. With the words "I'm tired of trying to hold myself up," came a very deep, familiar yearning in me really to step aside and allow myself to be taught another way, and I said, "It feels like the pain in my body is giving birth in me to a new kind of relationship with myself." Lance said, "How does that feel inside, to be taught another way?" In a flash, a memory came of me 30 years ago in a classroom as a postulant in the convent. We were being given a talk by our spiritual mistress. She was telling us that if only we followed all the directives in the little black book she was giving us that day, we would discover God's will in our lives. I remember clearly the deep yearning and hope that brought. If I could follow all these outside ways of behaving, then I would find the spiritual in my life. This particular morning the same yearning was there, but a very different realization surfaced: "My yearning to let go into more holiness has to be a letting go into this fear in my body and the heavy weighted-down feeling in my own muscles. This is my key to spiritual growth, the owning of my own brokenness. This yearning for freedom and holiness comes right within my own body." As I paused with the body-feel of these words, I was aware how they could never convey the texture of their feeling. The feeling was literally that nothing could come between me and my continued growth into more wholeness. "Thanks be to God" seemed to say it best!

Some Final Reflections

We have often wondered if there would be any noticeable difference in our boys as Lance and I continue to Focus together. Lately, we have noticed a definite "softening into himself" in David, our 18-year-old. It seems more than the ordinary "growing up" that we see in kids his age. In part, our sense of this change comes from Lance being softer with the boys as he learns to be more gentle with his own unfinishedness. We value very much our 15- and 18-year-old boys seeing their father a part of what could very easily seem to them a woman's journey. Growing toward more wholeness, becoming more at ease in oneself, is for both men and women. Seeing their father involved in Focusing gives them special permission and courage to do the same as they grow into their identity as men. It gives them a concrete model. So for our teenage boys, this new pattern modeled by *their father* says to them: in the future when I am hurt or afraid, I will remember what Dad did when he was confused and weary. It is O.K. to be vulnerable! For boys to witness this model toward painful issues so different from the usual one of dominance or control is to break through generations of old cultural patterns. They will know their dad pointed out another way.

As the years go by in our marriages, most of us inevitably get caught up in scripts we write for ourselves, our spouses and our kids, trying to manipulate and fix almost every aspect of these relationships. We demand that the other do things "my way or else." All our manipulative, controlling tricks come out of the bag as we apply them to the situations we have no control over.

What has dawned on us as Focusing Companions is that Focusing dramatically changed this destructive pattern in our marriage. Together, the regular owning of what is real, more than anything else, has nurtured the bodily wisdom of our original attraction to each other. This one simple learning seems to turn everything around. We see this as the single most important step enabling couples to grow together! It is never too late for couples who want to make a change. It is never too late to grow more whole together. Our sense is that we *can* reverse so much of the heartache that exists in marriages today.

No matter how old we are, no matter how many mistakes we have made—and we have all made them in one form or another—it's never too late to own what is real in ourselves now, letting the ripples of that inner wholeness touch those we love. Even if we did not Focus with our children when they were young, how many opportunities we have now as college-age children come home and as married children return. They still can be influenced by our growth. It is always time for fresh beginnings. The miracle of change is possible. We have found that this miracle of change can happen if both of us are faithful to the learnings we have just shared with you. For us, it feels like a grounded pathway to peace within ourselves, in others and in God.

Chapter 10

Focusing Companions: Discovering Together the body/Body Life of Spirit

WHOLENESS (HOLINESS) FLOWS OUT OF OUR OWN INTEGRATION and the experience we acquire from nurturing each other in non-dominative relationships which say: "In order to be somebody and to feel good about who I am, I don't have to fix myself or anybody else."

As you have read in Lance and Marianne's chapter, there is absolutely nothing comparable to the empowerment that comes between two people than what happens when they allow themselves to be graced through mutual Focusing.

As I wrote earlier, this is because the hope or feel of a future in any relationship does not lie in everything being all okay according to the scripts we bring to that relationship. Rather, hope lies in the discovery that we can feel good about ourselves even when we are not yet whole (or "perfect") and when the external things are not yet okay. How? Because that sense of a promising future is the gift we receive when each person can own the truth of their script, allowing its real meaning to be given. It is the body-feel of that unfolding story inside and between us that brings the hope. The "felt" story is usually so different in its "feel" than the script we have written. These scripts we all bring to relationships are what get in the way. They usually involve in some way trying to fix the relationship and each other, instead of together owning these scripts in such a way that their true stories emerge. Being together in this truth always feels safe, caring, non-manipulative, life-giving, honest, intimately connected, trusting—all qualities we hunger and search for in relationships of commitment.

We learn as Focusing Companions that the most important teacher in life and in any growing relationship is not some guru, venerable tradition, rule book, or outside model, valuable at times as these may be. But our most significant and primary source of wisdom comes in simply owning and listening to whatever is real inside us. Held in a Focusing way, sooner or later it will guide and teach us. In a relationship, this changes the quality of its feel and of the way we carry our own agenda. In an earlier chapter I said that most people, to some degree, live a lie in their relationships. Focusing companionship turns this untruthfulness upside-down, but not through confrontation. It comes through the body-feel of "graced" truth. This feels so different from mutual resignation, a cold war, or always planning out the next confrontation or explanation. However, until you actually experience it, the mind cannot conceive how hope is not somehow connected to being fixed, or resolving all the issues. But there is empowerment in the wholeness that comes from owning whatever is real in our bodies. Being at home in our bodies with this realness invites Spirit. Doing this together creates a community of grace.

In the quote I used from Gendlin earlier, he describes this atmosphere well when he said: "Every 'bad' feeling is potential energy toward a more right way of being if you give it space to move toward its rightness."[1] Focusing companions give each other and their relationship that "noncontrolling space," so that every important feeling, especially the so-called "bad" ones, can move in the direction they know is right.

This was brought home to me very poignantly when, after years of criticizing Pete's compulsive workaholism, we were sitting together in a Focusing Companion session. Pete was focusing on some of his feelings about what this was doing to his writing, our relationship, his creativity, and our living/working environment when the words came, "It feels like you telling me what's wrong with me all the time makes me fight against these feelings in myself. I feel like rejecting everything connected with this whole thing in myself, instead of holding it and listening to it."

Those were breakthrough words and the closest he had ever come to even admitting the worsening problem. As he sat in this safe climate where none of this confrontation was going on, they stirred to the surface. Staying with this over the months in Focusing Companionship, so much of the story underneath this destructive behavior has finally been given a chance to speak. Just as with Marianne and Lance, the Focusing Companionship has literally saved us on the brink of disaster. But for me personally, it has not only intellectually convinced me, but deeply touched me in how pointless and deadended my continuing explanations have been for 25 years. Pete needed from me the support to care for, not reject, all the feelings around his need to control through work, because an important piece of his self-identity and worth was invested there. I was not giving him that support when we "talked it over like two adults" and I pointed out the problems it was creating. It only made him want to push that part of himself further away, making the problem worse, until we accidentally stumbled on the Focusing Companion way of Focusing together.

Prior to that, we would Focus together each day after breakfast, each doing his own Focusing, then sharing afterwards. At any time during or outside these regular Focusing times, we were always available and willing to help each other Focus if something came up and either of us needed help. But one was guide, the other Focused. There was never time set aside for *mutual* Focusing and guiding, because morning Focusing was limited to fifteen minutes and there were no time constraints on "emergencies." After any long session, we were both too tired to do anything more. As a result, the Focusing relationship never felt mutually vulnerable and supportive enough to surface the deeply-protected issues, that is, not until Pete experienced me along with him being mutually vulnerable as an equal focuser. Even better, if my Focusing then was on the pain, isolation, frustration, etc., that I felt in our deteriorating relationship, and if the sharing came after genuine shifts inside me had occurred, then this had a deep impact on opening up Pete to his role and responsibility in this. Prior to and outside this companion-setting, Pete had drawn up his defenses and I was trying to break through them. Inside the companion-setting, Pete did not need walls and I did not need to attack. Moreover, the habit-protected places in both of us that were harming the relationship could be drawn to the surface in this atmosphere. We both could feel that unconditional, non-manipulative acceptance of each other "as is," not "should be," and this helped us befriend those deeply-embedded stories so they could risk beginning to speak. When a Focusing Companion can feel the other(s) let go of their agenda for him/her, then that person can finally relax into what is real and needs listening to inside. Prior to that body-experience, protective walls need to be kept in place.

Within this personal discovery, Focusing Companions learn how the process of "graced community" goes forward so we can then guide others to find it for themselves. The teacher is within us, as is every person's unique body-awareness of gift (grace). Indeed, the process (of community as gift) *IS* the message and Christianity teaches that the message is the *PROCESS*. Growing into greater unity is possible because, as St. Paul put it, "we live in Christ." To experience this, though, together we need to be with whatever is real in our bodies in a safe, supportive environment, waiting and listening to the teacher within. Creating this caring, nonmanipulative climate so the body/Body's guidance can be heard is the indispensable role Focusing Companions play in building communities of grace. To find and listen to that inner resource within each of us, that body-sense of the Spirit guiding us into the next step in life, is why Focusing Companions come together. God-consciousness grows out of such body-spirituality.

As we enter the last decade of this century, it is my dream that what we are discovering as Focusing Companions will become an effective catalyst for empowering couples to assume leadership in the development of a spirituality that touches what is real inside us and in life today. This new spirituality must be able to bring about critically-needed family and environmental changes, especially in the lives of children. In the Catholic world, as the active role of religious communities and priests declines, a socially-effective spirituality must emerge from the world and values of married life.

This new spirituality must be one that not only is psychologically and theologically healthy, but grows out of and directly connects with the struggles, pain and joys of married and family life. It must be a spirituality that can bring God's grace directly into what is real in relationships of intimacy, providing direction and healing for the wounds we bring to such commitments. It must touch the fears, hidden agenda, and challenges that any long-term relationship faces. Parents with young children are especially hungry to learn how to keep their marriages growing and together, as well as enhance their parental role in a way that is healthy and spiritually sound.

We have been given a priceless gift and direction for the future in the mutual vulnerability of Focusing together. When such vulnerability can happen between parents, finally, it will touch children. This is an extraordinary and completely surprising step, taking us far beyond what we had already learned from using Focusing in a ministry, counseling, or spiritual direction model, valid and helpful as these have been and continue to be.

Something far more significant happens when one person in a relationship is not "teacher" or "expert" and the other "learner" or "client." When journeying together in *mutual vulnerability*, there is a common sharing and acknowledgement of inner brokenness and need. Then, under such circumstances, the being together moves beyond a relationship of power and dependence into one of equality as invitation for grace. By mutually owning what is real in our bodies *as a community*, we open the unfinished struggle of that relationship to God's grace.

This is a vital and significant step beyond private Focusing, beyond ministry or service Focusing and into community Focusing. Inexperienced as we may be in the development of this next step, it becomes immediately apparent that a precious, exciting model for "relationships of grace" is now surfacing here. Whether there is some special conflict among us or we are simply enjoying a regular Focusing Companions session together, the mutual vulnerability of body-openness breaks down the body-feel of hardness and defenses with which we armor ourselves when we feel threatened. It helps us move beyond trying to fix ourselves and others or to manipulate those around us to secure our agenda. With this loosening of the dominance body-feel, we can make contact with one another at a much deeper level. We are more "in" each other rather than on the outside, separated, alienated, and alone.

Something begins to shift inside our bodies with this loosening, as we experience in such softening a growing security and trust, together with a diminishment of the need to stand our ground, protecting ourselves from vulnerability. Fear eases because the focuser is no longer trying to control anything or anyone, including him/herself. The guide has let go of the same control. Nobody is fixing anybody. Instead, they are both connected within the intimacy of a real presence to each other which rarely, if ever, do we permit to happen within, let alone between ourselves. This shared Real Presence is what Eucharist as the Life of the Body of the Whole Christ is all about—living in the body and its feelings (the flesh and blood) of each other *as one Body*. Present formats of Eucharist distance us and disempower us from this experience of Eucharist.

Married couples know the feel of body barriers at all levels of their communication. They live in this world every day. The health of their marriage depends upon continuous growth both personally and as a relationship, especially in body openness. They know that nurturing and growing in their body availability to each other and their children must have top priority if their relationship is ever going to last, let alone mature. Carrying negative feelings like resentment or anger, experience soon teaches them, is deadly to mutual vulnerability and any kind of caring openness in their communication with each other. For example, there is something so sacred in the quality of body-presence to a child—in play, helping with homework, taking time to teach something—which says: "You are valuable and worth my time." Its feel of availability and openness to the limitations of being a child blesses that child with the self-esteem which makes the risks of growing in later life possible.

We learn our most important life-values through our body from the feel of other bodies. What message comes into the very tissues of a child's body when parents are so wounded that they cannot be present, or live so rushed and with other priorities that they do not take time to guide the child by their body-presence into discovering and prizing his/her own unique spirit. All of this depends on a quality of body-communication, which in turn depends on whether or not we can be congruent with the feelings we carry in our bodies now.

Gendlin's research in Focusing clearly shows that the key element in processing feelings, so that bodies are open and can connect in passing on self-esteem to each other, is grace. Perhaps this is too much of a religious word for some people, but the "gift dimension" of the process, both in the "felt-shift" in one's own body as well as the quality of body-availability to others this makes possible, must be recognized as essential.

Without this indispensable ingredient, self-esteem programs degenerate quickly into some new rehash of dominance.

Most people in long-term, committed relationships, especially married couples with children, are already motivated to become Focusing Companions because they instinctively know what I have just said, although they may not know what to do to work through the barriers. If we are ever to make any significant change in the level of violence and destruction in human relationships, the time has come for those whose lifestyle involves such a commitment to assume responsibility in developing a new body-spirituality for family life.

Just imagine the impact on children in a home where their parents were Focusing Companions! Imagine the impact on a neighborhood if some of these parents gathered to use Focusing skills to help troubled and delinquent kids! What would happen in our schools if children grew up knowing Focusing, and gathered together after school in order to help one another as Focusing Companions. Imagine the preparation for marriage and parenting they would get if their school and church environment supported what they were learning at home. What an impact this would have on their role in the community as adults!

This is not just "peer counseling" for the "less fortunate or disadvantaged." This would be body-learning in *creating "graced" community*—quite a different model from the more traditional one of "dominance," "charity," or "service." In this scenario, the more-advantaged do not dole out their skills, charity, and education to the less-advantaged.

What we in our culture, and especially our children, are most deprived of is the body-feel of an alternative to the only model we know—namely, control, manipulation and dominance. Most of us do not have any body-feel for the alternative—God's grace. The model for support groups and community-building at all levels that can come out of what we are learning as Focusing Companions has the potential to break this deadly pattern if we can reorganize ourselves and reach out to those already eager to bring health to their marriages and family life.

This missing body-feel for an alternative to the myth of dominance destroys us all, but most especially our most sensitive and promising children when they feel hopelessly trapped.

In her pain and frustration the aunt of the young 16-year-old who took his life expresses her anguish and questions in a letter weeks after the funeral:

It's three weeks later, and I'm still stopped everywhere I go by people wanting to talk about his suicide. "What happened?" they ask. "Why did he take his life?" "He had everything going for him." "What went wrong?" This isn't supposed to happen in a white, middle-class family where their 16-year-old son had such a promising future. When someone from the drug scene or from an abusive family takes his life, we seem to "understand." But when this happens to a college-prep honors student, the mind reels! A whole community anguishes at the senselessness of it all. The fear is rampant. "If it can happen in a "good" family, why not in ours? is the unspoken question I see in their eyes.

In reflecting back on these past three weeks, next to the deep ache and sadness I feel at the loss of my godchild is a sense of shock I feel at the insanity I see all around. How very *primitive* we are in the way we handle pain—from the medical professionals who try to numb the pain with muscle relaxants and tranquilizers to the therapists who were called in immediately to help parents. Their endless words, as they themselves felt out of control and were so eager to make the pain stop: "You know it's not your fault. You did the best you could. You shouldn't blame yourselves. At some point, we can't take responsibility for our kid's actions. You have three other children who need you, so look toward the future and don't look back." Some tried to listen, but quickly reverted back to talking when "nothing" seemed to happen, obviously ill-at-ease in their own confusion at "what to do." They couldn't "fix" such pain, so they panicked.

Endless words in the face of such tragedy! All clamoring for control where everything felt so out of control. In fact, the parents **were** blaming themselves. In retrospect, they were saying, "How blind we were. There were signs all around, and we just didn't realize what was happening." No one was there to help them own the excruciating terror *they* felt. All reverted back to the myth of dominance.

As the days went by, I realized how painful it was for me to watch not only the professionals let us down, but also the church, good friends, and even our own families. Who among us knows how to journey inside with us? Who knows how to help us own what is real in ourselves? How long must we continue to deny our feelings under the disguise of "good intentions"?˙ Everyone scrambles for answers when there are no answers to tragedies. No words will ever make any sense or bring this boy back.

The questions kept screaming inside me: How is it that in 1991, within a successful, sophisticated family who really love each other, there can be such tremendous ignorance? Why do so many still not know what's missing? How is it that we still don't know that the answers lie right within the very pain we're all trained to deny and run from? How can we have come so far and missed so much? How can we let people know that the answer lies right within the pain they fear so much, that there is a process already in place to teach us a way to be with how we feel?

The misinterpretation of the role of pain is the killer! We seem so ready to try *anything* rather than pay attention to the teacher that lies waiting within our own bodies. We escape in talking about feelings, hoping that just mentioning them will ease the pain. The church tells us that God takes young children because He has a special plan and saw they were good. It's a plan they tell us we can't understand because it's a mystery. If we don't go with the church, all manner of New Age gimmicks are waiting in the wings to help us. We can even contact the dead through a variety of "channelers." They all attempt to comfort, but miss the mark, because they are saturated with control from beginning to end. How far out do we need to go before we will stop and come to our senses? The self-inflicted death of a child has to be the most bizarre symbol of a culture gone wrong! When will the craziness that is destroying us stop?

As a mother who is teaching my own children to Focus, I was particularly distraught as I saw how we as mothers try to protect our children from pain. In a conversation with my sister, I heard what I think has been the huge stumbling block for parents. She was telling me that driving her 14-year-old daughter to school one morning, she was warning her that she might hear comments from the kids about her brother's death. She told her: "Just ignore them, kids can be cruel at times." I listened as it dawned on me how often I've heard similar statements from parents. Before we can ever teach our children how to listen in a gentle way to their pain we too must learn how to care for our own pain, and fears. We need to learn how bodily to hold our own fear of rejection, misunderstandings, and loneliness. If we always look upon pain as the enemy, it's only natural that we will try to protect our children. It's instinctive for us to protect our children. Wouldn't it make more sense to teach them a process like Focusing so they would know *how* to be with hurting feelings? Instead, we try to cover all bases where we think they may get hurt. As we continue to deny our feelings and those of one another, one tragedy after another piles up. If we don't find another way and find it soon, our inner wars will continue to be waged at the price of our children's lives. My nephew gave up in his struggle to find his own spirit when the system around him felt too overwhelming and he knew of no alternative.

* * * * *

Children who have learned to change and grow by not doing violence to themselves and others have found the kingdom of heaven and God within. They know with a "body-faith" that change is possible, and that the kind of change which brings wholeness and peace comes as a gift, not through dominance. This is what Focusing as Companions helps us discover together. It is a rite of passage, a liturgy, a ritual of profound conversion away from the powers of self-alienation, of shame, of fear and human destruction into the empowerment of graced community. We find a community of gift and hope inside ourselves as well as in relationship to all that surrounds us. "In truth, in very truth I tell you a grain of wheat remains a solitary grain unless it falls into the ground and dies; but if it dies, it bears a rich harvest."[2]

Focusing Companions tap into a Real Presence. The walls, the armor, the separations that we construct in order to protect ourselves begin to loosen and crumble. Within this Real Presence we are joined together in an intimacy which our bodies know as sacred and as gift. More deeply rooted in the *Body* through our own bodies, we can grow to love ourselves and others. From this union inside ourselves and with one another a new presence is born in our midst—softer, gentler, more open, wide-eyed, fragile, yet filled with promise and hope for the future.

Sound familiar? Yes, not unlike the feel of a child. As I wrote earlier, the Gospels tell us, "He called a child over, placed it in their midst, and said, 'Amen, I say to you: unless you turn and become like little children, you will not enter the Kingdom of Heaven.'"[3] Jesus introduced the child as model, not to extol innocence but childhood openness and vulnerability. And, as you recall, I commented that this is what Focusing Companions really become when journeying together in mutual vulnerability. Bit by bit within the safety of this special relationship, they take off the armor that blocks grace getting through to their feelings in the body. But to do this means breaking with old cultural traditions and patterns in spirituality that neglected and negated the body and its feelings.

The ancient clerical and religious life out of which the Christian spirituality we know emerged, both as an expression of that world and as a means to perpetuate it, is fast disappearing. Today people still have the same basic needs and hungers as they did in the past. But they no longer find nourishment in a disembodied clerical spirituality that feels unreal and irrelevant to their lives. The Catholic Church in particular is confronted with a practical problem of leadership in developing a spirituality of human interpersonal relationships that can replace the model from the past. The reason is that the present clerical and religious leadership have rarely experienced nor do they have widespread support to live in small, long-term, committed interpersonal relationships. This is deadly for their spiritual growth because it provides them with no trusting, intimate and long-term companionship within which they can safely enter into their bodies and own their feelings day after day.

"Professional" religious people are still "married" to some expression of service or ministry. They are married to their religious order's mission wherever that may take them, or to their image of Christ, of God, etc. They have been encouraged and trained to be vulnerable to their image of Christ, but rarely with one another. Where outside of marriage is the experience and the commitment that will provide us with a new model of spirituality, a model flowing out of "graced relationships" rather than a rehash once again of the outworn versions of dominance we have inherited from our religious and patriarchal past?

The world of parents struggling not to pass on inherited wounds to their children, and couples agonizing as they endeavor to hold their partnerships or marriages together is the real womb of today's spirituality. These relationships, under tremendous stress, but still prized, are the fertile ground within which a relevant "spirituality of relationship" can be created. The mutual vulnerability of couples and small communities Focusing together will reveal within these broken and suffering bodies the healing power of God's grace. A spirituality that offers hope for the future must emerge from this experience of trying to create and live a new quality of interpersonal presence, first of all in our families. If there were cultural support for the development of Focusing Companions just among small groups of friends, this too would touch many, many lives, particularly if those involved were in service or ministry roles.

In my Focusing Companion ministry team of two men and one woman, in addition to the ordinary differences of opinion, personality, ways of working, etc., that inevitably arise, habit-protected places that block effective ministry are healing. As the Thompson's have written, the key that allows well-protected places to change inside us is the body-feel of unconditional acceptance by another. Marianne's words were: "It's this freedom in me (to accept him as he is) that somehow gives Lance the space to allow what's in him to surface and be owned." And as she wrote further on: "Our minds could not comprehend what was waiting for us on the other side of control." This applies just as much to the renewal of churches, health care, ministry, service, education, rehab work, etc., as it does to a marriage and family life. Healthy religious communities, both east and west, won't happen either until they discover what "awaits them on the other side of control." In fact, more and more people are looking for this alternative to control in whatever they are going to call "church" in the future, because they know all this is preparation for the real challenge that lies ahead.

Some day, enough people on this planet will be ready to transcend old ethnic and denominational, as well as cultural animosities and differences in order to develop an environmental, global spirituality that is rooted in the common body-experience of "grace" *which we all share as human beings.* That experience can save our planet! Spiritual values discovered within the same body we all share can bond us together in protecting our planet's fragile ecology.

The simplicity and transcultural experience of Focusing, coming out of the common foundation of our body's consciousness, is the most hope-filled gift I know of that promises the world's children a future on this globe. It is a priceless treasure of God that comes at a time when we all need it so desperately. But, like many unexpected gifts, it still waits to be discovered while we slowly move toward recognizing the absolute necessity of a global spirituality as the foundation for our very survival.

For Christians, unless we begin by honoring and respecting our own body with its wisdom and direction as a living cell in the Body of the Whole Christ, we will not know how to respect and listen to the Whole Body of humankind. Focusing helps people find self-esteem in the acceptance of who they are, warts and all. It enables them to connect their hunger for the sacred, a Higher Power, and greater Wholeness (holiness) with the way they treat themselves and the world around them.

This is all very basic stuff that Focusing Companions learn from the inside rather than as an outside ideal, theory, sermon or one more impossible "should be" that make us feel even more helpless and a failure.

During the coming years, effective ways must be found to encourage parents to become Focusing Companions. This will model Focusing in the home, where children can then be taught a way of owning their real feelings by being gentle and caring as they listen for the story in this part of themselves. Gradually, within generations that follow us will arise the foundation for a spirituality of environmental wholeness as we learn not to betray our bodies. As children learn to find and be true to their body-spirit, then as adults they will have no need to escape into the ideology of domination to fill the vacuum. When we are bodily grounded and experience empowerment in our bodies, life itself carries all the meaning we ever need. We do not need to substitute behaviors of manipulation to feel good about ourselves. Living in the body/Body carries its own overflowing fullness of meaning because it is our life of Spirit.

When such spiritual values can be communicated in and through a process like Focusing, where children are taught to feel the gift (grace) in their bodies, then cultural, ethnic and religious diversity will no longer be seen as obstacles to the growth of a global, environmental spirituality. When people from diverse backgrounds realize that such spiritual experience is *our common "body heritage"* and is environmentally healthy, they will simultaneously realize that this in no way betrays whatever has been healthy in their own spiritual tradition.

Focusing provides an ongoing inner environment for the body-experience of gift (grace). It is simple, practical, teachable and easily passed on to adults as well as children in widely-diverse cultures. Focusing provides concrete steps and tools that allow our bodies to feel the gift of change in human relationships. Rather than merely discussing ideas or opinions about the need for change, Focusing helps us let go into the body sense of whatever is real—fear, guilt, anger, loneliness, etc. Then, change in how we carry such feelings can happen. Stuck feelings are the underlying engine of destruction that first must be opened to healing if people are to sense their tied-in-ness to each other and their environment.

Without a spirituality grounded in the body, enabling us to own and not deny or neglect the untold stories within such feelings, then fear, security needs, greed, etc., will continue to dominate and destroy our relationships on this planet. Focusing teaches us how to allow God's grace into our feelings. Talking and thinking, even with the best of intentions, do not do this. *There is an alternative* to the myth of dominance and control that has so infected cultures, spiritualities, relationships and self-experience up to this point in human history. I fervently believe that the number one priority during this coming decade and for the new century we will soon enter must be to spread the "Good News" of this alternative to younger generations. Their creativity and faith in themselves will then be sparked to pass it on once again to their own children. By doing this, a new life-giving spirituality will be born on our beloved planet earth.

Once young people discover this "amazing grace" right within the very feelings they run from, it will just make good sense for them to want all their relationships to be part of this miracle as well.

Chapter 11

The Voice of Sexuality from Inside the Graced Body

Why Are We Afraid to Bless, to Share, to Love Each Other With What In Us Is Not Yet Perfect?[1]

AS I LISTEN TO THE AGONY AND BEWILDERMENT OF CHRISTIANS struggling to find guidance for all the issues of human sexuality on our agenda today, nobody seems to pay any attention to the fact that the people voting on these issues at Church synods and conventions, or who write documents for the Vatican, are themselves products of a very dysfunctional and body-alienated culture. How do these individuals discern guidelines for the sexual behavior of other bodies when they have probably disowned their own and have no spirituality that allows God's grace to speak within them through the owning of their own sexual needs and feelings? Most of us need to do our own homework first.

We all come out of a church that uses an asceticism of control to enforce morality. This also has become the assumed secular model we take for granted. When there is trouble, increase the control—add more police or tighten up enforcement. Today, religion as well as civil governments still invest much of our human and financial resources in this outmoded paradigm.

My view is that for religion to provide healthy moral and spiritual leadership in society, religious people need to learn an asceticism and spirituality of gift. This is a spirituality that allows God's grace to guide us through the very brokenness within our bodies. It allows the story in our fears, our shaming, and old wounds to be heard. Before any of us take on the enormous challenge of coming together in order to articulate the particulars of a sexual morality both consistent with the life and meaning of Jesus, as well as the human process of wholeness, we must first listen to the story of brokenness in our own bodies through which the Spirit speaks.

For those who believe that Jesus is the way, the truth and the life, not only for ourselves but our planet, then the most powerful witness they can give is to be growing into wholeness themselves. What better opportunity for this than within the challenging and changing world of human sexuality. To exercise this needed leadership, Christians must discover that learning to be at home in their bodies empowers their sexuality in the Spirit. Not only individual Christians, but married couples, families and church leadership need this empowerment to live their own truth before they can presume to give guidelines to others.

This is a confusing time for everyone because we are inundated with everything around us directed toward the body. We are told we must share feelings, we must put on this kind of lotion, we must eat this type of food, we must wear this perfume, never be too fat or too thin, wear this brand of clothing, and on and on. Most advertising incessantly harps on the body day after day. Such all-encompassing body preoccupation is actually a fixation, an addiction to pursuing things *outside* our body as the solution and answer to all our inner needs. It engenders compulsive, obsessive behavior and, of course, is the exact opposite of what we mean by the body process of owning in a Focusing way the truth of what we feel in our bodies.

This obsession with things outside as a remedy for the inner feel of our unfinishedness is the exact opposite of a healthy congruence with whatever is real in our bodies. It is the antithesis of that quality of responsible, inner presence that brings about self-possession and allows our own unique spirit-life to move forward toward wholeness. Our body-fixated culture is actually preaching a gospel of body denial. It refuses to believe that there can be graced movement in our feelings, within the very brokenness from which we flee. This is where the inner life of Spirit in our spirit comes into our awareness. Our culture denies any answer or response that comes from within our body. There are only the outside, the external, material products which it hucksters.

This endless message with which we are constantly bombarded tells us there is no "story" to be listened to within our feelings. There is no inner process to be honored. Least of all is there any gifted answer that will come to us if we but wait and listen in openness and faith, not running from whatever is real inside ourselves to grab the first quick fix being marketed. But, of course, there is no easy money to be made on the world's best market, our feelings of unfinishedness, if we say too loudly that answers only come from *inside* ourselves. We never hear about carrying that unfinishedness in our bodies as an invitation to God's *free* gift of Grace.

Few know how to find a healthy approach to their body in this confusion. However, some things are becoming more clear. For example, at this time in history, the externals of human relationships are vastly different from what they were in Biblical times. Moreover, we are living through a turning point in human experience where there is clearly an evolution in human consciousness. It involves both the knowing capacity of our bodies as well as our minds.

Therefore, we cannot risk being alienated from our bodies as we seek to develop the social and religious support that will create communities of grace for the future. How else can Christians understand the continuing Incarnation and presence of Jesus in our midst? Surely not by disowning our human, sexual body that is His Presence here on earth? Jesus was and is the profound revelation that graced sexuality and spirituality are one in our human body.

But, as Robert Bly would put it:

When men and women come together,
. . . how much they have to abandon!
Wrens make their nests of fancy
threads and string ends, animals
abandon all their money each year.
What is that men and women leave?
Harder than wrens' doing, they have
to abandon their longing for the perfect.[2]

The stakes are just that high before a new Body, not yet born, can ever come to birth. This Body groans toward a unity, a fullness, a oneness in all this confusion, not by perpetuating the old system of control (which is what we abandon with this obsession for the perfect), but by laboring toward a graced wholeness as we learn to "own" and love ourselves and each other in all our unfinishedness.

What caused us each to live hidden?
A wound, the wind, a word, a parent.
Sometimes we wait in a helpless way,
awkwardly, not whole and not healed.
When we hid the wound, we fell back
from a human to a shelled life . . .[3]

* * * * *

In the month of May when all leaves open
I see when I walk how well all things
lean on each other, how the bees work,
the fish make their living the first day.
Monarchs fly high; then I understand
I love you with what in me is unfinished.

I love you with what in me is still
changing, what has no head or arms
or legs, what has not found its body . . .
And lovers, tough ones, how many there are
whose holy bodies are not yet born.[4]

"Then I understand, I love you with what in me is unfinished. I love you with what in me is still changing. . . ." Those few lines capture so clearly what we have missed. We run from the terror of it, and in so doing never love in grace, in truth, in the unfinishedness of the human, limited persons who we are and always will be. When is it that we plan to have this magical, perfect love life? What a strange paradox that by rejecting the body-feel of our incompleteness in all its human expression, we close off our only invitation to God's grace—our unfinishedness. Then we must fall back on control, on performance, manipulation, charades and all the power-brokering that blocks us from intimacy. No wonder our bodies in their always-incomplete sexual wholeness cry out in pain and desperation for intimacy! We have painted ourselves into an impossible corner, not only by denying the body-feel of unfinishedness that we are, but in refusing to bless, to share and to gift each other with what in us is not yet perfect.

All this comes about because in our culture we have lost the body-feel for grace, which can only be known by owning that in us which is unfinished. We are left with sexual bodies programmed and conditioned to block the very life-giving, healing energies we need to experience that intimacy which only happens in relationships of grace. Reject the unfinishedness, the wounds, hurts, and fears in our sexual bodies and we reject what in us is most needing of God's grace. Shamed, we perceive our incomplete humanity as a wall, not a doorway into the world of gift that it actually is.

Sexuality and beauty, more than anything else, are meant to give us a body-feel for the two worlds about which Robert Bly writes. One world—of hiding, repression, using others; a world of lies, deception and dominance hides the doorway of passion and the beauty of our bodies as a special, privileged path that is meant to carry us into the other world of gifted nakedness between ourselves. It is a realm of graced nakedness, the birthing place of a new Body in the mutual vulnerability of truthfulness together.

We do not discover this rich realm of God's amazing grace just because we happen to be born Irish or Italian Catholic, come from a devout Methodist family, have gone through Baptist Bible or parochial school, go to church every Sunday, or do whatever else we assume connects us with Christianity.

Rather, we make contact with this whole world and its revelation in Jesus—even if we do not understand it—when we connect with our own body in utter truthfulness. When the game playing is over, it is then and only then that we stand on the threshold of a new world, a world that lies just beyond the gamble of roulette we play with life, as we are swept up into the roles we play for dominance by the roar of the cheering crowd.

All the beauty and attraction of the human body is meant to draw and lead us into this world of grace. All that pulls us into orgasm is meant quite literally to explode us into this gifted sphere where we break through a "glass darkly" into the light.

But, oh, how we need a special nurturing from childhood in order not to disown our unfinishedness, our fears, the shaming and wounds we carry in our bodies, wounds that leave us with sexuality as just one more way to control and numb our hurts. Then, all we can hear is the addictive energy of lust desperately trying to cover up our pain. Loving each other sexually, which is, of course, the only way we can love, is not necessarily synonymous with genital sex. Loving each other sexually in the world of gift, graced loving, flows out of a social climate within which people are encouraged as children to own their bodies—all of what they feel. Adolescents, let alone young lovers contemplating marriage, cannot be expected to integrate their sexuality into life-giving relationships as adults in a society that denies them as children a process for owning whatever is real in their bodies.

Sexuality is meant to be an integral part of the body-feel we have of our own spirit, whether we are two or ninety-two. We suffer a cultural deprivation of this body-feel of Spirit in our sexuality, especially through religion and education, because they disconnect us from our bodies. This is what creates the problems of sexual integration. An atmosphere of educating and valuing only our rational thinking ability alienates us from the lifelong process of discovering, nurturing and living in the sexual body-feel of our own spirit. As we journey through all the stages of life, Spirit waits for us at each stage as a special step into wholeness if we are encouraged to be guided by our own unique body-spirit.

The Body-life of Spirit is known only through our body, a sexual body within the body-feel of our own spirit. The personal, social, spiritual and environmental consequences of breaking this sacred covenant with our bodies is disastrous. I firmly believe that Christianity will become more and more an irrelevant anachronism, as human evolution moves forward, unless Christians create a spirituality rooted in the Incarnation—our sexual body "in Christ." Everything else is simply more verbiage, even with the best of intentions and the loftiest of ideals. The proof is in what happens to human sexual bodies on this planet. Do they become more whole, less violent, less destructive of others and the environment around them? The present impact of the world's religions, when evaluated from this perspective, clearly indicates some radical change is necessary in all of them.

Early in life before puberty and adolescence, children must be guided into discovering their sexuality as just one of many fascinating body-feelings for life and sharing. Childhood presence to a broad spectrum of body-feelings through Focusing helps children experience developing sexuality within the context of many options. Sexual feelings become part of a bigger picture, a larger world. The body-feel of sexuality in this wider texture of feelings that unfold into who I am places developing sexual feelings in perspective within the body.

The body-feel of an unfolding me in all that the child allows him/herself to feel as it tells its story in a Focusing way brings the guidance of their own unique spirit "in the Spirit" into play. When, through owning their own vague creative urges, a child discovers the "right" expression for this part of who they are, they can feel in their bodies the gift dimension of their own story unfolding. So, too, the owning of their sexual feelings is part of this same body-openness to grace. Graced direction can come into the whole area of their sexual development and expression. This way, not only do sexual feelings become part of a whole panorama of body-feelings to which they are accustomed to listen and open to grace, but new priorities become possibile. Choice enters more feasibly into the equation as a graced story within these feelings brings the freedom to choose.

As I wrote earlier in the booklet, "A Bio-Spiritual Approach to Sexuality," a process like Focusing expands self-awareness in the body by making room for *all* our feelings. It gives our emotional life space in which to be owned and nurtured. Our erotic and genital feelings, as part of this openness, then have an opportunity to move out into the consciousness of the whole body. Without this spiritually and emotionally healthy process, genital feelings become trapped in the groin, because they are not known as part of the entire inner landscape of body-feelings with which one is familiar. We cannot relax with our sexual energy when we are unable to feel it in a context. With no room to expand into the rest of the body's feelings, genital arousal easily becomes hyperactive.

When these feelings are locked up in the genital area, they literally get claustrophobic. We become preoccupied with needing relief from this build-up because sexual energy has not been given room in which to expand within our body's awareness of itself. Focusing opens up more space inside. It provides the option and freedom to be fully in our bodies as sexual without necessarily expressing ourselves genitally. Focusing provides the practical steps of an inner body awareness that frees us so the innate wisdom of our entire body can permeate genital arousal with its own order and balance. This is very different from repressing genital arousal. Without any space for making room and owning, we invariably become entangled in addictive sexual patterns.

This is as true within the "acceptable" framework of marital sex as outside it. Readily-available sex, in or out of marriage, is not what brings sexual integration. Even the first step of a Focusing Inventory teaches a simple way of gaining access to the body's knowing that sexuality is more broadly based than a preoccupation with genital pleasure. Then, in Step Four, by letting go into the felt-sense, we discover there is even greater breadth to our sexual feelings as the story within them unfolds.

The key that brings integration is the congruence we have with all of our feelings, with all that our body carries. Through congruence we grow more whole in all areas of our life. Unless this is happening through some regularly-used process like Focusing, experience has taught me that couples can have sexual intercourse regularly for years and not grow one iota, either individually or in their relationship.

Recall that by congruence I mean our ability consciously to feel our feelings physiologically (not just sexual but all the others as well), and allow these feelings to symbolize themselves accurately. Unless sexual feelings, like any others, are owned and listened to in this way, then sex can become as incongruent an act for manipulating feelings as is any other process-skipping device that blocks the story in those feelings from unfolding. Sexual feelings, like all the others, are there as doorways to wholeness within the Larger Body, or, in Paul's language, "in Christ." Thus, Focusing not only introduces an alternative beyond dominance or control as the path toward sexual integration, but it opens a doorway on spirituality through the body itself.

If genital sex is the only "felt" item on the menu, simply because the hormones are doing their job and nothing else is ever allowed to be felt, there is hardly much freedom of choice. A Focusing way of living in our body broadens and graces the choices of which we can become aware. Sexual energy and expression is opened out as potentially a much more life-giving, constructive and creative presence. The pleasure of sexual energy and creative contact with others has options far beyond mere genital expression. The hunger we have to connect in a life-giving way with the world around us is nourished and given a wider creative outreach by owning whatever is real in our bodies as a way of spiritual living.

This kind of living inspirits our sexuality. Our sexual energy invigorates as well as begets new life around us. We are born again and again as our presence to our own sexuality reveals more and more of who we are and are becoming. Anyone who lives this way, even in a limited area of their life, knows the body-feel of new energy that floods in, of sudden insight, of things confused suddenly coming together, or new options opening up when they allow themselves just to "be in" the dance, the sculpting, the sport, the music, the sunset. They know how integrative it feels, how whole and connected this fleeting moment seems—like the body pleasure of real, connecting sex versus just the release of sexual tension.

But somehow, especially in religion, we must grow beyond our fear of letting go into the truth of ourselves, of owning whatever is real inside if we are to plunge through into the world of grace. Because religion has taught us to break our sacred body covenant, then all feelings become suspect, and ultimately in the name of religion we deprive ourselves of the body-feel and pleasure of grace. What then do we have left but the power of raging hormones and a path to addictive obsession with our genitals. What irony that in the name of morality and religion we undermine the very body awareness of grace necessary for sexual integration and for the birth of new communities of grace.

How Profoundly Sexual Are All Our Expressions of Life-Giving and Loving

I stood up from weeding my garden to better listen to an unfamiliar sound. Looking around, I could see nothing, but heard something coming closer and closer down the gravel road. Then, suddenly, out from behind the hedge of trees blocking my view came Grandma pulling the new red wagon she had bought for the grandchildren. It was my neighbor, Nancy, and proudly sitting bolt upright in the little cart, like the queen of Sheba surrounded by an entourage of family dogs, sat one of the visiting grandchildren. Nancy did not see me, but as I watched I could feel, even at a distance, her own special way of being life-giving, of communicating her own beautiful sexuality to those around her.

I smiled as I walked into the house, recalling how Bob, her husband, had made a point earlier of emphasizing that they had found the new wagon in Intercourse, Pennsylvania to help celebrate their 40th wedding anniversary when all the grandchildren would arrive. I wonder as they grow older if they realize how deeply sexual the wagon, new sandbox and other loving preparations for these family reunions really are. All that I have said earlier in this book about being programmed to disconnect from our bodies and therefore from the body-feel of our own unique spirit forces us into identifying sexuality only with genital sex. Even though in later life we may vaguely suspect differently, we are still habituated to thinking along the lines of this narrow perception. We feel ill-at-ease when talking about the careful planning of a meal for someone, or the holding of a child on our lap with warmth and care, the time and thoughtfulness of searching for just the right gift, or even remembering a birthday with a special card as "sexual" expressions of ourselves.

I wonder now, as I write, if Nancy realized that taking her granddaughter down the road for that wagon ride was just as profoundly sexual as that moment years ago when little Katlin's mother was conceived. I suspect she does, not to write or talk about it like I am doing here, but in her body. I can feel it in the joy and deep satisfaction that comes across when the house is full of returning children and grandchildren during the holidays. Bob, too, has his own masculine way of communicating the same message. The quality of presence is infused with their own unique feminine and masculine sexuality . . . smiles, thoughtfulness, doors opened, care with diets, phone calls and countless other ordinary things.

I think there is a deep wisdom in the human spirit that knows, despite our cultural conditioning, that the key to sexual integration is *presence*, and that sexual expression is so much more extensive than its genital component. How else could we continue to grow as human beings when illness or other circumstances prevent us from expressing ourselves genitally? We know we do not cease being sexual without genital sex, nor does the expression or communication of ourselves to others stop being sexual just because the expression is not genital.

Life-giving and loving can and do go on through our bodies irrespective of genital sex. They do not come to a halt because we choose celibacy, or because life circumstances deprive us of the genital expression of loving and giving, as beautiful and appropriate as these can be.

The psychological carrier of sexual integration is the continuing ability to be congruent with the energy of our sexuality in the creation of human wholeness. This always involves relationship and a quality of presence that is life-giving. Focusing creates such an "in-relationship" environment, whether to oneself or others. There is surrender to the power of grace in genuine Focusing which reveals the hidden story in our sexual feelings. This bodily-felt truth, meaning, or story is owned in our bodies through Focusing and becomes an integral part of who we are. There is a new wholeness being born through gift every time we allow ourselves to focus. We can tangibly feel this birthing process in ourselves and in others whom we lead in Focusing. This is the key ingredient in the integration of our sexuality.

No human life, especially a Christian one, is a vocation to sterility. We need the body-feel of begetting new life through our sexuality. We need to experience within a wide spectrum of communication that our sexual presence is nurturing and life-giving and is not restricted just to healthy, loving, genital sex, which even in marriage is a very small portion of a couple's communication with each other. A Focusing relationship feels physically life-giving and nurturing in our body. It feels like we are giving birth to ourselves, to the other(s) and to the relationship, the new Body, that is being born. Such experience permeates our bodies with a deeply-felt sexual satisfaction and pleasure. It responds to a profound human need in both male and female to generate life, regardless of age.

We are meant physically to feel this in our bodies from the time we are old enough to own our body feelings on into old age. This gives our sexual feelings that room to be felt and owned within the totality of body feelings as we connect to the world around us. Sexual feelings become part of an entire body presence that gives and receives life, like Nancy pulling her little granddaughter down the road in the wagon. Each of us needs to feel in our bodies that we are passing on life because this is the critical body-awareness that integrates the energy of our sexuality. The body-experience of passing on life is at the heart of this birthing of a new Body of grace.

From around the age of six or seven when relationships become important in a child's life, sexuality needs to be situated and discussed in the home, church and school within the context of teaching children how to own and listen to *all* of their feelings. Gradually, through a process like Focusing, they come to recognize that whenever they feel things, it is their body telling them there is a story that needs listening to in these feelings. When they honor and respect their body's way of talking to them, then the feelings change and they notice they can have more fun at play, concentrate better on their homework, notice other people's needs, be a better listener, etc. In other words, the quality of their presence to themselves and others becomes clearer and sharper, widens out and is not as confused and narrow as before. This is important for all of us to notice. It is especially true for adolescents, the widowed, divorced, singles, celibates, those going through menopause, and men in mid-life reevaluations, where owning sexual feelings allows them to tell their unique stories at this time in life. This always situates such feelings in a context, opening up options and choices. No matter what our life situation, we need concretely to feel that our sexuality can be owned and present in us, fully alive and vital. This is without regard to genital expression. Such broadened sexual presence begets new life.

In my experience, I have never heard more people describe this body-feel of giving life than I have found from listening to people who guide others in Focusing. It feels sexually life-creating to be so close when accompanying another in this non-manipulative, noncontrolling, intimate fashion. Finally discovering a way to be caring and present without fixing feels like one is plunged right into the intimacy of the gift dimension of life itself—sacred and awesome territory that fills us with profound satisfaction and fulfillment. Literally before our eyes we can see and feel a birthing, just as Elizabeth at 13 could experience this with eight-year-old Kirsten.

Focusing can provide children with a body-feel for the kind of presence that begets new life around them, even at an early age. Going into adolescence with this familiar habit of owning all of their feelings, they are then prepared to treat newly emerging sexual feelings as they do the rest of their feelings. Moreover, sexual feelings—like others when owned in a Focusing way—tell their story and then become part of the way in which a young person can be present to themselves and others. Such feelings become part of this freer and deeper quality of presence that a child gradually realizes brings life to others. The energy and drive of sexual feelings—like the energy that is in pain, frustration, fear, excitement, etc.—is processed through Focusing and integrated into a positive quality of presence that children can then bring to the world around them. We all need to live this way, no matter what our age, because it changes the way our body carries feelings. This in turn changes the quality of our presence to ourselves and others, which is the carrier of the tremendous energy all our feelings possess. They can go in the direction of self- and social-destruction, or they can move toward congruence and new life, depending upon whether we are taught to disown or own the energy in our feelings. This is the important role of community in sexual integration.

People long to be guided by a loving, trusting community into owning whatever is real inside themselves. To repress, to subjugate, to deny, to punish rather than to own in Christ's Body our realness is profoundly to reject both the possibility of receiving grace as well as the gracious gift and Giver as well. The control choice is a radical rejection of grace, albeit often done in the name of God, asking Divine intervention either to control or remove our feelings.

What Focusing and bio-spirituality offer is a freedom to experience the presence of God's grace within our body-owning of whatever is real. Owning the truth of myself as I carry that in my body allows my *graced story* to unfold. This creates its own order, an order far more enduring, community-building, and integrating than any formed through our attempts at control. There is an innate body-spirituality within every experience of congruence. It is our body's way of touching grace.

A Christian bio-spiritual approach to sexuality involves commitment to guiding each other in learning how to risk being congruent with whatever is real in us. Through this leap of faith, we discover that within our unfinished humanity there lies direction, meaning and an enormous energy for life and love. When we are helped by one another to experience this, then we carry whatever we feel about ourselves not as an embarrassment or enemy to be run from, but as the life-giver and lover we are all meant to be, just as we are right now.

A true faith community gifts children with this body-feel for themselves right within their own feelings of incompleteness, insecurity, lack of confidence, fears, hesitations and all that goes with being powerless and vulnerable in an adults' world. With the gift of being supported in owning all their body-feelings, children can then risk the responsibility involved in continuing to grow in this congruence. Right within their feelings and in their sexuality they will know a graced story at work in their growing bodies, guiding them in the sexual expression of themselves. The other alternative—unowned needs and feelings—also has its momentum, but the energy buildup is destructive, eventually breaking through in some form of violence.

Christians have a very privileged faith dimension to bring to their sexuality, because the believing community can risk guiding its members into owning their sexuality with whatever immaturity or woundedness each carries. This they do together in faith as an owning of the broken Body of Christ. Then all will experience being empowered in this vulnerability by the Spirit of Christ. Such faith-filled journeying together will not only create a more mature, responsible and integrated expression of sexuality in the community, but a shared joy in the pleasure of God's grace.

The lack of sexual integration in a healthy Christian community of growing people of all ages will be recognized not as shameful, something to be run from or ignored. Nor will it be the occasion to use religion or God for more effective control. Instead, a healthy, faith-filled approach to sexuality would guide children (as well as any one else) into owning whatever is real inside each of us as the lifelong challenge of saying "yes" each day to growing more whole in Christ. This congruent owning—often in fear and pain—would be the Christian community's embrace of the broken Body of the Whole Christ and a celebration that in this Body of the Lord, which we all are together, lies the power of the Resurrection. Our humanity itself is what carries forward the continuing Incarnation of the Resurrecting Body of the Whole Christ. The extraordinary energy of sexuality, when integrated into the graced life of this

Body through Focusing, solidly joins and grounds both spirituality and sexuality in our body.

Intimacy, sexual integration, and a maturing faith in the Body of the Resurrection, as it is known in our own bodies, all depend upon this visceral feel for begetting life. This grows in us through the quality of presence that wholeness gives birth to inside ourselves. The Resurrection Body of the Whole Christ is this growing congruence in each of us. This is the graced resource out of which needed sexual guidelines can emerge. The "hope to which we are called" is God's gift given in and through this quality of our presence to one another. As Karl Barth put it in his *Commentary on Romans:* "By participation in the Body of Christ, the powers of the age to come are released into the bodies of those who make it up, just as they were in the healing miracles of the incarnate Jesus."[5]

The Birthing of a New Body: The Place to Look for Guidelines in Human Sexuality

While writing this chapter I went to Oaxaca, Mexico for a couple of weeks in May. One evening, sitting in the park, with these pages in gestation, I penned the following words while watching a beautiful, young, American couple on their honeymoon. With thanks to Robert Bly, I wrote:

Young Lovers

The Mariachi sing of love and death
wandering the portales,
And the laughter of children
playing in the park
brings her face to his.
Her head thrown back against his shoulders,
His strong arms enclose her,
And their eyes are full of hope and life.

The breeze catches her summer skirt.
His handsome face sees only her beauty
in the cooling evening,
and I wonder with Robert Bly. . . .

Will this holy moment
of the wisdom passion holds
fade,

and be lost
like gardenia blossoms
in the tray of a passing Indian girl?

Or will they come to understand
before it is too late
that we love each other
within the healing miracle
of what in us is most unfinished?

Will they learn to love each other
with what in them is still changing . . .
what has no handsome face, nor perfect lips,
no dancing hair;
what has not yet found its body?

Are they the lovers,
the tough ones,
whose Holy Body not yet formed
will someday in our midst
be born?

Or will the shadow of childhood's past,
the shame of owning truth
and incompleteness
rise to snuff out his carefree tapping of the
music's rhythm on her bare shoulder?

Or will his playful fingers
cease to wander
into the melody of their own love,
as she responds with inviting giggles?
Is it soon to disappear?

Are they the ones to understand
their passion now, a kiss, their touch . . .
just being together
in all their young unfinishedness . . .
is their new Body
being born?

Do they know
this is the gift we give each other?
This, the gift we love with . . .
or were they told to dream another
dream?

They stretch
and walk around the park,

but soon are back again
before my thoughts have left them.

I watch and pray
that they may feel this birthing body
and its hope and promise.
Or will they cry themselves apart,
knowing only their unfinishedness
and not
its mystery and hope?

Around the corner from the Zocalo,
high up on the altar of the Compania,
Ignatius smiles amid the crumbling
of the church his sons once built.

Across the plaza balloons rise
from laughing, playing children
to touch the knowing looks of Clare and Francis
framed against a new moon
on the aging face of the cathedral.

And two young lovers hold each other
as the Mystery settles in
to spend yet
another night in our midst.

Are They the Lovers, the Tough Ones . . .?

When I returned to California, I found these words that
Marianne had written earlier in the year, describing this new
Body being born with Lance as her Focusing Companion after
19 years of marriage:

There is something very deeply sexual in the process of
owning what's real in ourselves that has it's own power to
draw us *into* the other. Right within the heart of surrendering to the truth of who we are lies the erotic. For me as a
married woman, sexual fulfillment begins within the setting of Focusing Companionship with my husband, Lance,
and then comes to its natural climax within sexual intercourse. It's like being vulnerable to each other in Focusing
is extended right into physical intimacy, so there is a deep
sense of integration rather than feeling used by another.
For us, vulnerability in Focusing feels like good foreplay.
The level of surrender feels enhanced within the letting go
into our scary places. That letting go is physical invitation

to come together. The owning of our *mutual* vulnerabilities draws us into being more of who we really are.

As we are being led in this direction, there is an incredible realness to the sexual energy that comes *right out of* the owning of what feels negative inside us. There is a tangibly-felt connection with the desire to be physically penetrated, along with a profoundly deep sense of being *penetrated by gift*. The felt experience almost puts to shame the words to describe it. It feels like *every* nucleus in our cells is inviting and surrendering to grace. The sexual energy feels like a new Body is literally being born.

We feel that before any real intimacy with another is possible, this intimacy must first be felt with oneself! Owning the truth of who we are brings about an incredibly intimate feeling toward oneself. When this same quality of surrender is extended to each other, then our union of two bodies feels like a bridge into greater oneness. We are part of a continuing creation. Within the climax, there is a fleeting embrace of a Greater Whole.

The "More" between us becomes a life-giving gift, not only to us but to our children, and through us to the Larger Body. Within this kind of letting go into each other there isn't the need to use the other's body for one's own pleasure. Together we are with one another in the same way as we are during Focusing—open to Gift! The gift of the other is given in the same way as the gift that comes to us in Focusing—in surrender. Being real together without any strings attached stirs a desire of oneness with the beloved. Freed from the need to fix one another, we are ready to allow the other inside—as he or she is! We are open to be changed by the other. As we become disposed for Gift, we are open to the graces of a maturing wholeness. Our relationship becomes more and more of what we call "the in-between." It's a new identity; *more* than the two of us alone!

The exchange between us *comes* from gift and *leads* to a gifted union. There is a keen sense of being graced, so the feel of some "More" that we create together is totally *new*. *Our* identity is toned with a completely new sense of who we are *together*. It's a body-feel that says: "We didn't *do* this." For us, Ed's words describe the feel of this so well. "With a loosening of the body-feel of dominance, we can make contact with one another at a much deeper level. We are more 'in' each other, rather than on the outside separated, alienated and alone." Something does begin to shift inside our bodies with such loosening, and a new sense of genuine security and trust enters into our relationship. Being connected within the intimacy of real presence to one another brings such a gifted dimension into our physical union.

Because of the need for chemotherapy several years ago, I abruptly entered menopause without the gradual onset that most women experience. I was told, not only by my gynecologist but by friends, that this would be a tough time sexually. There would be many physical changes as hormones readjust, and I could expect my whole level of sexual feelings and desire greatly to diminish. Over the following months, as I sat in a Focusing way with the sadness I felt over the early loss of ovulation each month and with this whole change in myself, I was shocked by what began to happen in me. Right within the owning of these feelings there developed a new sense of desire and intimacy. What happened in me wasn't what I expected at all!

As I learned another kind of intimacy with myself, my desire to be with Lance heightened. I can't help but wonder if Focusing could be a new way of entering oneself during menopause as it is during any period in one's life? My suspicion is that it is!

There is an incredible reservoir of gifted surprise within our bodies. When hurts, fears, confusion, even our catastrophic expectations can be gently entered into over a long enough period of time, then together we become a new Body. Again, after 19 years of marriage, it feels inside like it did when we were newly in love—soft, exciting and hope-filled."

> And two young lovers hold each other
> as the Mystery settles in
> to spend yet
> another night in our midst.

* * * * *

How we fight the vulnerability of owning our own body with all that it feels! How we rail and threaten with ideologies, theories and rules for the body to cover up our unwillingness to enter the "inner nest . . . never quite round . . . made by the other imperfect bird."[6] Dare we trust that in the mutual vulnerability of owning together what is real in our bodies, the Spirit of God would be present to guide us? Indeed, this represents a leap of faith which public pronouncements of the Christian churches seem never to have heard. But quietly in the ranks, despite all that we have inherited, in the "freshness of deep down things (where) generations have trod (and) nature is never spent . . . the Holy Ghost over the bent World broods with warm breasts and with ah! bright wings."[7]

Let us listen and learn the language of grace in our bodies and then we will know the answers for which we search.

When the right thing happens,
the whole body knows.
The road covered with stones
turns to a soft river
moving among reeds.[8]

Before this can happen though, we all have so much to abandon. Old men must venture down from their Roman towers, the seminary professors from behind their books and desks, church politicians, left or right, must leave their power brokering behind, and millions of frightened, wounded, ordinary folk must set forth without the safety net of their own version of the myth. Then, when we stand stripped of the myth's facade, with nothing but what is real to share, we may, finally, say to one another,

Come with me, we will walk alone,
away from the buildings and the high places.
I love to go with you,
and enter the valley where no one is king.[9]

Chapter 12

A New Body Can Be Born

TODAY WE NEED . . . EVOKER(S) OF PERSONS . . . TO instill moral values not by didactic preachments, but by opening a way of personal experience that will validate itself integrally and uniquely in the intimate depths of each individual. The ethical conduct of life in our civilization can then be altered on the basis of these experiences and be illuminated by the enlarged awareness of reality which they bring.[1]

Many years ago when I was 15 or 16, along with cousins, uncles and my father, we were enjoying two weeks of camping and fishing in the high Sierras. The elevation was somewhere between eight and ten thousand feet where magnificent, craggy peaks glistened against the intense blue sky. Here and there, patches of lingering snow contrasted their pure whiteness against the summer's lush, green outcroppings of grass and profusion of wild flowers. Small clear lakes rested in saddles between granite and volcanic rock whose stark, jagged lines were softened by the twisting roots and branches of dwarfed and wind-sculpted junipers. I was in a world of Japanese bonsai scattered across this rooftop garden of the world.

Wandering alone and aimlessly in this scenery one lazy, summer afternoon, I climbed to the top of a mountain where an unusually large emerald-green meadow stretched out before me. Zigzagging through the lush grass ran a sparkling stream and on all sides the granite cliffs were turning gold from the late afternoon sun. Shadows and patterns of darker green nestled in pockets along the lower canyon walls.

The whole effect overwhelmed me. I recall, even now, how I felt a deep sense of awe and reverence, physically needing to respond to some presence that was more than just the beauty before me. What I did was move toward a fallen log at the edge of the meadow, drop to my knees and bend forward with my head down, eyes closed in a position of semi-prostration. I felt enveloped in an awesome Presence that seemed to come out of me as well as everything that surrounded me. Although it is impossible to describe, an unspoken life mission or invitation broke through to a conscious level of awareness inside me. Perhaps these words convey some of it:

> Whatever you hunger for is right in the rock being a rock, the grass being grass, the tree a tree. The flower has only to be a flower to be whole, to be in harmony with everything else.

> But how does a person just be human?

> Unlike the trees and flowers, people are confused about what it means to be human. So you will have to spend your life looking for the answer yourself.

> Look not with your mind, but with your body. If you can find a way to live in your body and not reject any of it, then you will be guided into discovering the wisdom you sense in nature all around you.

> Your own body is the key that will tune you in to this vast and awesome Presence, the source of all wisdom.

The next thing I recall was that I once more became aware of myself and my surroundings. Almost like awakening, I adverted to where I was and what I was doing. I began feeling self-conscious and somewhat embarrassed. Bent over behind the log, having not yet opened my eyes or moved, I also sensed someone or some other presence—and this frightened me. Opening my eyes, I cautiously lifted my head from behind the log, to find myself facing a huge buck that had grazed to within three feet of me on the other side of this fallen tree. I do not remember who was more startled by this eyeball-to-eyeball encounter. Neither of us could move from shock. Then the buck snorted and fled into what I quickly became aware was the darkness of evening.

How long had I been there motionless, that this deer could have fed right up to me? Where was the sun and late afternoon light? Shaken and confused by the entire episode, I arose, reoriented myself, and hustled back to camp before everything turned inky black.

A bewildering experience for a young boy. Certainly not one to talk about if you did not want raised eyebrows directed your way. However, immersed as I had been in this inexplicable Rip Van Winkle-like experience, a clue about the human body was etched deep in my bones that afternoon. This body-feel has been neglected and sadly ignored at times, but never lost. Like the special airport electronic equipment which fine tunes a pilot in on the right glidepath, this homing instinct has always been my ultimate arbiter in life-direction. Even though there has never been any religious or cultural support to nurture this body-listening, that long ago experience of my body as the bridge into the Mystery and meaning of life has always remained to guide me. There is a trust that was put in place by that experience, one that I have returned to and physically felt again and again as it connects me with this Presence—my own body "in" some Larger Body.

All my years of formal education and religious formation battered mercilessly at this priority, taking their toll but never extinguishing that body-feel for the right path. So when I finally let myself go through Gendlin's Focusing for the first time, what had still survived in me from that precious afternoon rose up inside, cheered and wept for joy. Someone else not only knew, but understood with depth and precision! Since then, nothing has helped me more to be true to that childhood invitation than Focusing.

Today I can join many others in saying that research and experience now teach us that we must create a culture in which all of us, starting in childhood, are helped to experience ourselves as a living, integral cell of some Larger Body-Process. I know of no more simple, practical, teachable approach to this experience than through Focusing. When anyone experiences the gift dimension of what Gendlin calls the "felt-shift" (the gratuitous symbol interacting with the felt sense), they have the body experience of what in Christianity would be called "grace." Experientially, gift and giver are connected. I know today that healthy human living in the Spirit has always been and will always be the journey of living in all that is real in one's body, with the doors wide open to that gift. We all need to discover experientially early in life that as integral cells of this Body, we are meant to receive not only its energy and life as a gift to us, but by living in such openness we are also given our identity. It is within this journey that we discover who we really are, and that we are not alone. Without this body-feel of Presence (or whatever one might want to call it), the pain, fears, self-doubt and incomprehensible in life drive us back into the dead-ended pattern of trying to fix and control everything.

We need to carry whatever is real in our bodies in openness to this Presence because the revelation of our own identity is there waiting to be given. Ultimately, this is the revelation we all long for, not some information about the nature of God, but an answer to the question, "Who am I?" We deeply yearn for the body-feel of "our story" unfolding within the energy and wisdom of this Larger Body.

To celebrate life by letting go of trying to figure out and fix everything is to **be** a community of grace. This for me is congruent prayer. As a Christian, I find this deeply satisfying and profoundly rooted in my tradition, as a new body can be born in us, literally from this faith. We are never too old to come home to ourselves.

Slowly being given an identity apart from fixing or having answers feels so grounded in the mystery of life. It resonates so passionately with leaves that burst into crimson and gold as fall days grow shorter, with the sacred quiet of winter's snow as it gentles the tired earth to rest, and with the swelling energy of new life when I touch the budding branches of pear trees in March or watch adolescents awkwardly reach out to one another on a date. It all feels so organically one.

And yet, would it seem paradoxical to you if I said that I have always prized education, the challenge of research, and the fine tuning of the intellect? My grandfather was a medical doctor, my mother a teacher, and their love of the human mind's capacity to probe and break through into new understandings rubbed off on me at a very early age. I love the adventure of the new worlds books have opened up for me, just as Grandpa's telescope, microscope and magnificent library did for him. There have never been enough hours in the day for me to explore through books the many facets of the world around me from biology to art, music to architecture, psychology to geology.

And yet from the time of that walk in the high Sierras, my bones have also told me there is a further knowing beyond the answers any of us can find in books or come to with our minds.

Words like Paul's "knowing beyond all knowledge," clearly distinguishing the limitations of cognitive knowledge as compared to some kind of gifted body-knowledge, are like symbols that touch the felt-sense of that afternoon's message with an "aha!"

And then, as I would nurture that "aha," a thousand voices from my mentors and from the university where I was teaching would rise up in chorus to chant:

> It is our ability to understand rationally, to manipulate and fix the world around us that raises us up above all other inhabitants of this earth. You are denigrating and rejecting centuries of human effort and dedication to in any way diminish the mind's supremacy in its valiant effort to explain and better comprehend whatever we don't understand about life and the world around us.

So it has taken me a lifetime just to discover there are assumptions in the above, which may not be true to begin with, let alone that an even more important factor in healthy human living on this planet, which I call the "gift dimension of life," does not even have a place in this kind of thinking.

In our culture, this essential component of healthy human growth is not even recognized as existing and real. Therefore we have no vocabulary for it except the unacceptable religious word—grace. We do not know how to share our body-feel of gift from and in the larger Body. Developing and sharing together a body-feel for this gift dimension of life, especially in our own personal growing as well as in relationships, is virtually nonexistent, even in organized religion. Children, whether in a religious or nonreligious setting, are not guided into recognizing, nurturing and developing a trust in this body process as the key ingredient in their social and personal growth. No wonder we have such a violent society. We feel embarrassed, awkward, scared, or unpatriotic in this pluralistic society to even mention this crucial and necessary component of every human being's maturation process. However, the body-feel of gift does not have to be acknowledged, described and nurtured only in a religious setting or with a religious interpretation. The fact that all of us as human beings need the Larger Body's wisdom, healing and life energy to grow more whole and discover who we are can be taught and described in nonreligious language without theological interpretation. Therefore, in or out of religion, we can begin to help each other live in such a way that we are open to receive these gifts. This is essential if we are not to continue social and planetary suicide. We must create a more global approach to spirituality, recognizing what we all share as human that must be nurtured and passed on to our children, aside from whatever religious interpretations we might want to give to this precious dimension of human life.

In the words of Robert Frost,

Something we were withholding made us weak
Until we found out that it was ourselves
We were withholding from our land of the living,
And forthwith found salvation in surrender.[2]

Could it be that what we are withholding is body-faith rooted and only known in the language of body—our feelings—rather than in logical, cognitive concepts which we can manipulate and control with our minds? Could this not be just as true in religion as well when those concepts are about God? In our attempt to understand, predict and control, are we too frightened to risk owning all our feelings, because we learned long ago that such feelings do not reveal their story with the kind of predictability we want? Perhaps that is just too much vulnerability, so we practice "safe religion."

Yet something rooted in the common dream of our bodies tells us that unless we own all that we are, nurturing and listening to our own organism, we have no solid foundation for understanding ourselves nor the universe in which we live.

This new Body that is struggling to be born in our body is not metaphorical, mystical fantasy or religious pathology. Given the technology we have to destroy each other and our environment, I believe the organic feel of our own body in a larger Body/Process is imperative for our very survival. Without the conviction in our bones of who we are in relationship to everything else that exists, and that there is a benevolent gift of healing always available if we will not disown whatever is real in our bodies, fear and insecurity will continue to overwhelm us and turn us down the path of violent self-destruction.

Human survival, let alone growth, depends more on the body-feel of grace, wonder and presence than it does on understanding, prediction and control. Unfortunately, most of religion has made this visceral experience as remote and unattainable as has the scientific method's too-narrow perspective of the human journey. One ponders why religions have kept the accessibility of the body-feel of gift such a closely-guarded secret, because as the eminent theologian Karl Rahner often said, experientially from our limited vantage point the knowledge of gift and giver are one. Good reason from inside the body for the psalmist to sing out, "Hear, all you nations . . . my heart whispers sound sense."[3] We can trust holding, nurturing and listening to our heart, even if it feels broken, lost or frightened because:

> . . . God is as close to us
> as we can risk being close
> to our real selves.[4]

A new body can be born.

Chapter 13

Our Body: Common Ground for a Global Spirituality and Community

IF RELIGION HAS KEPT THE BODY-FEEL OF GRACE SO SEPARATED FROM our own growth process, little wonder that the curious and genuine seekers of our times have trouble even identifying that for which they are looking. Recently I was asked to listen to and comment on a well-received talk, "Spiritual Response to the Global Crisis," by the eminent futurist, author, and theoretical physicist/psychologist, Peter Russell. I have long been an admirer of Mr. Russell and have used his video, "The Global Brain" in my own workshop. But I have always told these groups of my puzzlement as to why a man of such vision and breadth of learning would title it "Global Brain" rather than "Global Body." Clearly, what his video describes is the evolution of "body/Body consciousness."

When I heard his more recent talk, I realized that like many other brilliant and sensitive thinkers trying to respond to the issues of our day, he really does not appreciate the evolution of consciousness in the human body, but still restricts it to greater cognitive understanding, or at least uses only language that gives this impression. In his remarks, after a brief recounting of some of the major problem areas that threaten the health of our planet—e.g., the ozone layer's depletion, pollution of fresh water, climate changes and food production, top soil erosion, etc.—he goes on to describe what he calls a "spiritual response" as the ultimate and long-term answer to these problems. Drawing from the Buddhist approach, he describes how people always try to find satisfaction for their needs outside themselves in more land, wealth, ideas, relationships, money, etc. He speaks of this as an illusion, and that only an "inner shift" from this "exploitative consciousness" to a "compassion- ate consciousness" can bring about lasting change.

Whether we are at peace inside ourselves, he says, and therefore have no need to misuse the world around us, depends on how "we choose to see things." How one grows into seeing things differently is the result, he believes, of "freeing the mind." This freedom comes from living in the present moment (through meditation, presumably). This changes our percep- tion from seeing persons and situations in terms of satisfying or not satisfying our needs to "being in life with them," a journey- ing together on this planet peacefully. This change he calls the spiritual challenge of our time.

Although so much of this resonated positively in me, nonetheless, I was left with even more puzzlement than with the "Global Brain." Something felt off. Listening carefully once more to the tape, it hit me.

Once again it was *the body* that was missing, as well as clear simple guidelines that ordinary people can use to change the negative feelings that affect the way we see things. Where people need help is in owning their real unprocessed feelings about material things, relationships, money, their self-esteem and all the other things we carry in our bodies that drive us to exploit and manipulate the world around us. We do not choose to feel things differently. That is pure gift. To some degree we are able to choose what we think about, but freedom here may also be very limited if our feelings are involved. Guiding people into living in openness to receive this gift is the spiritual challenge of our time. It is the only response to our global crisis or any other relational problem that will bring about lasting change in the way "we perceive things." I do not know Buddhism from the inside, but I suspect that those who do know this truth as well. Probably, most ancient spiritual traditions refracted through contemporary Western eyes get out of focus in some way. I suspect that is the problem here and not just a semantic one.

I do not think what is needed is some method to "free the mind," but a way to be deeply in touch with the truth of what- ever is real in our bodies so that what skews our way of seeing things—namely, our feelings—can change. With this body change we begin to see things differently as well. True inner freedom grows when my story as it is carried in all of my body is honored and cared for. We do not neglect or demean the consciousness of our body in its feelings any more than we would the marvel of our body's ability to think. All that makes us human must be nurtured to mature in balance and harmony, both within ourselves as well as with the world around us.

The reason that I choose to give this example of Peter Russell is that he represents for me a deeply-concerned, sensitive, articulate and influential Western academic, influenced by much that we need to learn from Eastern approaches to spirituality, but not yet in touch with this missing piece. I would summarize it this way: The challenge of developing in various cultures a global spirituality which can move ordinary people away from violence and exploitation is not just a question of recognizing our human potential for "compassionate awareness," but in recognizing the human potential in our bodies to *experience* this healing and transformation

a) as a gift,

b) coming to us from some Higher Power, some greater Body-Presence or however one wants to describe or image this experience,

c) because we are integral, living cells of this Larger Body,

d) and because we did not reject or disown our own body and its needs, instead deliberately allowing whatever was real inside (physical sensations, feelings) to be owned.

Sometimes this process might take place within a growing feel for being in some Larger Body, Power or Presence (related to religion or not), or it may be more consciously directed toward some person or group who creates the safety and support for such vulnerability. It makes no difference, the point being that we have the potential *to experience gift in our body* through some awareness of both gift and giver.

The task ahead of us in responding to this global spiritual crisis is to help anyone we can reach, especially childen, to acquire a body-feel for this gift dimension of life. Once they are taught (and this can be done in the public schools) how to care for their feelings by allowing this gift to come to them in their own story as these feelings unfold, we will have helped them find the most basic and necessary foundation for healthy human spiritual growth—let alone greatly diminished the violence around us. They will have been given the body-feel for how to dwell in their potentially-destructive feelings so that these can change. Then their creative and positive talents have space and energy to grow.

All of us, but especially kids who want to grow into a promising future, want to feel hope in our bodies. We need help to discover that this hope is the body-feel of gift (grace) telling us that tomorrow can be different, at least inside us. It lies in the body's experience that change is possible, even in what feels hopelessly stuck with no way out and no answers. Focusing gives us not just talk about a better tomorrow or in some afterlife, but it gives us the experience in our gut right now that those very feelings of despair can change. This does not mean the externals necessarily change, but when our feelings can tell their story, then the way we carry this life issue changes. New motivation is discovered, creative options, alternatives and different possibilities emerge, increased energy is released, often an improvement in physical health as well as a new way of looking at this issue and others simply follow from the felt shifts in the body.

Inner transformation that will impact the way we live on this planet must involve the *whole* human organism, which includes the consciousness of our body through its felt sense, as well as our cognitive process and will. The narrow educational paradigm that permeates the culture of most developed countries must expand to include the body-feel for the gift dimension of life and its relationship to change, as well as greater inner and outer wholeness. To continue as we have done in the past is to culturally enshrine a "process-skipping mechanism" of enormous proportion—one that is already lethal.

The experience of growing wholeness, gift and a changing self-identity is available to most human beings within the Focusing process and, I believe, can form the basis for a global spirituality. Caring people everywhere are first and foremost human beings with the same need for a healthy, spiritual growth-process, irrespective of religious or cultural background.

Focusing is an important step toward a global spirituality because in the common experience of bodily owning our discouragement, our helplessness, or our human limitations, we are at the same time discovering the gift of hope and the alternatives that are there as well. The common, shared experience of together living within some power greater than ourselves, gracing us with direction and energy to grow beyond our differences and fears, could form the solid foundation for a new, psychologically-healthy global spirituality and a giant leap forward in human evolution.

Unless we all find some mental health process, some spirituality that allows us to process what our bodies know and carry inside, as well as let go into receiving this gift, then we fall back into that kind of fixing mentality that easily sets us up for addictive behavior and ultimately back into the control and power game that with today's technology threatens us all. There is a profound and exciting opportunity through Focusing for the healing of ourselves—the fixers—and in that healing and growth to give birth to a new and life-renewing global spirituality for caring people. Let me discuss this further, particularly as it relates to addictive co-dependence. Many caring people have simply fallen into presuming it to be a healthy way of embodying their altruistic or religious values.

Part of this world for many of us is a Christian education and culture that has indoctrinated us with being fixers of the world's ills. The ideal that has been set up for us from the time we were children was that the better the fixer, the better the Christian. We were told to strive for this total gift of ourselves and the fixing of other people's problems. Moreover, the psychological underpinning of our values was built on the experience that we were valued in terms of what years ago a psychologist called "extrinsic valuation." We were acceptable, we were good people, we were lovable if we measured up to these ideals, these standards, these expectations. The bottom line in this culture came through loud and clear, that acceptance was conditioned on performance that pleased the power brokers of our small world.

If you grew up in a family, or school environment, or later in young adulthood generously invested your talents in a company, a service organization or a religious group, and experienced that you were "loved" only if you did this and this and this—only when you measured up—you got very mixed signals about who you were as a person. Then what can happen at some point—sometimes middle age—is that you discover "I don't really know who I am now since I can't measure up to playing the role expected of me." There is a frightening emptiness inside. We can be controlling things and fixing things for years, not realizing how we really feel about ourselves. Then something happens where we cannot control or fix. It may be that the last child leaves home, or we are told it is time to turn our job over to someone else, or one simply grows too old or physically infirm to be an efficient fixer any longer. Then we truly have an identity crisis—we do not know who we are any longer. Fear and a lot of anger, even rage, emerge toward family, teachers, church, whoever we believe has deprived us of ourselves. That is one part of a rather common experience for many people who have tried to lead good and generous lives. The other part I want to discuss is seldom reflected on because we are in the midst of this new experience.

Prior to the Second World War, most people lived in relative isolation from the rest of the world. They were in touch primarily with their family and friends in a local city, neighborhood or rural community. Radio had broken down this isolation to some degree, but our perspective still focused primarily on our immediate surroundings. Then came television. Something radically changed which is making a big difference inside us. Suddenly we have coming into our living rooms all the insoluble and horrendous problems of the whole planet. We look at the emaciated bodies of dying children in some part of drought-stricken Africa, the slaughter of innocent people in some Third World country, the bombing and deaths in northern Ireland, the corruption of whole governments by drug czars, and on and on. All the world's problems that need fixing are dumped on us every evening as we watch the news. The question is, how do caring people with the cultural conditioning I have been speaking of carry this in their bodies? Never before in human history have the planetary problems of the entire globe been literally deposited into the laps of millions of people each day. Then the local news comes on and gives us all the problems of our city and state. Then we look around and realize we have problems within our family, perhaps unresolved personal problems as well.

What we are faced with now can be put this way: How can a sensitive, caring person carry all this bodily without *global burnout*; that is, unless they have found a way of daily processing their frustration, pain, sense of helplessness or being overwhelmed by it all? The buildup day after day can be just too much, driving sensitive people to turn off feeling anything by frantically reaching out in addictive behaviors to misuse work, religion, drugs, relationships—almost all facets of life as they try to numb the pain. Much of this is done without awareness of this buildup. Moreover, if the person has been pre-programmed (as we have described earlier) into an identity primarily as fixer, then the problem is compounded even further. This addictive tendency is now fed a totally out-of-control daily megadose of insoluble problems covering the entire planet.

I am not saying that our former isolation was better than our present awareness of the earth's fragility and the immensity of human suffering. Not at all. A return to that limited, fragmentary awareness is not the answer. In fact, the radical shift in perception that has so suddenly come upon us resulting in the breakdown of the human organism, individually and collectively, is precisely the needed challenge that will force us into recognizing the inadequacies of our present quality of life, mental health practices and inherited spiritualities. We are being forced, because our survival depends on it, into searching for a global spirituality that transcends the limitations and parochialism of the past. This global spirituality must be rooted in a cross-cultural experience of our bodies' shared process of wholeness as gift. The present crisis is an opportunity unparalleled in human history. Our collective pain will either destroy us or thrust us into the discovery of a transdenominational and transcultural path to greater unity and caring for each other and our environment. We now face that choice.

We must find a global mental health process which at the same time is intrinsically a spiritual process, because it teaches us how to carry in our bodies the truth of how we are living on this fragile planet and what we are doing to ourselves, one another and our environment. At the same time, it must open to us, within this very terror, the hope and the alternatives which are also there. Focusing is the most practical step in this direction of which I know because it clarifies and supports the essential psychological-spiritual dynamics of human wholeness common to all people. Out of Focusing can come a global faith in the power of life to emerge from death, of light to be born out of what appears as only darkness. A global faith can grow in the realization of universal longings, hopes and dreams we discover in our common humanity, where before we only saw differences. This global faith can give birth to a trust in our shared common hunger for wholeness which we can learn to care for and nurture in one another.

I intentionally use the phrase "global spirituality" because finding answers to so many impossible problems that confront us individually and collectively is not just a question of calling more meetings, drawing up more plans, even of cooperation. People need to experience hope in their bodies where the energy for sacrifice, commitment and change lies. We all need to feel a connection to each other deeper than our rights, and our agendas, let alone greed. This same body-feel needs to tell us that answers are possible or we will not give up anything, assume the burden of responsibility nor risk the unknowns in any important venture into change. When solutions appear impossible, a global body-faith in the gift dimension of our shared human journey must be there, alive and waiting, to move us through the impasse. Otherwise all we do is set up endless meetings to make sure we protect our piece of the pie or hold conferences where visionaries can wax eloquently at the taxpayers' expense. Our bodies must open us to direction and answers from some power greater than our own vested interests, if personal and planetary wholeness is to evolve.

As television moves into more villages and homes, millions of people from diverse cultures and religious backgrounds will experience the overwhelmingness of the collective global problems that seem beyond anyone's ability to remedy. Then collectively, we will need to experience the gift dimension of human life as well or we will despair in a "get what I can now" policy toward each other. We need to know in our bodies that we are one and that there are directions and answers which can come to us from a power greater than ourselves; to feel hope together, irrespective of our religious or philosophical interpretations of that experience. This, I believe, is absolutely essential if we are ever to move beyond the myth of dominance and resolve the problems that it has created which threaten us all.

In the sharing of this common experience of hope, direction, and meaning (which can emerge through Focusing within the frustration and helplessness we feel), the ground of a common spirituality transcending inherited traditions can be born. The time has come in human history when we must experience such a shared spirituality in order to find new ways of treating ourselves, each other, and our common problems. At the same time, this does not preclude continuing to prize whatever in our own traditions does not block this more universal good.

What Gendlin identifies as the felt sense and the Focusing process provide all of us (simply because we share a common humanity) with a universally accessible experience of empowerment in vulnerability through gift (grace). This can then guide us creatively and caringly through the seemingly overwhelming issues that confront us. Together we can learn to let a power greater than ourselves mature us and enlighten us as we are given healing and unifying ways of relating to ourselves, one another, our planet and the whole cosmos.

The Body of this planet, which includes our body, hungers for hope and for the experience of life as meaning-filled. The Body/body cries out, asking a future for our children. We can no longer wait. All excuses pale before the clearing issue. At last we know it is the truth of ourselves and God in our bodies, not clothed as "our God" nor as "our self-image," that we fear. Why should the world's children, generation after generation, have to inherit such a legacy? Why must they be born again and again into the horrendous suffering the myth of dominance brings down on all of us who inhabit this planet?

Chapter 14

An Overview: The Body Dynamics of Our Inner Journey

The brave new world to be explored by the
twenty-first century is the immense labyrinth
of the soma, of the living, bodily experience
of human individuals. And we of the latter
third of the twentieth century have been
appointed discoverers and early cartographers
of this somatic continent.[1]

As you come toward the end of this book, it is my hope
that you have taken a long time to read it, especially if you
were unfamiliar with Focusing. I know I would feel very close
to you if, perhaps, something I wrote had triggered your curi-
osity or resonated with something that invited you into your
own body in a Focusing way. I write this to you because I
know the only way to get the message of this book is for you to
discover it within your own experience. Without your own
body-feel for what I have written here, these pages are just another collection of words and ideas.

Even at best my words can only serve as a symbol (in the
Focusing sense) that might resonate with something you already know and to which you are willing to listen. If that
happened because you have not just read for ideas, but *felt*
your way though this book, then it has served its purpose. By
providing a setting for you to enter more into your body in a
Focusing way, then both of us have traveled along a very sacred path. Together, we have entered holy ground and begun
to share through our bodies how we are part of the most momentous event in human history—the holy story of a new Body
being born in and through our body's struggle for wholeness
(holiness). It is from this new Body in our bodies that we dis-

cover the body-life of Spirit. This gifted revelation is not something complicated or esoteric for only the privileged few. The steps are simple and in all of us, if we want to   listen and follow them.

Step One:

First, we have to own our body in such a way that it can guide and speak to us. I have described at great length what many of us are learning from this owning process and how it reveals new meanings in so many areas of our lives.

Step Two:

Second, all we ever need to start with is whatever is real and upfront right now in our bodies. We do not need to master complicated wisdom traditions from other times and other cultures to grow more whole at this moment in our lives. We will find the spiritual dimension in life by owning whatever is real in our bodies now if we do it in such a truthful and vulnerable way that its unique, personal meaning can be revealed to us as gift. We do not impose meaning on our experience but allow it to be given. Nor do we let someone else thrust their meaning upon our experience nor abuse us with their feelings in such a way that we cannot listen to our own. Rather, we live in our own body in such an open, in-touch way that our life's meaning can be given to us. Owning our story unlocks for each of us the secrets of the Larger Body, of the universe, of The Mystery and of a cosmic saga in which we play a cherished and inimitable role. We count, and are meant to know that in our bodies.

Step Three:

Third, by helping each other to "own" in mutual vulnerability whatever is real inside us, the grace of community, of a new body/Body (individually and together) is given to us. The "missing piece," as I wrote in Chapter Four, is that access to the unification process (holiness) at every level—personal, family, social, cosmic—is within our own bodies when we are willing to create relationships of mutual openness to grace. Communities of life *are* communities of grace.

Why Bio-Spirituality Is Needed: A Summary

Over and over again, people tell me, "I've tried many different things but always felt something was missing. Now I know what it was—my body. That's the missing piece. I was never helped to recognize grace in my body. It was only an idea in my head."

Personal and social growth does not happen without a healthy spirituality grounded in the body and in a community of "believers" (not necessarily traditionally "religious") who acknowledge the reality of grace and the human potential for experiencing that gift in our bodies.

Diverse cultures and religions may give these essential components of human development and wholeness different names. But "bio-spiritual" is my word for describing these indispensable ingredients in the body-life of Spirit. Psychologically, we know it is absolutely necessary that life's personal meaning and connection with some Higher Power come to us through the process of congruence in our bodies. The agony of bypassing this drives entire generations and cultures into pain-killing addictions.

Unfortunately, we live in a world in which the predominant religions, including Christianity, still do not teach their spiritualities within the body's struggle for wholeness. For this reason they have relatively little impact on the violence and destruction we continue to inflict upon ourselves and the world around us. As new generations reject the old rituals that once brought felt meaning to many, then a vacuum is created in the body. Without meaning we are lost, and the pain of this eats us out from the inside, not only creating emotional and physical disease but setting us up for all kinds of addictions to numb this suffering.

Millions reject the old expressions of religion, education, even politics, because they are no longer meaning-filled. They commonly use such expressions as, "It doesn't mean anything to me any longer."

Meaning does not come to us primarily through the concepts we acquire intellectually. Meaning is graced or gifted to us personally as something we feel in our body. Meaning that brings purpose, energy, goals and motivation into our life comes out of a felt-sense in the body. Words, concepts and theories cannot capture it completely. It is more than any clear explanation.

This is why healthy spirituality has to be grounded in the body. And we solidly ground meaning that endures not by a lot of talk or by stirring up emotions, but by rooting it directly in the body's own process of wholeness. This process is: 1) socializing (community-building within us and around us); 2) experientially connected to the body-feel of gift (grace); and 3) experienced as given to us by some Higher Power.

Bio-Spirituality approaches the experience of this Higher Power (or God) out of the body's hunger for unity, completion, and healing of the pain that spawns violence and destruction, as we attempt to find meaning in life and ease the suffering of the wounds and incompleteness we carry inside us.

Christian bio-spirituality is guided by the belief that Jesus is God's revelation, proclaiming that there is an alternative to the myth of dominance as the model for how we relate to ourselves (especially our own bodies), to others, and to the planet on which we live. Christian bio-spirituality pulls together all those who share the dream of a spirituality rooted in the Body of Christ, our bodies, and in a faith that, together in Christ, the impossible becomes possible. Despite seemingly insurmountable obstacles, in Christ we can change and create real communities of grace.

This movement has begun. Ahead lie many exciting and hope-filled years, spelling out in concrete, practical steps how we can begin within our own bodies to create an openness to God's grace, finding hope and encouragement in the body-feel of that gift. Then we must look at how this good news can come into the lives of children in the home, at school, church, temple, synagogue, or mosque; how parents, husbands and wives, neighborhood friends, ministry teams and other small groupings can become Focusing Companions and grow beyond the old patterns of dominance.

For Christians, this movement has deeply-felt roots reaching back into the Gospel because it means replacing the dominance model that infiltrated Christianity with the experience of a new alternative—graced communities of faith. This is a dream that now can be made practical and workable. It is a hope that can be brought into the everyday lives of ordinary people. But the body-experience (not just the teaching) of everyone's absolute dependence on God's grace, including a leadership that is open to grow and change in an atmosphere of mutual vulnerability with everyone else, cannot be lost again as the foundation of *graced* community. Psychologically, it is also the foundation of a spirituality grounded in the human body where both unity within us and around us has its roots. I say this, not just because it happens to be consistent with the life and meaning of Jesus, but because today we know psychologically it is requisite for human wholeness, individually and collectively.

Special Learnings That Move Us Into The Alternative: A Bio-Spirituality

Over the years those of us who value our Christian roots and for whom Focusing has become a way of life have noticed a three-fold pattern of development emerging. *First*, we observe that bio-spiritual growth moves us away from adoring a "God-object" and draws us toward a deeper experience of our own wholeness process as our most intimate awareness of sacred presence. Objectifying God, which is the mind's instinctual way to control what it knows, feels less and less right. It is nowhere near as nurturing and real for us as is the awesome experience of grace in our body, which grows through Focusing.

This Presence is not a something or someone, and we find ourselves no longer comfortable with making God into some sort of person-object. Instead, this unique, personal, bodily, felt experience that permeates our entire being (and which words cannot adequately describe) gradually takes the place of our former "God concept." It feels more accurate to describe this unifying, intimate, gifted, life-movement within our embodied knowing as "the sacred," as "the Presence," "the More," as the "being in Christ" of St. Paul. It is a "being-in" rather than "pointing-to" type of experience, much as one might point at a tree or talk to another person.

Regular Focusing over a period of time brings to awareness that there is continuity and pattern in this integrating body-movement. It not only feels freeing and healing, but is so sacred, loving and caring, and incredibly penetrates into the very essence of one's being. And it all seems to come about as a gift within the changed way we now treat ourselves. Instead of trying to *fix* our weaknesses, to dominate and change our fears and hurts, treating all this troublesome stuff in ourselves as the enemy, we take an entirely different approach. Now, through Focusing, we caringly and gently own how we actually carry any feelings around in our bodies. We listen to them as they try to teach us something. We honor them as friends, not enemies. We wait and listen, (as Elizabeth told her teacher she does), to the feelings we have been taught to call "bad." As our hurting, scared and angry inner places unfold to tell their stories and we can feel the movement toward wholeness grow not just in our bodies, but within our entire being, we find ourselves truly blessed in this ongoing incarnation of God-in-us.

A *second* growth-enhancing pattern we notice is that this inner experience of what happens as we change the way we treat ourselves—especially the things we do not like inside—opens new and creative options for relating to the world around us. The question soon surfaces: "If this can happen in me, why not in my son or daughter, my spouse, friends, or members of my church or support group?" Then we begin exploring how this might be passed on to others, which usually confronts us with the fact that the only way we have learned to make it happen is by exercising some kind of control. So we slip into pushing, imposing, nagging, pressuring or in some way manipulating, usually without even realizing what we are doing. How deeply engrained are our old patterns of "getting things done." But there is another way.

Few of us in pain or confusion will reject someone we trust who takes the time to walk with us, especially if those accompanying us do not need to fix us in order to feel good about themselves. There is a kind of wisdom and peace-filled sureness in such a person that invites us to be present to our terror or pain just as he or she is being with us. In time, it comes so naturally simply to slip into a Focusing relationship with another in pain and help them to move into this quality of presence to what is real in themselves. All this can happen when we let go of the dominance way of trying to make things better for them and for ourselves. Our own experience of taking care of ourselves in this way becomes our teacher and in time helps us learn to relate in the same nonmanipulating way with others. It takes time, more for some than for others. But old dominance patterns, so pervading our relational behavior, can gradually be healed by our own Focusing. This, in turn, prepares us to begin the changes necessary in how we will relate to others, especially those in whom we have significant vested interests and for whom we already have written the script for how they should shape their lives.

Sometimes, with someone you trust whom you know cares for you, your invitation to Focusing can come in by the back door through a sharing of your own personal experience of this process. You can begin by describing what Focusing means to you, and then ask if that person would be willing to guide *you* with some simple steps that you can teach them. If the other person is open to this, you can briefly instruct them in the procedure, give them a single page with the steps as an aid, together with an assurance that you will guide them if necessary regarding what you might need while going through the process. All of us who focus have found that with some prior experience in Focusing to fall back upon, it is really the loving, supportive presence of another that helps when we are stuck or even afraid to focus. It is amazing what happens to uninitiated people who, perhaps for the first time, experience being part of the Focusing dynamic of "letting go and letting God." This can be a powerful invitation to explore Focusing for themselves.

Finally, there is a *third* pattern that we observe happening for many of us when our outreach results in another or a small group experiencing personal change through Focusing. When we regularly come together to help each other in Focusing, an experience of empowerment through mutual vulnerability becomes recognizable within the relationship. This new quality of interpersonal presence to one another, so different from our old patterns of dominance, has opened up the option of giving concrete structure to that experience as "Focusing Companions."

Key Ingredients of the Alternative

Over the years, key ingredients for an alternative to our inherited psychologies and spiritualities of control have gradually surfaced. Let me summarize them as follows.

1. Our bodies are the key to growing beyond all our dominance programming.

The main reason for this is that the mind cannot grasp the process of human wholeness. Only the body can know this process through experience. It is not simply a matter of getting our mental priorities straight so we can move in another direction. You do not move beyond dominance by getting better control over dominance with your head! We need to learn that there is another resource, an alternative to dominance within the body's capacity for knowing. The challenge is to explore our body-experience of vulnerability, the polar opposite of control. That is where we discover the resource that carries us beyond the myth of dominance.

2. Our body is not just a "something" we have or to which we can point to. It is also a process, a movement toward wholeness.

Elizabeth, John, Marianne, Gloria, Bill, Lance and hundreds more are learning that when they remain in a special way with hurting places, something moves forward inside them. They are beginning to choose the vulnerability of not running away from painful feelings, because they have begun to sense that these places can shift, and then they feel better. That's an important part of what the body is, this forward movement within the felt-carrying of issues. This is an experience of spirit-in-our-body. It is an awesome gift that we are only just beginning to appreciate as spiritual.

There is a body-life of Spirit we are meant to feel physically. St. Ignatius tried to guide someone making his Spiritual Exercises into this body experience of God as process. He called his spirituality Trinitarian, which attempts (using theological language) to describe God as an eternal process. But Ignatius, following the ancient Christian traditions, believed that the human person was made in the image and likeness of this eternal process—God. From his own experience, he knew that people could be guided into the body-feel of this, not as the immutable, totally-transcendent inner life of the Diety, but within the limited struggle for human wholeness in which we all participate. He knew as a mystic that the process of moving from incongruence to more wholeness is a gift and that this can be felt in our body. So he devised "exercises" or steps to guide people into this experience. Today, that same goal can be enormously enhanced by Focusing.

3. We need to develop a body-listening priority, rather than a head-thinking priority.

This is new territory for most of us, attending to how we carry things in a feeling way, respecting the potential for transformation that lies within our body's ability to move forward. It is difficult for us to realize that *the message is the process, and the process is the message.* This is the challenge of growing beyond the dominance model to one of grace in our body. When we listen gently and caringly to the energy for movement in our body-knowing, then we do not need control because the body rights itself, much as an air-filled container will bob to the surface of the water after being submerged. A gift is given at that point, which leads us to our fourth learning.

4. The body experience of our own process "is" our tangible point of entry into the Mystery of God.

This is the zone of grace as it can physically be felt in our body. It is within the sense of body-movement, or lack thereof, that we are drawn, as I earlier described, into the mystery of light and dark, good and evil. God is not some mental content apprehended by the mind. God-with-us is the gifted *movement that is spirit* within our body's unfolding. The story of spirit is written within the forward unfolding of our personal wholeness.

This was and continues to be the meaning and message of Jesus. There is an essential psychological teaching about the process of human evolution in the life of Jesus, apart from any theological interpretation of who he was. The profound owning of his body and feelings, as well as his deepening faith in the power of new life to break through these—even suffering, rejection and despair—is meant to give witness to the inexorable process all humans must enter into again and again to find harmony within and among ourselves, toward the planet that nourishes us and in some Higher, Gifting Presence in our midst.

5. Focusing is intrinsically community-building.

Focusing builds personal, social and planetary wholeness. Any harmonious and healthy group or global community grows out of the body's movement toward congruence, individually and collectively. The starting point is always in assuming responsibility for our own personal homework. Despite all of religion's lofty ideals, models and endless rules about everything, the bottom line is: "Whole people beget whole people. Fragmented people beget fragmented people." The first step is our own inner journey of community within ourselves.

6. Community (wholeness/holiness), both inside as well as around ourselves, is a gift—God's grace.

Community grows because we live as invitation for it to be given to us. We cannot make it happen. Focusing teaches through its steps, and as an attitude, how to be invitation. In a simple, psychologically-sound procedure that a child can learn, Focusing helps us to let go of fixing everyone and everything, including ourselves, opening us up to become invitation. Community can then be gifted to us. As we extend this movement of wholeness out into other people's lives, community can then be born around us. This is living in the Spirit, a spiritual life. Focusing brings structure and support to our body-life of Spirit with awesome precision.

7. Another way of relating is possible as an alternative to relationships of control.

There is an implicit acknowledgement of mutual need when entering into a shared Focusing relationship. It is found in the guide as a letting go of dominance by accompanying the focuser rather than directing. On the part of the focuser, it can be identified as a letting go of dominating or fixing whatever he or she may be Focusing on. The Focusing relationship has taught us that whenever both guide and focuser loose the reins of control (the guide letting go of fixing the other and the focuser letting go of fixing himself or herself), then this quality of mutual vulnerability becomes an invitation for a gift to be given.

8. Behind every act of violence—emotional, verbal or physical—lies unprocessed feelings.

These unowned feelings have not been defused by being given the inner space and time to tell their story. The result is always destructive and painful, often catastrophic, from rape, murder, war and the mass destruction of life and property to the smashing of someone's self-esteem by the violence of our words or actions. We all have the right to our feelings, but we do not have the right to abuse those around us with those feelings. If you stop and think back over an ordinary week in your life, it will hit you how often during that time you have been abused by the unprocessed feelings other people are carrying around and have dumped on you because you made some innocent remark, walked in at the wrong time, reminded them of an abuser from their past, and so on.

How are the unprocessed feelings of any of us who abuse others any different from the unowned feelings igniting the bloody fighting between the Serbs and Croats in Yugoslavia, the Catholics and Protestants in northern Ireland or the Jews and Arabs? It is all a matter of degree and to what extent the violence is publicized or has immediate international ramifications. It is all violence, however, and cut from the same piece of cloth in the unprocessed feelings carried in our bodies.

A few weeks ago, I was watching a mother and three young children shopping near me in the grocery store. She was obviously packing a very heavy load of unprocessed feelings because her verbal and emotional abuse of her children was in no way called for by the few annoying things they did. In fact, her verbal violence was so strong in its felt-impact that not only would her kids cower when she let go, but when I passed her I noticed myself flinching as if to protect myself from being physically hit. In a way, this is mild compared to the day-in and day-out grinding down of self-esteem that goes on in many marriages, classrooms and workplaces as the unprocessed feelings of those who have some kind of power over us perpetuate their devastating violence. Knowing now that there is an alternative, I have often asked myself: "Does any decent, caring human being on this earth really have any choice but to try some alternative to what we are doing to each other?"

One of the wonderfully freeing, community-building and life-giving experiences of being a Focusing Companion is that the guidelines for these sessions protect us from abusing each other with our feelings.[2] This is taking place not through denial, neglect or some other form of manipulation, but in the mutual support for each person's owning whatever feelings are real.

9. For Christians who bring their faith to the experience of becoming an invitation together through leading and being led as Focusing Companions, St. Paul's spirituality and meaning of Christ not only comes alive, but literally makes sense.

A new potential for interacting invites and disposes both people for the gift of empowerment, as Paul would put it, "in Christ." This new quality of interaction and presence, a mutual vulnerability, disposes both persons individually and in their relationship for their next gifted step into greater wholeness. As this gift of unfolding unity is nourished through continued Focusing together, old patterns of manipulation and control are literally replaced with new life in the Spirit. This profundity of felt-connection in Christ, and its deepening of faith, defies verbal expression. When two or three gather as an invitation "in His name," (Jesus IS mutual openness to God), "to wash each other's feet" in mutually vulnerable service to one another's personal journeys, then the grace and empowerment that create community happens. "Where two or three meet in my name, I shall be there with them."[3] A new, nondominative model for relating to each other in marriage, parenting, ministry teams, the refounding of religious communities, support groups, etc., can emerge. It is a call to healthy, life-giving, graced communities of the future in which we discover a quality of human interaction not based on dominance but upon grace.

10. Ordinary people can be helped by other ordinary people to touch what is real inside themselves as their starting point for spiritual growth.

We can help each other grow spiritually with this alternative, rather than imposing outside agenda, religious or other ideals, and all the "should be's" of education, culture and church. Experience has taught us that our daily owning of what is real in our body is the only starting place if wholeness/holiness is the goal of our spiritual as well as human journey.

The Christian spirituality we have inherited, and I suspect this might be true of other traditions as well, confuses and distracts us from the starting place of what is real right now inside us by substituting religious input—ideals, ideas, rituals, Scripture, writings of the saints, theology, an endless list of "oughts," etc., etc. Of course, there is a proper place for many of these in the overall education of a person within a certain tradition and history. Laws, too, have their role in protecting the common good. But never can information, whether it be in the form of religious traditions, sermons, history, teachings, rituals or theologizing, be substituted for the process of holiness in our bodies. The mission of Christ, of the Christian community, of any individual Christian, in fact, of any human being, is the call of human life itself as this draws us toward wholeness, unity, oneness, harmony within ourselves and with all that exists. This is never facilitated effectively as religious ideal or theory, but as a lifelong process in our bodies.

It took me a long time to realize that what I had been exposed to as spirituality completely missed the mark. Tragically, many so-called "renewal" programs still follow the same tired model. It is easy to see why, given the paucity of leadership in any other direction, let alone the centuries of programming that mold us into not even questioning the basic presuppositions of what we are doing. Moreover, nothing is more scary than one's *own* truth and the struggle to own in one's body whatever is real, especially when this frightens or confuses us. No wonder that without the support of others who have gone through such experience themselves, and therefore know how to guide, we run back into our heads, continuing to fill them with every likely piece of information that might bring us fulfillment. Emotional highs, too, have a limited life-span. New ideas excite for a while, as does moving rhetoric, but in the long run if our energy does not flow out of body changes that are actually transforming us into community within ourselves, then the ideas and ideals, no matter how eloquent, become as stale and boring as last week's newspaper.

Energy that brings continuity and a better future flows out of owning our bodies as an invitation to Spirit. Here is where new body-life in the Spirit can be born. Here, the mystery of who Jesus was and is today *can be felt*. And even that old Christian word, "Incarnation," finally makes sense.

11. A sound environmental spirituality must be grounded in the human body.

When we denigrate our body and its felt-sensing capacity, this cuts us off from God because God is revealed to us through all that makes up the human journey into holiness (wholeness). Focusing is intrinsically spiritual because it restores that sacred covenant God asks of us in giving us a body on this part of the passage. By more deeply connecting with our own body's spirituality and its ability to reveal God in us, we learn to prize and hold in wonder that same capacity in others and all of nature. We recognize that in destroying our natural environment, we shrivel ourselves and deprive our spirit of nourishment. The restoration of our sacred covenant with the material world, which is a profound spiritual as well as survival issue for our time, must be rooted, first of all, in a healthy spirituality of the human body. We are living, integral cells of the Larger Body, so its wholeness depends on our wholeness. We are literally the parts that make up the whole. The starting point for each of us is, first of all, ourselves.

Furthermore, with Focusing we have a practical, transcultural, transdenominational foundation for spirituality, because it is rooted in what we all share in common—the human body and its movement toward wholeness. Out of this mutually-encouraged and shared body-experience can come a more communal, global, body-spirituality with body-grounded values, direction and vision—because such values and perceptions flow out of what we all share in common—our human body and its universal hunger for wholeness. Hope for a global environmental spirituality that will nurture and care for our planet must be grounded in the body/Body we all share together. We belittle and often negate our well-meant efforts to preserve the health of the environment if our own inner body-environment is being neglected or abused.

Summary

The Body Dynamics Of Graced Community (Inside And Outside Ourselves)

As the gift of unfolding unity is nourished through continued Focusing together, we have found that outworn patterns of manipulation and control are literally replaced with new life in the Spirit. Gradually the body-feel of an alternative to the myth of dominance emerges. There seems to be a pattern here, which we have at various times called: "Steps for healing lifestyles, spiritualities and relationships of control," or "Steps for growing beyond relationships of dominance into communities of grace."

As a therapist, I experience these as essential steps in the healing process, regardless of their connection to a religious tradition. For Christians, I have found this tie-in helpful if it does not interfere with the process, but motivates them to enter the body-dynamic of their own inner journey. These steps are:

1) Owning the Brokenness:

If we lead one another into knowing and *owning in a bodily way our own brokenness*, rather than denying or neglecting it, then we can know with our "inward eyes" the Brokenness of Christ's Body in a way we have never experienced or understood before. We can experience our humanity, together with all its limitations and weaknesses, not as an enemy to be conquered, dominated, or run from, but as the indispensable human bridge giving us access to God's grace, our own identity, the meaning of life and The Mystery.

As Paul wrote, "I glory in my infirmities," because in owning them I know the power of Christ's broken, yet resurrected Body of which I am a living cell. The very things we are accustomed to fear and hide from others or ourselves, we begin to recognize as doorways, no longer walls. The human condition, our shortcomings, our very real limitations make sense when we let go of the myth of dominance. As Paul consistently tried to communicate, it is only against the truth of our needing, broken background that the vivid appearance of some power greater than our weaknesses can be experienced. If we are disempowered from owning in our body the truth of how brokenness sits in us in a feeling way, then we block conscious body contact with the graced resources of power that can heal and help us grow beyond those limitations. We do not *know* what grace feels like in our body. We only *understand* something of it as a theological concept. By owning whatever is real in our body, we invariably encounter our brokenness, and in owning that we embrace the brokenness of the Whole Body as we carry it within ourselves. In Christian theology, this Body is not only wounded but is gifted with the Spirit in Christ. Thus, this Larger Body, of which we are integral cells graced in Christ, can grow beyond its limitations into new life and wholeness.

In our culture, which is addicted to every conceivable painkiller, to advocate a healing process which plunges us right into pain is the most radically countercultural proposal anyone could come up with. Therefore, "caring-feeling-presence" is a crucial psychological support in helping any of us risk holding pain in our bodies long enough for it to tell its story and begin to connect with a body-feel for "the more." But it does take time and some kind of faith context for anyone to break the old patterns of denial, neglect, rejection, repression or whatever process-skipping habit we use to avoid this fundamental first step in growth. It involves breaking some addiction and that is a big step for anyone.

That is why the Pauline connection of our body as a living cell in the Body of Christ is such a powerful context within which Christians can find support to take this gigantic step. I have emphasized it constantly throughout this book, because I find the power of belief to be even stronger than the fear of pain. When this belief can be reinforced by the actual physical feel of the following second step, and what may have been largely an idea moves into body experience, then the old body patterns are being replaced by new patterning. Information and insight simply do not adequately provide an alternative body-pattern for addictions locked into the human organism. The body needs to feel safe enough to let go of the behavior and allow its replacement to come in. Psychologically, for an embodied pattern to change, one must use an embodied psychological process and this is what these steps make possible. People endlessly try to change embodied patterns with ideals and religious information, not realizing this is doomed to failure and is a waste of time.

2) *Discovering the Hope:*

When we can be faithful to owning this body of our bro-kenness, then, in the naked vulnerability of such truthfulness when we are gifted with "symbols" that connect, we experience in our bodies "that *hope* to which we are called"—the healing, life-giving power of Christ's Resurrected Body in us. The two—brokenness and hope—go together like two sides of the same coin.

The body-feel of the other side of the pain—the felt-shift, the change, the meaning unfolding, the story behind the pain revealing itself, the breakthrough into the Mystery obscured by the hurt, the sense of gift in all this—these can now come into body awareness. To know in the fear, the confusion or hurt that there is hope and a gift there, too, is to believe and have faith much deeper than anything our minds can give. Mind in-formation gives us more control, which is usually pointless for healing most inner pain which is beyond the help of manipula-tion. But faith that grows out of the gifted felt-shift in the body teaches us how to dwell in peace and openness to the story as it unfolds in whatever is real now.

The religions of the world, including Christianity, are still very primitive in their understanding of the process of whole-ness in the human organism. They still rely too much on an-cient asceticisms and spiritual practices often based on a very limited understanding of the body's struggle for holiness. For this reason, they have relatively little impact on the violence and destruction we continue to inflict upon ourselves and the world around us. However, I know these first two steps are integral to a spirituality grounded in the body-process of wholeness which ordinary people cross-culturally can use to heal the feelings that spawn violence. For Christians whose spirituality should never have slipped away from their bodies, it brings us home again to grow in a faith rooted in the Body of Christ, our own bodies, and into a communal experience that together in Christ the impossible becomes possible.

3) *Experiencing the Vision:*

If we persevere in helping one another bodily to own our brokenness, and in return are gifted with the same kind of tan-gible hope, then a new level of synthesis, a new *vision* of what this means can emerge. We gradually recognize that our own process of wholeness is a healing of the planet, the Body of the Whole Christ, the Cosmic Christ being born in us. The Pauline vision of the Body of the Whole Christ is a collective healing process. Cosmogenesis, in the words of Teilhard de Chardin, takes place in us, individually and collectively. The vision of our planet not destroying itself but becoming whole and one is a body experience we can have together as Focusing Companions. The vision is felt as possible and that gives us energy to persevere with the healing and care of our environment.

Once again, the body-feel of our own personal journeys of wholeness as the primary contribution we make to healing our environment and the Global Body fuels commitment, creativity, and mutual cooperation that is shared both ways—in personal growth and the birth of a caring community.

4) The Gift of Community:

Finally, when mutual vulnerability becomes the quality of interpersonal presence through shared Focusing, a *community* is born wherein we understand not abstractly but experientially how the "agape community" of loving service to one another is empowered through the Spirit as a new Global Body, a New Creation, not destroying itself through dominance but becoming Whole and One in Christ. Here, we find a sacramental community of grace and faith built not upon a model of control, but upon the experience of empowerment in mutual vulnerability.

Community is born in the experience and sharing of each other's process of wholeness as a healing of the planet. When a shared Christian faith is brought to this as the Gospel vision of healing the Body of the Whole Christ, ourselves, then small groups become living cells in the development of larger communities of grace. The whole Larger Body then is organically and solidly built on love.

A packaging and marketing culture like ours, which turns people's energy and time toward consumption and manipulates us through the media into feeling guilty that we are not doing our part to help the economy by buying more things, or that implies something is wrong or incomplete in us because we do not have such and such, needs a spirituality rooted in these body feelings if they are ever going to tell the truth. We need a spirituality that gets us in touch with the truth of ourselves and our real needs, not the artificial ones created for us. We need strong relationships deeply rooted in our bodies, like Focusing Companions, which bring us face-to-face with whatever is real in our lives, what our real body priorities are, and give us the space and time to discover and nurture our own spirit. This spirit shrivels and is starved in the midst of a world gone berserk over new things to acquire. Ironically, most violence in our society is not between the have's and the have-not's, but is perpetrated behind the headlines by people who are driven by the pain of a lost or blocked spirit-life. These four steps are the best investment I know of for peace in ourselves, in our families, cities, country, and the whole globe. But the question as always is, "Who is willing to make this investment?"

Appendix A

Academic Roots of the Bio-Spiritual Movement

by
Peter A. Campbell

BIO-SPIRITUAL AWAKENING IS SLOWLY DAWNING DURING THIS end-time of the 20th century. Philosophy, psychology, and theology together have blended their differing strands into the weaving of a bright, fresh pattern. A special convergence is occurring in our time, revealing an unparalleled threshold in human awareness. Let us glance back, for a moment, at some highlights of this movement's academic origins.

It was 1951 and the eminent French thinker Merleau-Ponty was invited to present a lecture at an international gathering of philosophers in Geneva. His topic: to sum up the results of philosophical reflection during the first half of the 20th century. His conclusion: *the denial of any dualism between body and soul is what characterizes the modern movement of human experience.*

Merleau-Ponty's fundamental discovery was "the body-subject," the flesh and blood character of "intentionality," of the human capacity to know, to reflect, to be self-aware. The human body itself is the source of meaning without there being need for any appeal to a distinct, totally "other" entity called "soul" to explain its existence or operation. In the words of Remy Kwant, "Merleau-Ponty tried to penetrate into the semi-darkness of our corporal intentionality, and he tried to explain how by its development freedom, thought and spiritual life came into existence."[1]

Now the stage was set. Someone had dared utter the unthinkable: "spirit comes into existence by the development of the body."[2] The language was embryonic and imprecise. It

233

needed to wait upon further refinements to be drawn from psychology, refinements which would spell out the exact meaning of that embodied "development" which we will outline in a moment. Merleau-Ponty did not deny spirit, but he did deny that it was in any way disembodied, somehow other than or distinct from the human organism. "The spirit is the 'other side' of the body itself, and this 'other side' cannot be separated from the body."[3] The human body is the intentional or knowing subject. The implications were staggering. It meant there was no separated "faculty" of the soul, an intellect or will acting like some watchful overseer directing the body's more gross and fumbling movements. The body itself was reflective, even in its most basic sensory awareness.

Merleau-Ponty brought body into spirit and spirit into body in a way that no one previously had imagined. It was a stunning and significant breakthrough, one which still brings consternation to many traditionalists in the fields both of science and religion. European thinkers would further develop this theme. But the next truly significant step toward a more comprehensive "bio-spirituality,"—the discernment of spirit-process within the body's own movement toward wholeness—would have to wait until the impact of this insightful breakthrough had traversed the Atlantic and taken up residence on the pioneering frontier of North American Third Force psychology.

Carl Rogers and "Congruence"

The key names here are many. But two stand out above the others: Carl Rogers and Eugene Gendlin. Rogers was a practical therapist, a scientist and scholar who loved theory but always measured its speculative interpretations against the day-to-day pain and struggle for growth in his clients. Early in his career he stumbled, almost by accident, upon a crucial piece of data about how people change. It was a pattern of observation Rogers noted at first not so much in his clients as in himself. He found, in his words, "the curious paradox that when I accept myself as I am, then I change. I believe that I have learned this from my clients as well as within my own experience—that we cannot change, we cannot move away from what we are, until we thoroughly *accept* what we are. Then change seems to come about almost unnoticed."[4]

The experience and explanation were so simple and direct. When Rogers could *be* his feelings, they changed. Here there was no cumbersome piling of one personality theory upon another, no dividing of the person into drives and fixations that could be sorted and analyzed. Past models of change had stressed some sort of shift in thinking or ideas as the principal method for reorganizing personality. Rogers' learning emphasized "being in," "accepting," or "owning" one's feelings as the key to actual change, rather than merely "interpreting" them. His was a radically different step in this first rough mapping of bodily-felt knowing.

With brilliant depth and clarity, Rogers realized that "being in," "accepting," or "owning your feelings" involved far more than merely thinking or interpreting them right. His work was to begin the first truly organic rather than cognitive exploration of this bodily-felt component in the process of therapeutic change. The full significance of his learnings would later develop into the clarification of *"congruence"* as *an ability consciously to feel your feelings physiologically and allow them to symbolize themselves accurately.*

The identification of congruence represented a major step forward in an understanding of how the body knows. A direct psychophysical link between cognition and sensing finally was opened for exploration. Forty years later, the extraordinary implications of this exceptional breakthrough still are rarely appreciated. It is, perhaps, the single most important discovery along the path toward an effective healing of the myth of dominance and the inevitable addictions that in one form or other soon follow.

This is because the psychological component in addiction can be traced directly to a specific lack of congruence, especially when the failure to be congruent endures for any length of time. Addictive behaviors become the natural and inevitable substitute that incongruent people use to dominate instead of accepting, owning or being in their feelings, especially those feelings they find frightening.

While developing "client-centered" therapy, Carl Rogers emphasized the relation between counselor and client as a therapeutic encouragement which could facilitate congruence. However, much like electricity, while Rogers knew *that* congruence worked, he did not fully understood *how*, or what actually happened within the person that made it all possible. The next creative step toward uncovering an answer and further revealing the body's unique way of knowing would fall to his gifted graduate student and, later, professional colleague at the University of Chicago, Eugene T. Gendlin.

Eugene Gendlin and "Felt-meaning"

Right from the start, Gendlin acknowledged that most personality theorists simply did not know how people changed therapeutically. The gratifying fact was that many did get better. But how this occurred still remained a mystery. Like Rogers, Gendlin recognized that "thinking it right" had little to do with the actual felt-process which went forward in a person as their psychological condition improved. In Gendlin's words:

> An Adlerian therapist some years ago told me: "Of course interpretation is not enough. Of course the person doesn't change only because of the wisdoms which the therapist tells him. But no technique really expresses what makes the change itself. The change comes through some kind of emotional digesting; but then you must admit that none of us understand what *that* is."

> Therapists often miss this fact. They labor at helping the individual to a better explanation of what is wrong with him, yet, when asked how the individual is to *change* this now-clearly-explained maladaption, nothing very clear is said. Somehow, knowing his problem, the individual should change, yet *knowing* is not the process of changing."[5]

There it was in a nutshell! "Knowing is not the process of changing!" Information is not the process of wholeness. While clear explanations or some framework of personality theory may provide tools for analyzing a client's psychological situation, these same explanations and theories are powerless to effect any needed reorganization. The actual engine of transformation lies elsewhere. But what could it be?

Carl Rogers had uncovered the barest tip of it all. "When I can be my feelings, then they change." But what did this actually mean and how was it such a crucial ingredient in the very process of transformation itself? With the kind of creative leap that so characterizes many great discoveries in science, Gendlin isolated a further piece in the experience of congruence.

It had been both his and Rogers' observation that "meaning" refers to more than what can be thought in the mind. There is *felt meaning* in the body as well. Common sense experience alerts us to this fact. Often, when sharing some troublesome feeling with a friend, you find yourself groping for more precise words to describe how it actually feels inside. Your friend, too, may help and ask: "Is it like this or that?," offering other words than those you may be trying out to describe some vague sense you have about a person or situation. Then, either you or your friend happen upon the precise word that seems to connect exactly with how you feel. "That's it, I'm really *jealous* of her, and I never realized that was why I acted the way I did." At that moment, a noticeable "felt-shift" occurs inside as you sense a rightness in the word "jealous," together with its connection to some heretofore vague uneasiness in your body.

During this dialogue with your friend, you let anything that surfaces in the conversation like words, imagery, or memories bounce off or interact with your body-feel of the whole thing until something connects. It is rather like the game we played as children when we hid something in a room and said "warmer, warmer" or "colder, colder" as the seeker came closer to or receded further from the object. Sometimes a word will feel like it almost says how we are inside, but it is still just a little bit off. We taste the closeness, yet it still is not quite what we are looking for.

The significance of such experience is that a felt-meaning already exists in your body. Your body has its own "intentionality," as Merleau-Ponty would put it. It knows something in a felt-way, something that may be quite complex. Each word, image, or memory symbol that comes is measured against that feltness and either is rejected because there is no feeling change when the two come together or it is accepted in the very relief, delight, surprise or wonder that surfaces when the connection is made.

But what is this connection between symbol and felt-meaning? It was here that Gendlin made a profound breakthrough—one which finally unmasked key players in the organismic *process* of change.

Congruence as Story

Felt-meaning, according to Gendlin, is carried in an *implicit* fashion within the human body. In his words:

> Implicit meanings are *incomplete.* They are not hidden conceptual units. They are not the same in nature as explicitly-known meanings. There is no *equation* possible between implicit meanings and "their" explicit symbolization. Rather than an equation, there is an *interaction* between felt experiencing and symbols (or events).[6] (emphasis ours)

That was the key! *There is not "equation" but "interaction" between symbol and felt meaning.* With this careful observation, the true nature of congruence could unfold. Felt-meaning is not some vague shadow form of more clearly-defined, rational concepts already conceived in the mind. We are dealing here with a knowing that is dramatically different from what we traditionally identify as human knowledge. The emphasis in this experiencing is not upon *information* but on *forward movement* in the body's knowing. Felt-meaning (or felt-sensing) represents an organismic step not simply toward some new "content" of knowledge but into an actual experiencing of *the "process" of wholeness itself.*

Congruence is much like enraptured listening to a good storyteller. When small children clamor for a bedtime tale, one soon senses that the storytelling itself is more potent than the fable that eventually unfolds. Part of what draws us all to a story is the felt ongoing-ness of it, the flow, the being carried along. The actual details become secondary. They provide a convenient structure within which some more primal process can unfold. There is a fundamental urge for such "going-forwardness" which lies inside each person. The interaction between symbol and felt-meaning brings this into awareness through an evolving of congruence. But the actual goal of such body-experience appears to be an unfolding of some greater wholeness within the human organism itself.

To summarize, then. There is a knowing that is mental, like abstract reasoning which expresses itself through concepts and information. There is knowing that is more obviously physical, like sensation and emotion. But beyond these two there exists yet a third experiencing that occurs when symbol and felt-meanings *interact.* What makes this knowing different is that it refers not to a specific "content" of rational awareness, nor to any distinct physical or emotional sensation. Rather, it identifies an unfolding *"process of wholeness"* occurring within the entire human organism. Congruence as "story" is our most primal experience of forward movement into a deeper current called "Spirit," as this evolves within human consciousness.

A Process Called Spirit

Congruence highlights or displays the organismic interaction that moves consciousness forward. *It expresses "the other side of the body" which Merleau-Ponty identified as "spirit."*

Felt-meaning is incomplete and the way it moves forward toward completion is through interaction with some symbol. But the interaction and forward movement are in no way subject to rational control. Carl Rogers perceptively noted the phenomenon: "When I can be my feelings, then they change." This treasured body-movement into wholeness represents an organismic experience of "gift," of "grace" which is not reducible to some immaterial operation perceived by the intellect. Grace is experienced in and through the body's knowing! Nor is this something we can call up on demand. The nature of such gift totally transcends our rational effort to dominate and control.

The upshot of all this is that those seeking to preserve the existence of spirit have been looking in the wrong place. The Holy Spirit has been described in Christian literature as *"Donum Dei,"* "the Gift of God." Grace is a concept which the mind can understand. *But the "Good News" is that this treasured symbol represents an experience of gifted movement which can be known only in our bodies!* Christian theology today has a rare opportunity to explore the incarnational aliveness of grace as this gift of God animates and becomes the very lifeblood of human spirit itself.

Spirit, therefore, is recognized not within some immaterial functioning of abstract reason—the logic of problem-solving. It is identified as an embodied experience of gift which draws the storytelling that is each person forward into wholeness. Spirit appears in and as the evolution of consciousness itself. The significance of congruence, therefore, is that it opens for us *the embodied experience of spirit as a process of wholeness within ourselves.*

Human intentionality includes a multifaceted capacity for abstract reason, sensation and emotion. Since the functioning of these capabilities has seemed so radically different, rational operations have traditionally been assigned to intellect as a faculty of the soul, while more mundane sensing and emotional life have been relegated to the body. It was inevitable that so-called "higher" powers of intellect and will would become the realm of spirit, just as bodily functions were given over to the world of the flesh. By putting body into spirit and spirit into body, Merleau-Ponty has forced a reevaluation which cannot be understood by the mind alone.

"Spirit" has always been intended to identify that capacity which somehow transcends limitations of the flesh. What Rogers and Gendlin offer is a fresh perspective on where this transcendence actually lies within the human organism and how it expresses itself. It does not function as some nonmaterial *content*, labeled "the faculty of intellect" or "soul." Rather, it is an experience of *"self-process."*

"Spirit comes into being by the development of the body." Now, we can begin to make the necessary precision about such development. *Spirit becomes visible "as" the graced unfolding of congruence in the body!* There is no such thing as "a" self. What exists is either the gift of ongoing *self-process*, the congruent movement into greater wholeness, or there is blocked self-process, frittering existence away in the myriad addictions that litter our human landscape.

It is eye-opening to realize that psychology has had to struggle with the quantitative language which breaks life into separable particles, just as early philosophers and theologians divided the person into body and soul. What Gendlin and Rogers have done is move away from any description of personality in terms of "thing contents"—drives, fixations, needs, etc.—and brought attention directly to bear upon the "embodied spirit" experience of self-process.

There is an important characteristic of this unfolding wholeness named "Spirit." It is innately social. Either we pass it along from generation to generation as an inviting, gift-filled sharing of congruence, or we hand down the model and pattern of dominance, the breaking off and frustration of this covenant with our body's story which inevitably brings on the dispiriting tragedy of addiction, a breakdown in community, and the destruction of our environment. Either we create a climate in which felt-meaning can move forward, or we produce an atmosphere wherein we become blocked from listening to our own bodies, the body of human community and, inevitably, of the planet itself. Gendlin refers to the spirit-threatening hazard of such frozen process as *"structure-bound experiencing."*

Addictive control, incongruence, blocked process, and structure-bound experiencing are all facets of one and the same dis-spiriting experience. They mean that in whatever area there is blockage, we find little development of congruence within a person, no ongoing story of wholeness, resulting in a dearth of the aliveness named spirit. There is no vibrancy of change, just the structure-bound repeating of stale patterns, like playing old tapes from the past.

Bio-Spirituality and Christian Theology

Bio-Spirituality represents the first serious pastoral and theoretical shift away from any dualism between body and soul in Western spirituality. This shift has occurred not because of some speculative synthesis. Rather, it has grown out of an experience of congruence (wholeness, holiness) as this unfolds within the human body. What makes the bio-spiritual movement different is not the appearance of new or unusual ideas. Instead, the very ground rules of discussion and exploration have been shifted away from ideas and explanations toward what might best be described as some kind of "resonance" with *a bodily-felt process of congruence* that expresses what we have heretofore called "Spirit."

Even back in the 1960's, theologians like Karl Rahner and Edward Schillebeeckx were struggling to break beyond the limiting confines of a theological method that narrowed perception into dualistic thinking. Rahner had already recognized that one could no longer speak of spirit and matter as separate, distinct "somethings." In his mind, the two overlapped and so penetrated one another that he could not write of one without the other. Indeed, it was the experience of such overlapping that already spelled the death knell of that neat and tidy theology which locked everything in its proper place. Rahner had already come to view matter and spirit as *"moments"* in a process, dynamically evolving together and into one another.

There was a deeper unity behind the oversimplified dualism of his predecessors who had failed to take evolution and, therefore, the body which knows it into consideration.

> What happens when we combine the ideas of the unity and the duality of spirit and matter, keeping in mind that both realities are moments in a dynamic history? *We can then say that matter of itself essentially develops toward spirit.*[7] (emphasis ours)

Karl Rahner lacked both an adequate language as well as a process for facilitating wholeness out of which he could theologize. Yet, despite this handicap, he clearly recognized that any ironclad dualism which kept matter and spirit locked in separate compartments, was totally ill-suited to describe the human person. Rahner was a prodigious forerunner of the bio-spiritual approach in theology. While remaining an academic to the end, his heart and spirit impatiently stretched beyond his outdated method and language. He left behind the legacy of an abstract eloquence to hint at what his body was already beginning to tell him.

> The material world is to some extent the one body of a manifold self-consciousness incorporating that body into the relation to its infinite source. And if cosmic consciousness has reached its first step in (humankind), it must continue to develop. Through (the) body (humankind) is allied to the whole cosmos and communicates with it. In their role as reference point of the spirit, body and cosmos together press on to ever greater consciousness.[8]

When we use the word "spiritual" in this book, it always refers to *a bodily-felt awareness,* not an abstract concept or idea. Furthermore, it involves surrendering into the truth of oneself as this is experienced in a bodily way, allowing some power greater than myself to bless me with another step toward wholeness (holiness)—*personally, communally, and globally.* The individual experience of congruence is inextricably bound into a larger communal and global framework. But at the crucial point where we are challenged to move beyond thinking and experiencing everything as though it were somehow separate, our language, thought patterns, and theological method quickly break down. *The human mind, it seems, is incapable of providing a language for the whole!* Here one enters the realm of body knowing, the living process of incarnation wherein we have no language other than that which the body provides. This is the domain of bio-spirituality.

Bishop John A.T. Robinson reminds us that ". . . without any exaggeration, the concept of the body forms the keystone of Paul's theology. . . . The body is that which joins all people, irrespective of individual differences, in life's bundle together."[9] Robinson, like Rahner, lacked a satisfactory language for describing his experience of the whole. But he, too, intuitively recognized the bio-spiritual perspective. For him, Christian revelation tied body and wholeness together in ways that the mind could never fully fathom.

> To say that individuals are members of a person is indeed a very violent use of language—and the context shows that Paul obviously meant it to be violent . . . when (he) took the term *soma* (body) and applied it to the Church, what it must have conveyed to him and his readers was (to employ a distinction which itself would have surprised him) something not corporate but corporal. It directed the mind to a person; it did not of itself suggest a social group . . .

> It is surely clear that for Paul to do or suffer anything 'with' Christ speaks of no external concomitance, like the P.T. instructor who says, "Now do this with me," but of a common organic functioning, as the new tissues take on the rhythms and metabolism of the body into which they have been grafted . . .

> The force of Paul's words can today perhaps be got only by paraphrasing: "Ye are the body of Christ and severally *membranes* thereof" (1 Cor. 12,17). The body that he has in mind is as concrete and as singular as the body of the Incarnation. (emphasis ours)[10]

In an interesting footnote, Robinson describes Karl Barth's bio-spiritual sense for this same wholeness which he, likewise, could describe only with moderate success.

> Believers . . . are therefore, in their full-grown and no way attenuated individuality, one body, one individual in Christ. They are not a mass of individuals, not even a corporation, a personified society, or a "totality," but The Individual, The One, The New (Human) (Romans, 443)[11]

Robinson and Barth were attuned to the body sense of wholeness. Their writings indicate that both men experienced the painful inadequacy of language. They could already feel in their bodies what they were unable to formulate with their minds, struggling to express what they knew in their hearts but could not yet craft through their words. Theirs was a bio-spiritual journey during the time when the only tools available were words and explanations, ideals and expectations.

There has always been a basic problem in Christian culture and theology, which bio-spirituality seeks to remedy. It is the perennial substitution of theological constructs or concepts about God, in place of the embodied process of human wholeness within which we are meant to receive and experience the divine. Healthy Christian spirituality invites surrender, not to God, but to what is real and true in ourselves "in Christ." Congruence with what is real in our own body opens a doorway into the language and experience of congruence with a Larger Body. Our individual process of wholeness offers the indispensable stepping-stone into that wider communion with God which the mystic tradition has always revered in Christianity. But the question, as always, is not merely to describe an experience but to help one another engage in the process of actually getting there.

While the different knowing and exploration that we call "bio-spiritual" is neither uniquely Christian nor tied to any particular religious tradition, it most definitely supports an incarnational emphasis within Christianity. Bio-Spirituality has the potential, perhaps for the first time in Christianity's long 2,000-year history, to move this tradition beyond the influence of Greek dualism, finally putting it back in touch with its more holistic Biblical origins. This time, though, it offers the promise of including a far more sophisticated experience of the body's role in healthy human and spiritual growth.

The philosophical, psychological, and theological roots of bio-spirituality, which we have barely touched in these pages, lay a foundation for restoring the Pauline vision of the Body of the Whole Christ and bringing sound mental health into the spiritual journey.

Appendix B

The Focusing Steps
(As We Teach Them)

by
Edwin M. McMahon, and
Peter A. Campbell

The following pages provide a summary of the Six Focusing Steps *as we teach them*, together with some points which guides find helpful. Other Focusing teachers have developed different styles and emphases.

Focusing is a very personal, caring, and gentle way of being with yourself or another. You might even use the word *reverent*. It is not pushing to get somewhere. Even though you may think you know what needs to happen in another person or yourself, the body's wisdom rarely follows a path laid down by the mind. You are doing something quite different when you focus; allowing a process to go forward. You are leaving yourself open to be drawn in a direction you might never have previously considered.

During Focusing you want to find some way to be with negative feelings and issues that is different from the usual holding them at arm's length or trying to avoid them. Being "caring" with an issue means that at least for this Focusing session you try to remain open to all that is there without immediately seeking to control it, make it better, or make it go away. Feelings change *as* they unfold, *as* they are heard, *as* they tell their uniquely-felt stories.

The Steps of Focusing are taught in many different ways and with quite diverse emphases. In the following pages, we summarize the Focusing Steps as well as the way in which we teach Focusing throughout our bio-spiritual network. We also share some of the reasons why we have settled on our approach over others. The outline we follow covers four main areas:

A) *Why We Teach Focusing the Way We Do*
B) *The Six Focusing Steps*
C) *The Short Form Steps*
D) *Further Suggestions for Guiding*

A) *Why We Teach Focusing the Way We Do*

Many teachers of Focusing begin with the skill of Rogerian active listening as a preparation for learning to focus and guide others. We tried that for a number of years, but then switched to staying with and emphasizing the Focusing process itself.

When saying this, we in no way denigrate the value of active or "healing" listening. But we found that emphasizing the listening skill at the same time we were teaching Focusing tended to confuse people. Active listening takes an enormous amount of time and energy to do well and, in itself, is an art form. The problem we found was that while the person listened to often feels heard, he or she does not necessarily experience the feel of inner change that can come from Focusing.

When Ed trained with Carl Rogers, he found that he often spent an enormous amount of time listening, but with very little significant *movement* taking place within the client. In listening, the structure is not fine-tuned enough to draw the person who is sharing right into the body-priority. Instead, the one sharing can go around in circles, skirting the periphery of what needs to be held in the body, while the one listening simply has to accompany them on this merry-go-round. From our experience, teaching people silently to be in their bodies, listening to the body-priority, has a much greater chance of being on target than we have experienced with verbalizations.

Active listening sessions easily become training sessions for therapists rather than sessions within which people experience forward movement within the process of Focusing. As Ed so often says, he got a sense for reflective listening from Rogers, but he did not experience an inside feel for movement within the client until he learned Focusing from Eugene Gendlin, the originator of Focusing, who was an early graduate student and colleague of Rogers.

Our question has always been, "How can we most effectively teach Focusing?" Experience has shown that listening sessions can very easily turn into *sharing* sessions rather than *process* sessions for untrained people because they have no inner sense for what the process of wholeness is all about. Focusing gets right to the point. Also, when listening is given first priority, Focusing begins to take second place as people concentrate on refining their listening skills. However, simply by following the Steps of Focusing, untrained people can begin to process and guide others without having highly-developed listening skills.

There is another reason we begin with Focusing and do not emphasize listening skills until later. What people need in the beginning, even more than an ability to listen, is *some simple way to hold in their bodies and own negative feelings.* You can go on listening forever and neither the listener nor the one listened to have any idea what to do with or how to be with hurting places. Experience over the last 17 years has taught us what the priorities are. We plunge people directly into *"caring-feeling-presence,"*—how to be with scary places—and you cannot do that without Focusing. Again, as Ed reminds us, "In no way did any of my training with Carl Rogers ever help me develop the approach of "caring-feeling-presence."

To start with Active Listening is the therapist's way of looking at things. It avoids the basic issue of both people journeying together in the pain of one of them, without any of the supports you can get by talking. You have to plunge people right into their process—"What's between me and feeling really good right now?"

Secular priorities are quite different from those that we emphasize in a bio-spiritual approach. Bio-spirituality emphasizes an experience of grace in the body or "letting go and letting God," as this is often put in AA circles. Such a priority supercedes for us the learning of listening skills, valuable though these may be.

Behind all our priorities lies one that is most important for the use of psychological processes in spirituality. It is enabling people to let go into the truth of themselves, especially their brokenness, in order that they may bodily experience *grace* within the process of their growth into wholeness.

Moreover, it is through the experience of companioning or journeying together as the focuser takes the risk with the guide to be vulnerable and own that brokenness in his or her body that the *Focusing Companions* experience begins to surface. This is a stage of growing together where no longer is the relationship one of doctor to patient, therapist to client, teacher to pupil. Rather, it becomes one in which there is *empowerment in mutual vulnerability.* Ed says more about this in his booklet on *Guidelines for Focusing Companions.* Once again, though, we feel that this experience does not happen as effectively when people simply concentrate on the development of listening skills.

Let us turn now to our outline of the Focusing Steps.

B) The Six Focusing Steps

(Note: The following pages are meant to be used as a reference resource for learning to focus and guide others in Focusing. Once you have studied and worked with these pages a few times, then make your own simplified one-page version of the Long Form Steps, being guided by the careful wording and key phrases printed below. Your personalized single page will make it easier to follow the basic Focusing movement both for yourself and while guiding another. The more expanded version given below can then be used as a resource to fall back on when needed. The reflection and study necessary in order to compose your own briefer (but, nonetheless, complete) version of the Long Form Steps will greatly help you to remember the sequence of these steps.)

(In the text which follows, suggestions for what to say are in plain type, instructions and explanations are in italics.)

Preparation

(The aim of this preparation exercise is to help the focuser grow quiet inside. It is not for the purpose of relaxing or numbing feelings. If there is anxiousness or tension, the preparation exercise helps to quiet the mind's chatter so the one Focusing can attend more carefully to whatever feelings are present in the body. Do not encourage the focuser to "relax." This just triggers all their habitual numbing mechanisms for blotting out feeling. Use the preparation exercise especially when you sense a lot of thinking and chatter in the head. The rationale behind the preparation exercise is that the simplest way to get out of the mind is to get into the body. When your attention is on body-feelings, you cannot be thinking at the same time. If the focuser is clearly in touch with body-feeling, then dispense with the preparation exercise and go directly to Step #1.)

Take a few moments and allow your attention to settle down into your solar plexus area. Ask yourself, "How does it feel in here?" Notice any body language that tells you how it is inside right now. If you find something there, then just attend to it quietly for a few moments, noticing as much of the feel of it as you can . . . *(pause)* . . . If nothing special comes to your attention, then let your awareness move around inside your body until you come to another place where you notice any feeling and pause there, carefully noticing whatever it is like inside. For example, you might find an uneasiness in your breathing, stiffness in your neck, heaviness in your legs—something like that, where attending to some identifiable sensation or feeling for a few quiet moments will help you to move out of head thinking and into your body's language. *(pause)*

1. FINDING A SPACE BY TAKING AN INVENTORY.

(The purpose of Step #1 is to allow an opportunity for the focuser to identify whatever issues lie between him or her and feeling really good or free right now. Often, we go in circles, overwhelmed by so much going on inside us that we really do not know where to begin. We remain stuck and paralyzed, trying to figure things out with our heads and getting nowhere. Step #1 gets the body involved in setting priorities. It helps to identify and set things down one at a time so we are not just a jumbled-up mess inside. This first Step provides needed distancing so we are not so paralyzed by the whirl-

pool of emotion. On the far side of all the "stuff" between me and feeling really good, there lies a core OK-ness. It helps to touch this place, even though each of us still has to go back and work through all our unfinished issues. Otherwise, we remain chronically dis-eased and consider this normal.)

A. Now, let me know if something comes when you ask yourself: "Is there anything in my life right now keeping me from feeling really good?" *(Pause)*

(Notice the careful wording of this question. You, as guide, invite the focuser to ask him/herself if there is anything in "my" life right now keeping "me" from feeling really good? This is another way to emphasize that the one Focusing is the one who is in charge. The guide is not an authority figure to whom the focuser responds. This is an inner dialogue. The guide's role is simply to be a companion on this inner journey.)

(If the focuser does not respond after some time, the facilitator might ask: "Did anything surface?" If the answer is "Yes" go to [B]; if the answer is "No," say:) "Let me know if something comes when you ask yourself: 'Is there anything in my life right now that feels important enough to be with in a Focusing way?'" *(If something comes, then go to Step #3, "Is it OK to be with this?")*

B. All right, now see if you can put this whole thing temporarily aside by imagining yourself setting it on the floor beside you . . . (or on a shelf, or in a container like a box—whatever image helps you to take it out of yourself for the time being, giving you the feel of some space between you and this whole thing). . . . Let me know if you are able to do this or not. *(pause)*

(Setting issues down is a way of getting distance from them. This is not pretending that they no longer exist. The purpose of the Inventory is to find and acknowledge what is there at this time. The focuser will come back to whatever has been set aside in a moment.)

(If the focuser cannot put an issue aside, you might suggest:)

Take a moment to dialogue with it, letting it know you recognize that it wants to be listened to right now, but that you need a few moments to get a little space from it in order to feel its priority along with some other things. You promise not to neglect it and will come back to it if it is really Number One, but for the time being would it be willing to sit down over there? (If this does not help in putting it aside, you might ask:) Does this thing feel like it is the one that needs Focusing on right now, or does it feel like you could try again to set it aside and go further with the inventory? (*If it cannot be set aside, go to Step #3. If the person can set it aside, then say:*) "Take a moment to notice what it feels like to have this whole thing set aside for the time being." (*Pause*)

C. Now ask yourself: "If I could leave this whole thing there for good and not need to carry it around ever again, would there be anything else between me and feeling really good right now? Let me know if anything further surfaces.

(*If anything else comes, repeat [B] and [C] again and again, each time helping the focuser get a feel of all the things being set aside by changing the phrasing to:*) Now ask yourself: "If I could leave both of these things (these three things, four, etc.) aside for good and not have to carry them around again, would there be anything else between me and feeling really good?" Let me know if something further surfaces, or if you can feel a reasonably open space now inside? (*Once the person has found such a space, continue with:*)

D. Finally, take a few moments to notice whether there are a couple of other things in your life right now, not problems, which feel important to you . . . maybe a challenge, a dream, something you are looking forward to . . . something it would be good to identify. If you find anything like this, then set it aside next to your problems and let me know when you have done this.

(*The reason for this last statement (D) is to allow an opportunity for the focuser to be in touch with more than negative things. Focusing is for all of life's issues, not just for problems. The Long Form Focusing inventory lets people identify everything that is important, positive and negative. Step #2 then allows your body to set the priority of what needs to be focused on at this time. Sometimes, there is a surprise. A positive issue takes center stage.*)

STEP 2. FEELING WHICH ONE IS NUMBER ONE.

(The purpose of Step #2 is learning to trust the body's wisdom. Rather than thinking a priority with your mind, you attend not to the mental content, but the body-feel of an issue. You are looking for the "feeling" doorway, not the "thinking" doorway. Often, you carry very serious life-issues, but the one with the most body-feel may be some inconsequential, irritating annoyance that will not let go inside. The point of Step #2 is to be drawn into your body-knowing. That means you need to find the "feeling" thread into the tapestry of your inner life. When you have strong resistances to getting near a scary life-issue, your body will open another inner doorway for you—often through the body-feel of some lesser issue that will help you to be drawn inside. Once inside, your body eventually will guide you to the bigger issue, but in ways that allow you take one step at a time instead of being overwhelmed by it all.)

Now, returning to whatever you have set aside, ask yourself: "Which one feels like it is Number One for me right now?" For example, which one feels the heaviest, hurts the most, has the most energy, is most exciting?" Say OK when you have found it or if you have difficulty finding it.

(Again, note that the one Focusing asks him/herself which feels like Number One. The guide simply invites the focuser to check inside. The focuser is responding primarily to a question that he or she asks him/herself.)

(If the focuser has difficulty finding a Number One issue, or if two issues seem to have equal weight, you might ask if they would want to Focus on how it feels not knowing which is Number One. Or, you might inquire whether it would be all right to sit with the feeling of both issues together that seem to have equal importance. The body-feel of an issue is the important key to Focusing. Content is secondary. Help the focuser discover what stands out most prominently in a feeling way in all this. Once something has been found, then move on to Step #3.)

STEP 3. IS IT OK TO BE WITH THIS?

(The purpose of Step #3 is to respect your defenses and not ignore or repress them, as well as to recognize that defenses and resistances are doorways, not walls, if you know how to be drawn through them. You will know the answer to the question in Step #3 almost

immediately. You will either get a clear "Yes," or an ambiguous "Maybe," or a loud inner "No!" Often, we will feel significant resistance to getting near a scary, inside place. This is our body telling us something. Instead of ignoring or repressing the feeling of resistance and trying to be with Number One, turn, instead, and ask if it would be OK for a few moments to be caring and gentle with the feeling of "not wanting to get near this," "of wanting to run away," "of being scared at the prospect of looking at some dreaded inner place." The feeling of resistance has taken center stage. So, be with it and allow it to tell its story. More often than not, your resistance will provide a more effective doorway into your body-knowing than will the Number One issue itself. Some resistances and issues may need what we call a "caring-feeling-presence." We will say more about that in a moment.)

Before going further, check for a moment to sense whether your body says it is OK to spend some time with this, giving it a more friendly hearing, allowing it to tell something of its story. Let me know whether this is OK or not.

<u>If it is OK:</u>

(If it is OK, but you do not know whether the issue might need caring-feeling-presence, ask:)
Is this something between you and feeling good or is it something positive?

(Then, if it is something between the focuser and feeling good, suggest ways you sense might be appropriate for creating a climate of caring-feeling-presence [cf. below] before going into step 4. Be sure to end your suggestions with:)

Let me know when you are ready to go further.

<u>If it's not OK:</u>

(If their response to the question, "Is it OK?" is a "No," then say:)

All right, ask yourself: "Is it OK to be with_____ *(fill in what the person has said—e.g.),* "not wanting to get any place near it,' 'feeling too scared of it,' 'feeling it is too overwhelming to sit with,' etc.? Let me know if it is OK to be with the feeling of all your resistance to getting near this issue.

(If the answer is still "No," ask the focuser to check whether there may be some part of this whole thing that he or she could sit with. They may even need to go back to their inventory and select some less-threatening issue. If that is necessary, you might ask how it feels not being able to face or be with a particular issue. Often, the feeling of resistance itself is the best doorway into Focusing. Work with the focuser to create a "caring-feeling presence" before proceeding further.)

Note: Caring-Feeling-Presence

(If, when leading someone, you can tell that the issue being worked with is difficult for them, quietly suggest something that helps create a "caring-feeling-presence" so that it might be easier for them actually to let go into the body-feeling of the issue. Caring-feeling-presence means finding a different body way to be with stuck, resistant, scary inner feelings. Sometimes, it helps to be with them as "teacher" rather than "enemy." Perhaps you can hold them as you would hold a crying, hurting child. What will help you to have some kind of "kinship" with this place? Find a way that fits your temperament where you can put your arm around the hurting place inside rather than only having the body-feel of pushing it away.)

(Remember, the purpose of a more open, caring, gentle inner climate or body-attitude is to help the focuser approach what is real inside, rather than reject, repress, ignore or numb it with some "process-skipping" mechanism. There is a fine line here, so the guide needs to encourage the focuser whenever caring-feeling-presence is used, to remain with the body-feelings in this climate of openness and availability in order to own these real feelings (difficult though they may be) rather than using caring-feeling-presence as just one more form of "process-skipping," a substitute for being in touch with the truth of oneself.)

(Select one or two of the following suggestions, perhaps get feedback to discern if another is called for; allow time to do it; do not just read this page. Empathically, with the focuser, try to sense what is happening and adapt these suggestions creatively to his or her needs.)

If this place inside feels so hurting, scary, stuck or blocked that you want to run away from it, then take time to create an atmosphere of caring-feeling openness, gentleness or kindness in a way that it can feel that presence from you. Perhaps hold and feel it in the same way you might hold and feel a crying, hurting child; or use some word or phrase to create a feeling climate toward it that is the opposite of the way you usually treat it. Maybe imagine putting your arm around it or patting it. Notice where you feel this issue or feeling most in your body and then put your hand there to comfort, pat and caress it; or just let it know with your hand that you care and are there. You might want to try one or a combination of these approaches.

STEP 4. LETTING GO INTO IT, JUST BEING IN IT, SENSING THE WHOLE OF IT

(Step #4 involves attending not to what your mind thinks about an issue but to how it feels in your body. Most of us want to play God and control the feelings that we do not like. Step #4 is allowing them to be heard. Sometimes, you need caring-feeling-presence in order to do this. There is no way you can "think" the whole of an issue as it is carried in your body, but you can feel it. That is what Step #4 is about.)

Now, ask yourself: "How does this whole thing feel in my body right now? How am I carrying it inside me?" Allow your awareness to seep into your body, to settle in and sense how all this feels inside. Say "OK" when you can feel something of this in your body.

(The point of this last direction is to give you, the guide, feedback on whether a focuser with whom you are unfamiliar is or is not aware of body-feelings connected with whatever is being focused upon. Obviously, the suggestion is superfluous for a person who already experiences this connection or is successfully moving through the cycles of felt-shifts.)

(Note: Once the Focusing process is moving along and it becomes clear the focuser can feel issues in his or her body, it is no longer necessary to keep the directions for Steps #4 and #5 separate from one another. Steps #4 and #5 are artificially separated in order to give the guide feedback as to whether the one Focusing (presum-

ably a beginner) can actually feel anything in his or her body that is connected with what is being focused upon. If it is clear the focuser has a body-feel for what is being focused on, combine the directions for Steps #4 and #5 together. For example: "Take a moment to be with how all that (_____—*insert whatever symbol has been shared)* feels, and then let me know if something further comes that fits the way this now feels as you sit with it."*)

STEP 5. ALLOWING IT TO EXPRESS ITSELF.

(Staying with the body-feel of an issue in Step #4, sooner or later it will express itself in some "symbol" that fits and feels right. The symbol may be a word, a phrase, an image, a memory, perhaps a feeling, tears, a giggle—anything that comes and seems to connect in some way with the issue being focused upon so there is some easing or "felt-rightness" about the connection. Dr. Gendlin refers to such easing as a "felt-shift." This is the body's way of taking a forward step toward wholeness in the resolution of an issue. Sometimes in Focusing there can be a big felt-shift. At other times, it is more like a series of smaller steps, each contributing to forward movement. Focuser and guide need to discern whether each smaller step needs to go further at that time, or whether this is a stopping point for now.)

Now, staying with how this whole thing feels inside, sense if anything further comes (like a word or mental image, a memory or just some other feeling) which connects with how it feels—anything that resonates with or is on target inside. Take your time and let me know if something comes that fits the way this whole thing feels.

(If a symbol comes, continue the process as follows:)

A. *(When a symbol is shared, let the focuser know that his or her symbol has been heard by reflecting it back exactly as spoken. If the focuser just nods or says "OK," proceed to (B) and ask:)*

B. Is this something that feels right to let unfold a little further? *(If the focuser says "No," and wants to conclude his or her Focusing, go to Step #6. If the focuser says "Yes," and wants to continue, go to (C).*

C. Ask yourself: "How does all this _____ *(insert symbol if shared)* now feel in my body?" Take time to let go into and sense how all about this feels inside and let me know if anything further comes that fits the way this now feels.

(Repeat Steps A, B and C as long as the focuser wants to keep Focusing, or at least as long as you have time for this exercise.)

(Remember to repeat the suggestion to be caring and gentle with an issue whenever this might be helpful.)

(If the focuser comes to a bad-feeling place that does not shift, or if they want to stop in a bad-feeling place, try some of the following. Empathically work with the focuser, attempting to sense what is happening and adapt these suggestions creatively to his/her needs.)

1. Ask yourself: "How does the worst of this feel in my body?"

2. Ask yourself: "What needs to happen (change) inside me for this whole thing to begin to feel better?"

3. Ask yourself: "What would feel like a small step forward with all this?"

4. Ask yourself: "What would feel like a breath of fresh air in this whole thing?"

5. Imagine, for a moment, how it would feel inside if this whole thing were all OK. *(Pause to try to feel it.)* Can you feel this way all the time? *(If answer is "No" say:)* Ask yourself: "What needs to change inside me for this to feel better?"

6. Staying with how this place feels inside, ask it: "What are you trying to do for me?" Let me know if anything comes to answer this question. *(Variation:)* "How are you trying to help me?"

7. Ask this place inside: "How do you need me to be with you so you can tell me what you want?"

8. Would it be OK for a few moments to sit quietly and gently with not wanting to go further? *(Then, if nothing comes, encourage the focuser with:)* Leave this place inside, promising that you will return at another time, letting it know that you respect its schedule, that you will check in again later to see whether it is ready to speak or still needs further nurturing.

9. As you get ready to stop, just imagine taking this whole thing and putting it aside—on a shelf, or on the floor beside you, or in a bag. Notice what it feels like to do that, and just stay with this feeling for a few moments in an unhurried, quiet, gentle way before you stop. Let me know when you are ready

to stop or if something connects that wants to go further at this time.

10. *(Sometimes, when there are difficult feelings or issues, it can help to ask:)* "Would it feel right to stop Focusing for a few moments and just talk a little about what you are feeling right now? We can go back to Focusing after talking a bit, if that is what you want to do."

(Then, you listen and reflect with "healing" or "active listening." You respond not just to the content that is shared, but to how the person feels inside when sharing this content. It can help to ask yourself: "How is this person IN what he or she is saying?" Let the person know that you hear not just "what" they are saying, but "how they are in what they are saying." If during the course of this dialogue other felt-senses appear, you can invite the focuser to check whether he or she might want to be with them in a Focusing way.)

Finding out if it is OK to stop:

(Presuming the focuser has said nothing about stopping and you feel for various reasons—time, tiredness, your own feel of where he or she is at—that maybe this is the right place to conclude for now, we suggest the following approach:)

Check inside and notice if this place needs to go further at this time or whether this is a place where it would be OK to stop, at least for now? Let me know what you find.

(You follow along with the focuser's response, either continuing with A, B, C or going to Step #6, unless there is some serious reason not to. Notice that in the above wording, "continuing" is given priority over "stopping" so you do not load your question in a way that might indicate you want to stop. If it seems that "stopping" is the priority, many focusers will interpret this as an indication of the guide's need to stop, thereby becoming distracted and not really paying attention to what their own felt-sense is telling them or becoming too inhibited to express it.)

STEP 6. NURTURING PERIOD

(Step #6 offers some quiet time in which to be aware of any change in how the body feels after having focused on an issue. This is a time for quiet reverence, thankfulness, perhaps marking special

feeling places to which one might want to return at a later time. It is also a time for creating "kinship" with unfinished places that will need to be carried until the next Focusing, promising not to neglect them. For those who value the spiritual dimension of Focusing, this is a time for nurturing and being grateful for the body-sense of graced opening as difficult feeling places unfold into greater wholeness within the person.)

Let us nurture this place with some before-and-after checking as we close. Take a few moments, now, to recall how it felt in your body when you began to Focus. (*Allow a short pause for doing this.*) Now, come to where you are inside at present, sensing whether this place feels the same as when you started or whether it has changed in any way. Let me know what you find.

If it does feel better:

A. Before-and-After Checking

Noticing where in the body it has changed.

(*If the focuser indicates some change, then help him or her notice concretely where that difference is and how it feels in their body by suggesting:*)

Take a few moments to notice specifically in your body where there has been some change, like a loosening, releasing, easing.

(*Or, if this has been shared, use the earlier description of how the issue felt in the body when they began, as distinct from how it feels now*).

Let me know what you find. (*Pause and wait for feedback.*)

B. Savoring the Movement

(*If there has been some movement, you might say:*)

Now give yourself a little time to savor that movement, staying with whatever concrete change you can feel in your body. Take time to become familiar with the feel of this changed inner landscape so you can find your way back to it later. Perhaps, it might want to go further at another time or maybe you might want to return just to be nourished by the feel of this change. *(Pause long enough for focuser to do this.)*

C. Time to say Thanks

Grounding "spiritual" in the body.
(After you sense an appropriate period of quiet has been given for "savoring," then:)

Christian Incarnational Emphasis:

(If your orientation involves Christian spiritual guidance or helping someone who values the Christian dimension of what they are Focusing on, you might very quietly and as unobtrusively as possible insert:)

As you savor the feel of this movement toward more wholeness and healing, let yourself at the same time become aware that this is how God's grace feels physically in your body. *(Pause)* This is your unique body-feeling of God's life-giving presence inside you—a presence and power of healing as real, as close, as tangible as you are willing to let yourself feel and reverence that change inside yourself. *(Pause)* In whatever way seems right, you might want to give yourself a few more moments just to be gratefully in the Lord with all this. *(Pause)* Whenever you are ready, you can stop.

Alternative:
(For others, you might quietly suggest, with as little interruption as possible, the following:)

As you savor the feel of this movement toward wholeness and healing, in whatever way seems right, give yourself a few more moments to be gratefully and reverently in this place of gift within yourself—perhaps in a way that says, "Thank you." *(Pause)* Whenever you are ready, you can stop.

If it does not feel better:

(When something is stuck, blocked, going in circles, etc., help the focuser to be with how this feels in a caring-feeling way, or listen

to what it might want to say as it is held gently. This often creates an inner climate for it to speak. Therefore, when whatever is being focused on feels the same, perhaps even worse, or maybe some easing but a strong edge of unfinishedness that is not OK, you might suggest the following, slowly guiding with:)

Take a moment to let this place that feels so _____ *(use their words, if possible)* know that you hear it, that you are going to respect it and not run away if it needs to tell you something. Being present in this caring, open way, sense whether anything comes that helps guide you toward whatever is the right thing to do now. Let me know if something comes. *(Pause for feedback.)*

(If it says nothing, or you sense the focuser is scared and blocking and wants to stop, honor that by helping them conclude with something like the following:)

As you bring this period of quiet to an end, let yourself feel as much of the unfinishedness in this whole thing as you can, asking it the question: "How do you need me to be with you so we can continue our journey together, so you can be my teacher rather than my enemy?" Let me know if anything comes that feels on target.

(Even if this does not dispose the focuser for movement at that time, the attitude of remaining open to an unfinished place can tone the relationship for that possibility later on, because the question itself begins an inner reconciliation and usually feels more hopeful as a place to stop.)

C) The Short Form Steps

(Use the Short Form of Focusing whenever you have a feeling that is clamoring for your attention—a spontaneously-given Number One. Use it, also, when you want to check in and see how things are going without taking time to go through an inventory and set issues aside, one by one.)

1. Is it OK to be with this?

(If there is already a feeling that needs to be focused on, ask yourself:) "Is it OK to be with this?" *(Check to make sure your body says it is all right to spend time with how this issue feels inside. If the answer is "No," see if it is OK to be with the feeling of the "No" instead.)*

2. Letting go into it and allowing it to express itself.

Ask yourself: "How does this whole thing feel in my body right now? How am I carrying it inside me?" Allow your awareness to seep into your body, to settle in and sense how all this feels inside. Create a caring-feeling-presence if needed to help you own how it really feels in your body. Wait patiently to see if it wants to express itself.

(If a symbol comes and you can feel its on-targetness, then check to see if it would be OK to go further. If it is, ask yourself:) "How does this now feel in my body?" *(Give the new symbol time to be felt, time to express itself and unfold further until you are ready to stop.)*

3. Nurturing

(Take the time to conclude your Focusing session using the three parts of Long Form Step #6—i.e., before-and-after checking; savoring the movement; and taking time to say:) "Thanks."

D) Further Suggestions for Guiding

1. Your primary role for guiding someone in Focusing is to help the focuser stay in the body-feel of his or her issue, and to create a trusting, caring, more secure climate within which it is easier to risk Focusing. The guide or companion creates this environment by the quality of presence in the relationship, one which is not hampered by the guide's need for control and success as a helper. Such an atmosphere encourages and disposes for Focusing and is, in itself, a gift that heals and opens for further grace.

2. The nature of your response as a guide is not to make cognitive connections of insight but to support a forward movement of felt-meaning within the focuser's body. This means your interventions should be intended to help an or-

ganismic process unfold. You are not there to *talk about* an issue, but to help the person stay in touch with the *body-feel* of that issue so it can tell its story.

3. Be ready to skip Steps #1 and #2 if the issue to be focused on is clearly evident. For example, something upsetting has just happened. *Always* check, though, to determine whether it is OK to be with this particular issue (Step #3), and if it needs to be held in a caring way before going further. Then, go through Steps #4 - #6.

4. Remember, the focuser cannot Focus while you (the guide) are talking or giving directions. Be mindful of brevity and clarity. Say what you have to say in order to support the process, then get out of the way and be quiet so the one Focusing can continue.

5. Always give clear ground rules so the one Focusing knows what to do next, and how to let you know when they have done what you asked. This frees the focuser to concentrate on Focusing and you from worrying about whether it is evident how you are to be called upon if further input is needed.

6. If at any point you become unsure about what to do next, ask the one Focusing: "What does it feel right to do now?" If the answer is: "I don't know," then ask whether it would be OK just to sit with that feeling of unsureness for a while and sense whether anything comes from that.

7. The person Focusing is *always* the one in charge! If he or she wants to stop, stop! If such a person runs into something that is too scary to go further with and decides to back off, that is their choice. Let them back off. You, as guide, might suggest at that point something like: "Would it be all right just to be caring and gentle with the feeling of how scary this is becoming right now and the need to back away from it?" Help the person stay with whatever comes as a real felt-meaning right now.

8. If you are running out of time you might ask, upon arriving at a natural resting place, "Check inside to see if this is something that needs to go further now, or would it be OK to stop here for the time being?" Generally, we find it better to weigh the option in favor of proceeding further with Focusing rather than abruptly injecting a stop sign. What you regard as a natural stopping place may not be such for the one Focusing.

9. Remember, while Focusing is always therapeutic, it is never a substitute for psychotherapy. The Focusing guide is a companion, not a therapist, unless professionally trained and licensed as well.

What To Do If Someone Cannot Get A Felt Sense

This is the person who knows a problem area with the mind but cannot feel it in the body.

1. Have such a person ask him/herself the following question, paying special attention to how the body responds: *"I feel OK about this in my body, don't I?"* Allow time to do this, then ask: *"Did you feel anything in your body that answered that? Just stay with this—be in it (Step #4), and see if something comes that connects with this feeling. Let me know if this happens."*

2. Some people often have a *background feeling* that follows them around during the day. It is some way they always feel—sad, always rushing, feeling inferior to others, always trying so hard, etc. It often helps to focus on this background feeling.

3. Sometimes, it helps to pick two or three of the most important things the focuser has said if this person has talked about what is bothering them. Look for the most *feeling* statements. This may be a single word or phrase. Tell the person: *When I say what I'm going to say, don't you say anything to me or to yourself, just be quiet and feel whatever comes.* Then, slowly repeat the key words or phrases you have noted. Allow time for silence. Then, if the person catches

an edge of body-feeling, move into the next appropriate step.

4. Ask how the one Focusing feels about not being able to get hold of a felt-sense.

5. Sometimes, when the one you assist seems to be getting nowhere, if it feels right, invite them to stop Focusing and just talk about whatever they are trying to get close to. Respond with Healing Listening by reflecting how the person is "in" what he or she is saying, the body-feel that you pick up.

Do not engage in ordinary conversation in which you share your own opinions, comments, judgments, evaluations, etc. Rather, try to let the other person know that you hear how the issue feels in them, or if you cannot catch any feeling, at least reflect each point being made.

When doing Healing Listening, you might find it helpful to ask *yourself* the following question: "How is this other person IN what he or she is saying?" What you seek to become aware of is not merely the *content* being shared—*what* is talked about—but, rather, *how this person must be feeling inside the experience he or she narrates*. Scared, angry, upset, etc. You, as healing listener, then respond not to *what* is talked about, but to *how* this individual feels in what is talked about. Let the other person know that you hear their excitement, desperation, loneliness, frustration, jealousy, etc.

Then, when both of you catch the edge of some more prominent feeling which may arise during such sharing, you might ask: "Is that something that feels right to focus on?" If the answer is "Yes," then ask: "Does it need some caring presence before going further? Let me know when you are ready to move further." Then, guide into Steps #4 & #5, when they are ready.

Remember, the greatest gift we give to someone whom we accompany in Focusing is a caring presence that is non-manipulative. Technique can be very helpful, but in the long run is of little consequence if this presence is missing. Such presence enables the focuser to feel safe enough to own whatever is real in his or her body. Your own body-experience of what Focusing feels like from the inside, plus your body-feel for the "felt-shift," as well as having acquired a body-sense for how to create a "caring-feeling-presence" toward your own fears and hurts, will give you the most essential knowledge you need to guide in Focusing—even if you make technical mistakes.

Our experience is that when people feel accompanied and not manipulated, this is such a disposing grace, that if the above body-learnings have been acquired through your own Focusing, then they give you the on-target directions you need to support the process. It seems that when this presence and this body-wisdom come into a relationship, the process takes care of itself, despite our other shortcomings.

Endnotes

Introduction

1. Eugene T. Gendlin, *Focusing*, New York, Bantam Books, Inc., 1981.
2. *Ibid.*, p.77.

Chapter 1

1. Les Brunswick, "Focusing, Philosophy, and Social Change," in *The Focusing Connection*, September, 1985, p. 1.
2. *Loc. cit.*
3. *Loc. cit.*

Chapter 4

1. Lancelot Law Whyte, *The Next Development in Man*, New York, The New American Library (a Mentor Book), 1962.
2. Peter A. Campbell, Edwin M. McMahon, *Bio-Spirituality: Focusing as a Way to Grow*, Chicago, Loyola University Press, 1985, p. 7.
3. Whyte, *op.cit.*, p. 203.
4. *Ibid.*, p. 204.
5. Patricia Ann Scales, "Mandala Theatre: Creativity, A Somatic and Mystical Perspective," unpublished M.A. thesis, Sierra University, Costa Mesa, California, 1987.

Chapter 5

1. St. Paul, Letter to the Galatians, 2:20, *The New American Bible*, New York, Oxford University Press, 1990, p. 297.

2. This is well developed in John A. T. Robinson, *The Body, A Study in Pauline Theology*, London, SCM Press, 1963, especially p. 51.
3. Acts of the Apostles, 17:28, *The New English Bible* (New Testament), Oxford University Press and Cambridge University Press, 1962, p. 231.

Chapter 7

1. Eugene T. Gendlin, *Focusing*, Everest House, New York, 1978, p. 75.
2. *Loc. cit.*
3. St. Paul, Letter to the Ephesians, 1:18-19. *The New English Bible* (New Testament), Oxford University Press and Cambridge University Press, 1962, p. 329.

Chapter 8

1. St. Paul, Letter to the Romans, 7:19-24, *The New American Bible, op.cit.*, p. 239.
2. Select passages in this chapter are drawn verbatim from two other articles. The passages are not referenced in the text. The articles are:
Peter A. Campbell, "Focusing—Doorway to the Body-Life of Spirit," in *Creation Spirituality*, Volume VII, Number 3, May/June 1991, p. 24. Peter A. Campbell and Edwin M. McMahon, *"Process-Skipping": A Mechanism That Locks In Addictive Patterns and Blocks the Experience of Grace*, Kansas City, Sheed and Ward Publishing, 1991.
3. Eugene T. Gendlin, *Let Your Body Interpret Your Dreams*, Chiron Publications, Wilmette, Illinois, 1986, p. 52-53.
4. Eddie Ensley, *Prayer that Heals our Emotions*, Columbus, Contemplative Books, 1986.
5. Anthony de Mello, S.J., *Sadhana: A Way to God*, St. Louis, The Institute of Jesuit Sources, 1978.
6. Eddie Ensley, *op. cit.*, pp. 74-75.
7. Eugene T. Gendlin, *Focusing, op. cit.*, p. 75.
8. Tony Kreuch, "Dealing with Anger: A Christian Response," *Journal of Christian Healing*, Vol. 9, No. 2, Fall 1987, pp. 18-20.

9. *Ibid.*, p. 20.

10. *Loc. cit.*

11. *Loc. cit.*

Chapter 9

1. Marianne Thompson, *Teaching Children to Focus*, (an interview by E. McMahon and P. Campbell), Kansas City, Sheed & Ward Publishing, 1991. Monograph Series on "Focusing and Bio-Spirituality."

Chapter 10

1. Gendlin, *Focusing*, *op.cit.*, p. 75.

2. The Gospel According to John, 12:24, *The New English Bible*, *op.cit.*, p. 175.

3. The Gospel According to Matthew 18:2, *The New American Bible*, *op.cit.*, p. 38.

Chapter 11

1. This chapter is written to continue the development of a bio-spiritual approach to sexuality written earlier by Peter Campbell and myself. The reader might want to refer to that more-detailed treatment which I will not repeat here. Cf. McMahon, E., Campbell, P., *A Bio-Spiritual Approach to Sexuality: Healing A Spirituality of Control*, Sheed & Ward Publishing, 1991. Monograph Series on "Focusing and Bio-Spirituality."

2. Robert Bly, "Listening to the Koln Concert," in *Loving A Woman in Two Worlds*, New York, Harper & Row, p. 68.

3. *Ibid.*, "Winter Poem," p. 16.

4. *Ibid.*, "In the Month of May," p. 79.

5. John A. T. Robinson, *The Body: A Study in Pauline Theology*, London, SCM Press, 1963, p. 73, (quoting from Karl Barth, Commentary on Romans, p. 443.)

6. Bly, *op.cit.*, p. 68.

7. W. H. Gardner (editor), "God's Grandeur," in *Gerard Manley Hopkins, A Selection of His Poems & Prose,* Baltimore, Penguin Books, 1953, p. 27.
8. Bly, *op.cit.,* "The Horse of Desire," p. 65.
9. Bly, *op.cit.,* "Come with Me," p. 29.

Chapter 12

1. Ira Progoff, *The Symbolic and the Real,* New York, Julian Press, 1963, p. 39.
2. Louis Untermeyer (editor), "The Gift Outright," in *The Road Not Taken: An Introduction to Robert Frost,* New York, Holt, Rinehart and Winston, 1971, pp. 262-263.
3. Psalm 49, *The Jerusalem Bible,* New York, Doubleday & Company, 1966, p. 831.
4. Edwin M. McMahon, Peter A. Campbell, *Please Touch,* New York, Sheed & Ward Publishing, 1969, p. 40.

Chapter 14

1. Thomas Hanna, *Bodies In Revolt: A Primer in Somatic Thinking,* Freeperson Press, 1985.
2. Edwin M. McMahon, "Focusing Companions: New Model for Relationships," Kansas City, Sheed & Ward Publishing, 1991. In addition to 28 suggested guidelines to protect and sustain the Focusing Companion relationship, this booklet discusses norms for selecting a Focusing guide, and how to become a Focusing Companion.
3. The Gospel According to Matthew, 18:20, *The Jerusalem Bible, op.cit.,* p. 44.

Appendix A

1. Remy Kwant, "The Human Body as the Self-Awareness of Being (an Inquiry into the Last Phase of Merleau-Ponty's Philosophical Life)," in *Humanitas,* Vol. 2, No. 1, Spring 1966.
2. *Ibid.,* p. 56.
3. *Ibid.,* p. 55.

4. Carl R. Rogers, *On Becoming A Person*, Boston, Houghton Mifflin, 1961, p. 17.

5. Eugene T. Gendlin, "A Theory of Personality Change," in *New Directions in Client-Centered Therapy*, Joseph T. Hart & J.M. Tomlinson, eds., Boston, Houghton Mifflin, 1970, p. 135.

6. *Ibid.*, p. 141.

7. Karl Rahner, "Christology and an Evolutionary World View," in *Theology Digest*, Vol. 28, No. 3, Fall 1980, p. 216.

8. *Ibid.*, p. 217.

9. John A. T. Robinson, *The Body: A Study in Pauline Theology*, *op. cit.*, p. 9, 29.

10. *Ibid.*, p. 50, 51, 63.

11. *Ibid.*, p. 51.

Focusing Resources

from the Institute for Bio-Spiritual Research

From the Institute for Bio-Spiritual Research, Edwin M. McMahon and Peter A. Campbell offer this series of monographs, audiocassettes, and videos explaining Focusing, the psychological structure and experiential foundation for Bio-Spirituality, a healthy spirituality grounded in the body and in a Christian theology that experientially supports human wholeness.

Monographs and Audiocassettes ─────────

What Is Focusing?
Introduces focusing in simple, non-technical terms.
LL1500, 12 pp booklet, $1.25
LL7500, audiocassette, $6.95

What Is Spiritual About Focusing?
Discussion of spiritual maturity and a theology of body- knowing.
LL1501, 12 pp booklet, $1.25
LL7501, audiocassette, $7.95

The Focusing Steps
Essential steps of the Focusing process.
LL1502, 24 pp booklet, $2.00
LL7502, audiocassette, $14.95

Questions Often Asked About Focusing and Spirituality
Responses to frequently asked questions.
LL1503, 12 pp booklet, $1.25
LL7503, audiocassette, $6.95

The Inward Connection
Discovering the Link between Focusing and Healthy Religion An excellent introduction, especially for teens, college students and young adults.
LL1504, 16 pp booklet, $1.50
LL7504, audiocassette, $6.95

Teaching Children to Focus
An Interview with Marianne Thompson
Practical, down-to-earth sharing of how a mother introduced Focusing to her young children.
LL1505, 20 pp booklet, $2.00
LL7505, audiocassette, $6.95

Focusing and Prayer
Illustration of the power of "Focusing Prayer."
LL1506, 28 pp booklet, $2.50
LL7506, audiocassette, $8.95

Childhood Wonder
A Doorway to the Spiritual in Focusing
Explores the spiritual dimension of wonder and its potential for spiritual growth.
LL1507, 12 pp booklet, $1.25
LL7507, audiocassette, $6.95

Searching for God With Our Fingertips
The Body as Spiritual Guide
LL1508, 12 pp booklet, $1.25
LL7508, audiocassette, $6.95

The Grace of Forgiving Yourself
Through Focusing
Using Focusing to deal with guilt, resentment, anger and fear.
LL1509, 12 pp booklet, $1.25
LL7509, audiocassette, $6.95

Addictive Religion
Identifies psychological addictions that cripple people's growth in wholeness/holiness.
LL1510, 24 pp booklet, $2.00
LL7510, audiocassette, $8.95

Focusing and Self-Renewal
Explores our capacity to grow through a self-renewing perspective.
LL1511, 12 pp booklet, $1.25
LL7511, audiocassette, $6.95

A Woman's Prayer
Notes from a Focusing Journal
A collection of entries from a mother's Focusing journal.
LL1512, 16 pp booklet, **$1.50**
LL7512, audiocassette, **$6.95**

"Process Skipping"
Mechanisms Which Lock In Addictive Patterns
Practical norms for asking the right questions and finding what actually supports human wholeness.
LL1513, 32 pp booklet, **$3.00**
LL7513, audiocassette, **$8.95**

A Bio-Spiritual Approach to Sexuality
Shows how intimacy with oneself is the key to intimacy with others.
LL1514, 40 pp booklet, **$3.50**
LL7514, audiocassette, **$14.95**

Journeying Together in Spirit
A Conversation with Sr. Ruth McGoldrick, S.P.
Sensitive comments on Focusing with the sick, elderly and the dying, reflecting a wisdom that time and experience have seasoned.
LL1515, 20 pp booklet, **$2.00**
LL7515, audiocassette, **$7.95**

How Adults Can Listen to Children in a Focusing Way
Play therapist Gloria Bruinix offers unique comments on Focusing and children.
LL1516, 28 pp booklet, **$2.50**
LL7516, audiocassette, **$8.95**

Focusing: Doorway to the Body-Life of Spirit
Identifies the psychological mechanism that locks addictive patterns in place.
LL1517, 20 pp booklet, **$2.00**
LL7517, audiocassette, **$7.95**

Focusing Companions
Provides down-to-earth, step-by-step suggestions on how to become Focusing Companions.
LL1518, 32 pp booklet, **$3.00**
LL7518, audiocassette, **$8.95**

Focusing Monographs
Complete set of all 19 Focusing monographs.
SS1500, 19 booklets, **$29.95**

Focusing Audiocassettes
Complete set of all 19 Focusing audiocassettes.
SS7500, 19 audiocassettes, **$139.95**

Videos

Focusing and Bio-Spirituality
An introduction to "focusing," showing how it has touched and transformed people's lives. Includes personal remarks by the Institute directors, a mother focusing with her 12-year-old daughter, "Focusing Companions" working together, and a Focusing massage therapist summarizing her sense for the spiritual dimension of body-work.
LL8481 (VHS), 37-min. video, **$29.95**

Because It Works
Four experienced guides share what means the most to them in their experience of Focusing. An extremely practical tape, introducing theory, technique, and the broader spiritual dimensions of Focusing.
LL8482 (VHS), 46-min. video, **$39.95**

Spirituality and Focusing
A set comprised of *"Focusing and Bio-Spirituality"* and *"Because It Works."*
SS8481 (VHS), **$49.95**

Focusing Companions
(Part I)

Records an actual Focusing session: Peter guides Joan. With general introduction to the Focusing Steps and concluding remarks about the actual experience.
LL8483 (VHS), 48-min. video, **$39.95**

Focusing Companions
(Part II)

Illustrates how Focusing Companions can support one another on their personal journeys. Very useful for learning the skills of Focusing and guiding.
LL8484 (VHS), 44-min. video, **$39.95**

Focusing Companions
(Part III): New Model for Community

Panel discussion explores the experience of "empowerment in mutual vulnerability." Helpful for anyone who wants to explore a new model for relationships/communities of grace: in marriage, parenting, ministry teams, small groups, and more.
LL8485 (VHS), 46-min. video, **$39.95**

Focusing Companions

A set comprised of *"Focusing Companions, parts I-III."*
SS8482 (VHS), **$79.95**

Building Self-Esteem
at School

A fifth-grade public school teacher and a Catholic school principal explain how they use Focusing with their students. An exciting and innovative experience with two women changing the lives of children in the Denver/Lakewood schools.
LL8489 (VHS), 30 min., **$29.95**

Learning the
Focusing Steps
(Part I and II)

A practical tool for learning the six steps of Focusing within a Bio-Spiritual approach to human growth. These steps are first explained, then modeled in short (15-20 minute) segments. Part II includes a complete, half-hour Focusing session that puts the six steps together. Tapes may be turned off between steps for reflection, discussion or practice.
LL8490 (VHS), Part I: 105 min.; Part II: 120 min., **$125.00**
